Other Publications:

PLANET EARTH
COLLECTOR'S LIBRARY OF THE CIVIL WAR
LIBRARY OF HEALTH
CLASSICS OF THE OLD WEST
THE EPIC OF FLIGHT
THE SEAFARERS
THE ENCYCLOPEDIA OF COLLECTIBLES
THE GREAT CITIES
WORLD WAR II
HOME REPAIR AND IMPROVEMENT
THE WORLD'S WILD PLACES
THE TIME-LIFE LIBRARY OF BOATING
HUMAN BEHAVIOR
THE ART OF SEWING
THE OLD WEST
THE EMERGENCE OF MAN
THE AMERICAN WILDERNESS
THE TIME-LIFE ENCYCLOPEDIA OF GARDENING
LIFE LIBRARY OF PHOTOGRAPHY
THIS FABULOUS CENTURY
FOODS OF THE WORLD
TIME-LIFE LIBRARY OF AMERICA
TIME-LIFE LIBRARY OF ART
GREAT AGES OF MAN
LIFE SCIENCE LIBRARY
THE LIFE HISTORY OF THE UNITED STATES
TIME READING PROGRAM
LIFE NATURE LIBRARY
LIFE WORLD LIBRARY
FAMILY LIBRARY:
    HOW THINGS WORK IN YOUR HOME
    THE TIME-LIFE BOOK OF THE FAMILY CAR
    THE TIME-LIFE FAMILY LEGAL GUIDE
    THE TIME-LIFE BOOK OF FAMILY FINANCE

*This volume is one of a series that explains and demonstrates
how to prepare various types of food, and that offers in each
book an international anthology of great recipes.*

Hors d'Oeuvre

BY
THE EDITORS OF TIME-LIFE BOOKS

TIME-LIFE BOOKS/ALEXANDRIA, VIRGINIA

Cover: A delicate blend of seafood and vegetables in a rich fish sauce is spooned into the crisp puff-pastry shells known as vol-au-vent. The shrimp, mussels, asparagus tips, sweet red peppers and mushrooms used to fill the vol-au-vent were precooked separately, then heated together in the sauce.

Time-Life Books Inc.
is a wholly owned subsidiary of
TIME INCORPORATED

Founder: Henry R. Luce 1898-1967

Editor-in-Chief: Henry Anatole Grunwald
President: J. Richard Munro
Chairman of the Board: Ralph P. Davidson
Executive Vice President: Clifford J. Grum
Chairman, Executive Committee: James R. Shepley
Editorial Director: Ralph Graves
Group Vice President, Books: Joan D. Manley
Vice Chairman: Arthur Temple

TIME-LIFE BOOKS INC.

Editor: George Constable. *Executive Editor:* George G. Daniels. *Board of Editors:* Dale M. Brown, Thomas H. Flaherty Jr., Martin Mann, Philip W. Payne, John Paul Porter, Gerry Schremp, Gerald Simons, Nakanori Tashiro, Kit van Tulleken. *Planning Director:* Edward Brash. *Art Director:* Tom Suzuki; *Assistant:* Arnold C. Holeywell. *Director of Administration:* David L. Harrison. *Director of Operations:* Gennaro C. Esposito. *Director of Research:* Carolyn L. Sackett; *Assistant:* Phyllis K. Wise. *Director of Photography:* Dolores Allen Littles. *Production Director:* Feliciano Madrid; *Assistants:* Peter A. Inchauteguiz, Karen A. Meyerson. *Copy Processing:* Gordon E. Buck. *Quality Control Director:* Robert L. Young; *Assistant:* James J. Cox; *Associates:* Daniel J. McSweeney, Michael G. Wight. *Art Coordinator:* Anne B. Landry. *Copy Room Director:* Susan Galloway Goldberg; *Assistants:* Celia Beattie, Ricki Tarlow

President: Carl G. Jaeger. *Executive Vice Presidents:* John Steven Maxwell, David J. Walsh. *Vice Presidents:* George Artandi, Stephen L. Bair, Peter G. Barnes, Nicholas Benton, John L. Canova, Beatrice T. Dobie, Carol Flaumenhaft, James L. Mercer, Herbert Sorkin, Paul R. Stewart

THE GOOD COOK

The original version of this book was created in London for Time-Life Books B.V.
European Editor: Kit van Tulleken; *Design Director:* Louis Klein; *Photography Director:* Pamela Marke; *Planning Director:* Alan Lothian; *Chief of Research:* Vanessa Kramer; *Chief Sub-Editor:* Ilse Gray; *Production Editor:* Ellen Brush; *Quality Control:* Douglas Whitworth

Staff for *Hors d'Oeuvre:* *Series Coordinator:* Liz Timothy; *Head Designer:* Rick Bowring; *Text Editors:* Gillian Boucher, Norman Kolpas; *Anthology Editors:* Josephine Bacon, Liz Clasen; *Staff Writers:* Alexandra Carlier, Jay Ferguson, Ellen Galford, Mary Harron, Thom Henvey; *Researchers:* Suad McCoy, Mary-Claire Hailey, Margaret Hall, Deborah Litton; *Designers:* Derek Copsey, Michael Morey, Mary Staples; *Sub-Editors:* Kathy Eason, Katie Lloyd, Sally Rowland; *Design Assistants:* Sally Curnock, Cherry Doyle, Ian Midson; *Editorial Department:* Anetha Besidonne, Pat Boag, Kate Cann, Beverley Doe, Philip Garner, Aquila Kegan, Lesley Kinahan, Debra Lelliott, Linda Mallet, Debra Raad, Brian Sambrook, Molly Sutherland, Julia West, Helen Whitehorn

U.S. Staff for *Hors d'Oeuvre:* *Editor:* Gerry Schremp; *Senior Editor:* Ellen Phillips; *Designer:* Ellen Robling; *Chief Researcher:* Barbara Fleming; *Picture Editor:* Christine Schuyler; *Writers:* Patricia Fanning, Leslie Marshall; *Researchers:* Patricia Kim (techniques), Ann Ready (anthology), Fran Moshos, Tina Ujlaki, Valerie Whitney; *Assistant Designer:* Peg Schreiber; *Copy Coordinators:* Nancy Berman, Tonna Gibert, Bobbie C. Paradise; *Art Assistant:* Mary L. Orr; *Picture Coordinator:* Alvin Ferrell; *Editorial Assistants:* Brenda Harwell, Patricia Whiteford

CHIEF SERIES CONSULTANT

Richard Olney, an American, has lived and worked for some three decades in France, where he is highly regarded as an authority on food and wine. Author of *The French Menu Cookbook* and of the award-winning *Simple French Food,* he has also contributed to numerous gastronomic magazines in France and the United States, including the influential journals *Cuisine et Vins de France* and *La Revue du Vin de France.* He has directed cooking courses in France and the United States and is a member of several distinguished gastronomic and oenological societies, including L'Académie Internationale du Vin, La Confrérie des Chevaliers du Tastevin and La Commanderie du Bontemps de Médoc et des Graves. Working in London with the series editorial staff, he has been basically responsible for the planning of this volume, and has supervised the final selection of recipes submitted by other consultants. The United States edition of The Good Cook has been revised by the Editors of Time-Life Books to bring it into complete accord with American customs and usage.

CHIEF AMERICAN CONSULTANT

Carol Cutler is the author of a number of cookbooks, including the award-winning *The Six-Minute Soufflé and Other Culinary Delights.* During the 12 years she lived in France, she studied at the Cordon Bleu and the École des Trois Gourmandes, and with private chefs. She is a member of the Cercle des Gourmettes, a long-established French food society limited to just 50 members, and is also a charter member of Les Dames d'Escoffier, Washington Chapter.

SPECIAL CONSULTANT

Joyce Dodson Piotrowski studied cooking while traveling and living around the world. A teacher, chef, caterer, food writer and consultant, she has been responsible for many of the step-by-step photographic sequences in this volume.

PHOTOGRAPHERS

Tom Belshaw specializes in food and still-life photography, undertaking both editorial and advertising assignments.
Aldo Tutino has worked in Milan, New York City and Washington, D.C. He has received a number of awards for his photographs from the New York Advertising Club.

INTERNATIONAL CONSULTANTS

GREAT BRITAIN: *Jane Grigson* has written a number of books about food and has been a cookery correspondent for the London *Observer* since 1968. *Alan Davidson* is the author of several cookbooks and the founder of Prospect Books, which specialize in scholarly publications about food and cookery. *Jean Reynolds,* who prepared some of the dishes for the photographs in this volume, is from San Francisco. She trained as a cook in the kitchens of several of France's great restaurants. *Richard Sax,* who also prepared some of the hors d'oeuvre in this volume, was for two years Chef-Director of the test kitchens for *The International Review of Food and Wine.* He trained in New York and in Paris, where he served an apprenticeship at the Hotel Plaza-Athénée. FRANCE: *Michel Lemonnier,* the co-founder and vice president of Les Amitiés Gastronomiques Internationales, is a frequent lecturer on wine and vineyards. GERMANY: *Jochen Kuchenbecker* trained as a chef, but worked for 10 years as a food photographer in several European countries before opening his own restaurant in Hamburg. *Anne Brakemeier* is the co-author of a number of cookbooks. ITALY: *Massimo Alberini* is a well-known food writer and journalist, with a particular interest in culinary history. His many books include *Storia del Pranzo all'Italiana, 4000 Anni a Tavola* and *100 Ricette Storiche.* THE NETHERLANDS: *Hugh Jans* has published cookbooks and his recipes appear in several Dutch magazines. THE UNITED STATES: *Judith Olney,* the author of *Comforting Food* and *Summer Food,* received her culinary training in England and in France. In addition to conducting cooking classes, she regularly contributes articles to gastronomic magazines.

Correspondents: Elisabeth Kraemer (Bonn); Margot Hapgood, Dorothy Bacon (London); Susan Jonas, Lucy T. Voulgaris (New York); Maria Vincenza Aloisi, Josephine du Brusle (Paris); Ann Natanson (Rome).
Valuable assistance was also provided by: Jeanne Buys, Janny Hovinga (Amsterdam); Hans-Heinrich Wellmann, Gertraud Bellon (Hamburg); Bona Schmid, Maria Teresa Marenco (Milan); Michèle le Baube, Cécile Dogneiz (Paris).

First printing. Printed in U.S.A.
Published simultaneously in Canada.
School and library distribution by Silver Burdett Company, Morristown, New Jersey 07960.

TIME-LIFE is a trademark of Time Incorporated U.S.A.

For information about any Time-Life book, please write:
Reader Information, Time-Life Books
541 North Fairbanks Court, Chicago, Illinois 60611

Library of Congress CIP data, page 176.

CONTENTS

A Beneficent Beginning

An hors d'oeuvre ushers in a meal with a flourish and stimulates enthusiasm for what is to follow. Indeed, its very name—literally, "outside the work"—is inseparable from the idea of a meal as a sequence of courses: It leads to the work proper—a substantial main course and dessert or cheese, or, in more formal meals, a calculated progression of several courses. Being the initial offering of the occasion, an hors d'oeuvre is approached with an eager and attentive palate—and hence is especially rewarding for cook and diner alike.

The hors d'oeuvre presentations demonstrated in this volume do not encompass all first courses. Many meals begin with dishes that also can be served in larger quantities as main courses—salad, pâté, soup or pasta, for example; none of these is shown here. But the range of dishes designed exclusively for first courses is remarkably varied in its own right. Any food can provide an enticing hors d'oeuvre if it is properly prepared; vegetables, meats, fish, shellfish and eggs all appear in the chapters that follow. All are served in small helpings that do not sate the appetite, but their most important common feature is a careful presentation that makes them doubly inviting, both in themselves and as heralds of the rest of a meal.

Planning for an appealing balance
The food chosen for an hors d'oeuvre and the way that food is prepared must always be considered in the context of the whole meal. In general, a pleasing contrast is the rule. If your main course is a richly sauced dish, the hors d'oeuvre should be simple—slender spring asparagus, perhaps, garnished with nothing more than a little lemon juice. If your main course is something less elaborate, such as a roast, you can begin the meal by serving rich ingredients—brains, for instance—swathed in creamy sauces. If your main course is a complicated assortment of meats and vegetables, serve an hors d'oeuvre that emphasizes a single taste and has a homogeneous texture; a soufflé or mousse would be a logical choice. A hot hors d'oeuvre happily precedes a cold main course; a hot main course is set in pleasing relief by a cold hors d'oeuvre. The same sort of considerations of polarity apply to texture: If one course is crisp and chewy, the other should be soft and unctuous.

The art of presenting hors d'oeuvre depends on an understanding of visual balance, proportion and appeal. Ingredients as elemental as fillets of fish—and even ingredients as luxurious as sweetbreads—will look mean and dull if they are surrounded by a large expanse of empty plate. But these foods acquire new charm when they are artfully arranged on individual plates, strung on small skewers or framed by pastry casings. Vegetables, meats and seafood, smoothly puréed, make pretty soufflés, mousses and mousselines. And sauces can play an important part in hors d'oeuvre: Their richness may be more welcome at the opening of a meal than later on, when the appetite has lost its edge.

This book is designed to teach all aspects of hors d'oeuvre presentation. On the following six pages, the making of sauces, stocks and aspics is explained. The primary ingredients used in hors d'oeuvre are then dealt with in five chapters. The first focuses on vegetables, from those simply steamed or boiled and served with complementary sauces to more intricate creations, such as little vegetable containers filled with appealing stuffings. A chapter on meats shows how those usually reserved for main courses can be offered as hors d'oeuvre if the meats are marinated or made into tiny rolls, creamy mousses or dainty sausages. The next chapter is devoted to fish and seafood; it begins with the elegant fish presentations of Japan—*sashimi* and *sushi*—and continues with demonstrations of marinated fish hors d'oeuvre, frogs' legs, and those perennial favorites, oysters and clams. Eggs in various guises—in aspics, custards and soufflés—form the subject of the fourth chapter. And the final chapter of the first half of this volume addresses the preparation of various types of casings used in the presentation of hors d'oeuvre—for example, crepes, pastry casings ranging from simple short-crust shells to vol-au-vent made from airy puff-pastry dough and bread casings such as brioche.

The second half of the book consists of an anthology of the best published hors d'oeuvre recipes. They will serve not only as prescriptions for particular dishes, but also as bases for your own improvisations.

An accompaniment of wine
Just as a robustly flavored roast is often served after a subtle hors d'oeuvre, red wine normally follows white in the course of a formal meal. That rule coincides neatly with the requirements of hors d'oeuvre, most of which are best enjoyed with a white wine. White wine complements vegetables, white meat and fish, and sauces enriched with cream or egg; red wine, with its tannic edge, would seem harsh in such company. But an exception is made for an hors d'oeuvre based on red meat or coated with a red wine sauce, which may be more agreeably accompanied by a light-bodied red wine. Explore the wine possibilities with the same spirit of adventure that inspires you as you contrive the hors d'oeuvre, and many pleasant discoveries will reward you.

A Quartet of Classics

Among the sauces used to garnish simple hors d'oeuvre and unite the elements of complex ones are four classic preparations: white sauce, tomato sauce, hollandaise sauce and white butter sauce *(recipes, page 162)*. In each case, the secret of success lies in careful, gentle cooking.

A white sauce *(right, top)* is nothing more than a flour-and-butter paste—a roux—that is thinned with milk, then simmered long enough to remove any taste of raw flour. This basic sauce can be made in advance and refrigerated for as long as two days, then reheated. It may be enriched with additional butter or with cream or egg yolks, and flavored with grated cheese or with chopped or puréed vegetables such as *duxelles (page 22)* or tomatoes.

A tomato sauce *(opposite, top)* consists of tomatoes gently cooked with seasonings to soften their flesh. For a smooth texture, the cooked sauce is puréed, then simmered again to reduce it to the required thickness. Like white sauce, tomato sauce can be made in advance and refrigerated; it will keep for four or five days. It can be enriched with cream; flavorings can include garlic and onions as well as dill, basil, chives or oregano.

Hollandaise sauce *(right, bottom)* is an emulsion formed by inducing warm egg yolks to bind with butter over heat. It requires a delicate hand: The yolks can only bind with small amounts of butter at a time, and if they become too hot, they will curdle. To make them less sensitive to heat, the yolks should be thinned with cold water before butter is added; the butter itself should be cold and stirred in very gradually. And the operation must be performed over the low heat of a double boiler. Hollandaise is best served as soon as it is made, but it can be left over warm water for as long as an hour.

White butter sauce *(opposite, bottom)* is another delicate preparation. Butter is whisked into an acidic liquid—here, a mixture of white wine and vinegar, flavored with shallots—so that the butter forms a creamy emulsion with the acid rather than melting to oil. Like hollandaise sauce, white butter sauce should be cooked as gently as possible. It must be served the moment it is made to prevent separation.

White Sauce: Milk Thickened by a Roux

1 **Making a roux.** Melt butter over low heat. Add an equal quantity of flour, and stir the butter and flour together with a whisk until the mixture is smooth. Cook the roux gently for two minutes, stirring constantly.

2 **Cooking.** Add milk—about 2 cups [½ liter] for 2 tablespoons [30 ml.] of flour—increase the heat and whisk until the sauce boils. Reduce the heat so that the sauce barely simmers; cook, uncovered, for 40 minutes. It should have the consistency of cream—or be thicker if you plan to use the sauce in a stuffing.

Hollandaise Sauce: Blending Egg Yolks and Butter

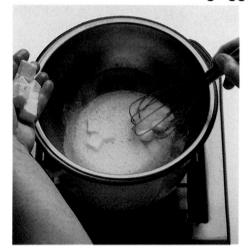

1 **Adding butter.** Put egg yolks in the top of a double boiler or in a stainless-steel bowl that has been placed over the rim of a pot half-filled with barely simmering water. Reduce the heat to low. Add a tablespoon [15 ml.] of cold water to the yolks and whisk them until they are smooth. Add a few cubes of cold butter and continue whisking.

2 **Adding lemon juice.** When the egg mixture has absorbed the butter, add more cubes and continue whisking. Add the remaining butter—in all, about 4 tablespoons [60 ml.] for each yolk—a few cubes at a time, whisking as they are absorbed. When the sauce is thick and creamy, after about 10 minutes, season and pour in strained fresh lemon juice.

Tomato Sauce: An Herb-scented Purée

1 **Seasoning tomatoes.** Chop onions fine and sauté them in a little oil in an enameled, stainless-steel or tin-lined copper pan until soft. Add quartered tomatoes, salt, a bay leaf, thyme and lightly crushed garlic cloves to the onions. Stirring occasionally, cook the mixture over low heat until the tomatoes disintegrate—20 to 30 minutes.

2 **Puréeing the tomatoes.** Set a sieve that has nylon or stainless-steel mesh over a large bowl. Use a pestle to push the tomato flesh through the sieve. Discard the seeds and skins, and the herbs that remain in the sieve. Pour the purée back into the pan.

3 **Reducing the purée.** Cook the tomato purée, uncovered, over low heat for 20 to 30 minutes, until it reduces to the consistency you prefer. To prevent sticking, stir it frequently—especially toward the end of the cooking time. Season the sauce with pepper and, if you wish, add chopped fresh herbs, such as basil or parsley.

White Butter Sauce: A Tingling Transformation

1 **Preparing the base.** Pour equal amounts of white wine vinegar and white wine into a nonreactive pan. Set the pan over low heat. Add finely chopped shallots to the combined liquids. Add a little salt. Let the mixture simmer until the liquid has almost disappeared—this will take 15 minutes or more.

2 **Adding butter.** Remove the pan from the heat and allow the contents to cool for a few seconds. Place a heat-diffusing pad over low heat and set the pan on it. Grind in some pepper. Add a few cubes of cold butter and whisk vigorously. Add more butter when the first batch of cubes begins to soften, leaving more space for whisking.

3 **Finishing the sauce.** Whisking constantly, continue adding butter a handful at a time until the sauce has the consistency of mayonnaise. Take the pan off the heat just as the last butter cubes are melting, but whisk for a few seconds more. Serve the sauce as soon as you have finished preparing it.

Accompaniments Based on Stock

Aromatic fish and meat stocks provide the bases for an important assemblage of sauces and coatings: The stocks can be turned either into the smooth, hot sauces known collectively as veloutés—"velvety" in French—or into the glittering aspics used for cold presentations. For all of these preparations, the quality of the basic stock is of primary importance.

Stocks are made by gently simmering fish trimmings or meat in water with herbs and aromatic vegetables *(recipes, page 163)*. Fish stocks can be made from fish bones, skins and heads. The most delicate meat stocks contain veal shank bones—which provide flavor and gelatin for body—supplemented by chicken pieces and sometimes by calf's feet or pork rind, which adds the extra gelatin that helps meat stock set to jelly.

Care in the cooking will ensure that any stock emerges clear. The stock ingredients should first be covered with cold water and the water brought slowly to a simmer; during this initial period, meat or fish will release albuminous scum, which must be removed so that it cannot cloud the liquid. Once the scum is removed, the only challenge is to keep the stock at a gentle, undisturbed simmer: Boiling will cause cloudiness, as will the agitation produced by stirring. Fish trimmings take 30 minutes to release their flavors; meat will take four to five hours. After cooking, solid ingredients are strained from the stock, and fat is removed from it *(box, opposite)*.

To turn a stock into a velouté, you need merely combine it with a roux *(page 6)* and simmer it to eliminate the taste of flour and reduce the liquid to the proper creamy consistency *(recipe, page 163)*. During simmering, any remaining fat and impurities from the stock will rise to the surface and can be skimmed off by the technique shown in the top demonstration. The completed velouté may be colored and flavored as shown on page 10.

Stock is turned into aspic as described in the box on the opposite page.

From Fish to Velouté Sauce

1 **Starting stock.** Put fish trimmings—here, bones, heads and skins of sole—in a pan; cover them with cold water. Bring the liquid to a simmer, spooning off any scum. Add a little salt, herbs and aromatic vegetables—fennel, parsley, thyme, bay leaves, garlic, celery, carrots and onions.

2 **Straining.** Partly cover the pan; simmer for 15 minutes. Add wine, return the liquid to a simmer and cook for five more minutes; add peppercorns and simmer for 10 minutes. Strain the stock through a colander lined with two layers of damp cheesecloth or muslin.

Veal Stock: A Versatile Foundation

1 **Starting stock.** To keep the meat from sticking, put a rack in the bottom of a deep pan. Add pieces of veal shank, meaty veal trimmings, and a handful of chicken necks and backs. Pour in enough cold water to cover the meat and bones by about 1 inch [2½ cm.]. Bring the water slowly to a simmer.

2 **Removing scum.** Remove all the scum that forms *(above)*, adding cold water to force more scum to rise. Then add salt, vegetables and herbs and barely simmer—partially covered and undisturbed—for five hours. Strain, chill and degrease the stock *(box, opposite)*. To make a velouté *(Steps 3-5, above)*, reheat the stock.

3 **Beginning the sauce.** To prepare a roux, melt butter in a pan over low heat; add an equal volume of flour and stir the roux with a whisk for a minute or so until smoothly blended. Ladle in the stock, then increase the heat and whisk continuously until the sauce boils.

4 **Cleansing.** To remove any impurities and fat, set the pan half off the heat. Keep the sauce simmering and, with a metal spoon, repeatedly remove the skin that forms on the surface of the sauce at the cool side of the pan.

5 **Finishing the sauce.** Continue to cleanse the velouté at intervals for about 40 minutes, or until no more fat rises to the surface. During the process, the sauce will reduce to the consistency of cream, and the pasty taste of undercooked flour will vanish. Before serving the sauce, adjust its seasoning.

Achieving a Limpid Aspic

Aspics made from meat or fish stocks must be sparklingly clear. To guarantee this, the stocks must be cleansed of fat and, in some cases, clarified. Removing fat is a simple task: When stock is chilled, the fat will rise to the surface and can be spooned and wiped off, as shown at right.

Now you will be able to see whether the stock is translucent. If it is cloudy—because all of the scum was not removed during cooking or because the liquid boiled—combine it with two beaten egg whites and their crumbled shells and whisk over high heat until the whites rise to the rim. Let the foam settle off the heat, then bring the stock just to a boil twice more. The protein in the egg will trap impurities, permitting them to be strained out. Gelatinous meat stock, chilled again, becomes aspic. Fish stock usually lacks gelatin; if it does not jell, turn it into aspic with the addition of commercial gelatin (recipe, page 163).

1 **Degreasing stock.** Make stock— in this case, veal stock. Let it cool, then refrigerate it until it is firmly set—eight to 12 hours. With a metal spoon, carefully remove the layer of fat that has formed on the surface of the stock.

2 **Wiping the surface clean.** To remove every last trace of fat, gently wipe the surface of the stock with a cloth or paper towel dampened with hot water. Store the stock in the refrigerator for up to four days or in the freezer for up to six months.

A Note of Color for Velouté and White Sauces

A velouté or white sauce used to garnish hot hors d'oeuvre can be endowed with color and flavor by highly pigmented spices and vegetables. Spices are easiest to use. Reddish paprika and yellow turmeric are preground and quickly dissolve when added to sauce. Saffron threads or the powdered saffron used here also dyes food yellow; the threads must be crushed and both forms must be combined with hot water to dissolve evenly.

Vegetables must be precooked to release their liquids, then puréed. Besides the spinach and red peppers shown, the possibilities include sorrel and tomatoes.

Spinach *(right)* is simply parboiled and drained before it is reduced to a purée in a food processor or sieve. Peppers *(below)* should be broiled to soften their flesh and make their papery skins easy to peel. Purée the peppers through a sieve, never in a food processor or blender, which would yield a frothy liquid. Tomatoes should be stewed and sieved *(page 7)*. Young sorrel needs no puréeing; after stewing in butter, it will disintegrate to a paste.

Spinach for a Vivid Green

Adding the purée. Trim off the tough stems of spinach. Parboil the leaves for two minutes, rinse under cold water, drain and squeeze dry. Purée the leaves in a food processor or chop them fine and force them through a sieve. Spinach has a strong coloring effect: Stir the purée into sauce a spoonful at a time.

The Golden Tint of Saffron

Coloring with spice. Put powdered saffron in a large spoon. Stir in hot water with a small spoon until the spice dissolves. Stir the solution into the sauce. A saffron solution will be reddish, but it will make the sauce yellow.

A Warm Red from Peppers

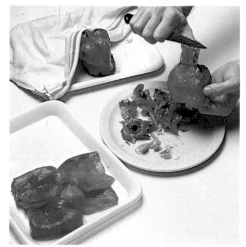

1 **Peeling peppers.** Broil peppers, turning them regularly so that their skins blister on all sides. Place them under a damp towel; it will trap steam, helping to loosen their skins. When the peppers cool, peel them and remove the stems, seeds and pulpy ribs.

2 **Puréeing the peppers.** Set over a bowl a sturdy sieve with a nonreactive nylon or stainless-steel mesh. Push the peppers through the sieve with a pestle. A pepper purée produced by sieving has more body and a more uniform consistency than one made by any other method.

3 **Embellishing the sauce.** Add the purée to either a velouté or white sauce in whatever proportions you please; neither the color nor the flavor of peppers is so intense as to demand caution.

Mayonnaise: A Rich Emulsion

Mayonnaise, a creamy emulsion of eggs, oil and flavorings, can be produced either in a blender or food processor, or by hand. The general rules of preparation are the same in both cases: The ingredients must be at room temperature, since the emulsion will not form if they are cold. And the oil must be added to the eggs very slowly; otherwise, the two will not bind.

Differences between the two versions are minor. Mayonnaise made in a blender or food processor must contain whole eggs: The liquid provided by their whites prevents the mixture from thickening too much. Mayonnaise made by hand uses only the egg yolks—the source of its famous richness. Oil may be added in a very thin stream to machine-made mayonnaise. But for hand-made mayonnaise, the oil must be added drop by drop at first to give the yolks time to absorb it.

Either version may be based on olive oil or milder vegetable oil and can be flavored in various ways *(recipes, page 161)*.

Taking Advantage of a Food Processor

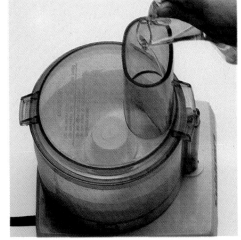

1 **Adding oil.** Combine an egg, salt, pepper, and vinegar or lemon juice in the bowl of a food processor equipped with a steel blade. Cover and blend for a few seconds. Without stopping the machine, pour oil in a slow stream through the feed tube until the mixture emulsifies and thickens. Stop the motor.

2 **Testing consistency.** Remove the processor lid and use a spatula to check the consistency of the mayonnaise: It should form soft peaks. If it is too stiff, fold in a few more drops of vinegar or lemon juice. If too thin, replace the lid, start the motor and dribble in more oil.

Using the Traditional Approach

1 **Adding lemon juice.** Put egg yolks, salt and pepper in a dry bowl placed on a damp, folded towel to steady it. Whisk the yolks about a minute, or until they appear slightly paler. Whisk in vinegar or, as here, lemon juice, squeezing the lemon over your hand to catch the seeds.

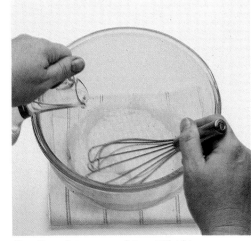

2 **Creating an emulsion.** Whisking continuously, add oil drop by drop. When the mayonnaise starts to thicken, whisk in the oil in a thin, steady stream. Increase the flow to a slightly thicker stream after half of the oil has been added to the bowl.

3 **Testing consistency.** Whisking rhythmically, continue to add oil until the mayonnaise forms soft peaks. If it seems too thick, you may dilute the mayonnaise with additional lemon juice or vinegar, or with warm water.

1
Vegetables
Imaginative Ways with Garden Bounty

The virtues of steaming and boiling
Choosing complementary sauces
Fashioning edible cases
Using filling for enrichment
Protective sheaths for deep frying

To make the nosegay arrangement shown here, hollowed red peppers were parboiled in an aromatic court bouillon, then filled with parboiled snow peas, asparagus, broccoli and leaves of raw Belgian endive *(pages 18-19)*. The vegetable fillings conceal pepper-flavored mayonnaise; the plates are garnished with leaves of chicory.

Refreshing and light, vegetable hors d'oeuvre make an excellent prelude to a meal. Vegetables lend themselves to any cooking method—steaming, boiling, braising, baking, broiling or frying—and, once they have been cooked, they may be enhanced by many sorts of sauces, accompaniments and garnishes.

The simplest offering consists of a single vegetable harvested at the height of its season, briefly steamed or parboiled just to tenderness, then served hot or cold with a complementary sauce. Fresh spring asparagus coated with a vinaigrette sauce is the classic example; leeks, broccoli and artichokes are only a few of the vegetables that can be used in the same way *(pages 16-17)*. For richer effects, the vegetable chosen can be served with mayonnaise, hollandaise, garlicky pesto, spicy green sauce or tomato sauce.

Steaming and boiling leave vegetables as close as possible to their natural states, their tastes and textures altered very little. Baking and deep frying *(pages 22-25),* however, work more dramatic changes: The vegetables emerge with crisp, golden surfaces that are pleasant contrasts to the tender flesh within. In deep frying, a crunchy envelope can be produced by a preliminary coating of batter—a delicate tempura batter in the Japanese style, for instance. For a thicker and heavier crust, the vegetables may be coated with layers of beaten eggs, herbs and flour, and cornmeal or bread crumbs mixed, if you like, with grated cheese. Similar ingredients may be combined to provide the gratin topping for baked vegetables.

The presentation of vegetable hors d'oeuvre ranges from the rustic to the formal. A selection of crisp-crusted deep-fried vegetables piled on a serving plate has a pleasantly jumbled look, for instance. At the opposite end of the compositional spectrum, such naturally hollow or easily hollowed-out vegetables as mushrooms, onions, tomatoes, zucchini, peppers and artichokes may be steamed, boiled or baked to serve as casings for savory fillings. For creations of this type, the choice of appropriate fillings is very broad indeed. Inventive mixtures of soft cheeses, grains, meats and seafood can all be used to fill vegetable containers. Or, for a particularly fresh and colorful effect, the fillings can consist of a collection of other vegetables, as shown opposite.

Steaming to Emphasize Fresh Flavor

Steamed just to tenderness over boiling water and served with a sauce, vegetables can make an incomparably light and delicious first course. You can use almost any vegetable in this manner: The only exceptions are extremely hard types such as artichokes and beets, which require prohibitively long cooking times, and fragile tomatoes, which would disintegrate in the moist heat. A single vegetable may be served *(top demonstration)* or several may be steamed together—arranged, if you like, on wooden skewers *(bottom demonstration)*.

Whatever the choice, care in the preparations will ensure that the vegetables emerge tender but not soggy. Choose firm, fresh vegetables. Small ones—such as button mushrooms or new potatoes—may be left whole. Larger vegetables should be cut into pieces ½ inch [1 cm.] thick or less so that they cook evenly.

The steaming time required for a vegetable depends on both density and dimensions. Hard vegetables such as carrots take longer to cook than softer mushrooms. Large pieces need longer steaming than small ones: Slices of zucchini, for instance, may take four minutes to cook, but the strands shown at right will cook in two minutes or less.

When steaming several different vegetables, allow for different cooking times. If you use both dense and fragile vegetables, either add the dense ones to the steamer several minutes before the others, or separately precook the denser vegetables. In any case, allow room in the steamer basket for circulation of steam: In a crowded basket, the vegetables will not cook evenly.

Steamed vegetables are often served with a sauce as simple as melted butter mixed with fresh lemon juice, but they make a fine foil for herbal garnishes. Basil-based pesto—Italian for "paste"—is used here with the zucchini strands *(recipe, page 161)*, and a simplified version of tarragon-scented béarnaise sauce is chosen for the skewered assemblage *(recipe, page 162)*.

Zucchini Julienne Tossed with Pesto

1 **Making the sauce.** In a mortar, pound garlic cloves and rinsed and dried fresh basil leaves to a coarse paste. Pound in salt, pepper, freshly grated Parmesan cheese and pine nuts. Stir in olive oil a little at a time, until the mixture is the consistency of heavy cream. Alternatively, purée all of the ingredients in a blender or food processor.

2 **Cutting up zucchini.** Wash and dry small, firm zucchini and trim off the ends. Using a mandolin adjusted to make thin julienne, cut the zucchini lengthwise into matchstick-sized strips by sliding each zucchini over the blade. When each one is reduced to a piece that is too thin to handle safely, cut it into strips by hand.

A Bright-hued Medley Cooked on Skewers

1 **Making béarnaise sauce.** In a nonreactive pan over medium heat, simmer white wine, vinegar, chopped shallots, tarragon and parsley, and salt and pepper until most of the liquid evaporates. Make hollandaise sauce *(page 6)* and whisk the flavored reduction into it. Keep the sauce warm.

2 **Preparing vegetables.** Trim peeled carrots into 2-inch [5-cm.] lengths and steam *(Step 3, above)* for 10 minutes. Trim asparagus tips. Clean mushroom caps. Cut circles in the stem ends of peppers, twist out the stems and attached seeds. Scrape out the ribs and cut the peppers into 1½-inch [4-cm.] squares.

3 **Steaming.** Pour water into a steamer or large pot to a depth of 2 inches [5 cm.] and bring it to a boil. Scatter the zucchini strips in a steamer basket and set the basket in the pot; the basket should not touch the water. Cover the pot and steam the zucchini for about two minutes. It is ready when lifted strands droop slightly.

4 **Serving the zucchini.** Immediately transfer the zucchini to a warmed serving dish. Spoon a generous amount of the pesto sauce onto the zucchini. Using two wooden spoons to keep the tender strands from breaking, lightly toss the zucchini with the sauce. Serve immediately.

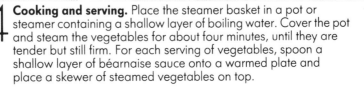

3 **Threading skewers.** Thread the vegetables onto wooden skewers, alternating the vegetables in a pleasing pattern. Use a twisting motion to thread the mushroom caps without splitting them. Place the skewers in two layers around the edge of a steamer basket, leaving space in the center.

4 **Cooking and serving.** Place the steamer basket in a pot or steamer containing a shallow layer of boiling water. Cover the pot and steam the vegetables for about four minutes, until they are tender but still firm. For each serving of vegetables, spoon a shallow layer of béarnaise sauce onto a warmed plate and place a skewer of steamed vegetables on top.

Boiling for Tenderness

Any vegetable that can be steamed for presentation as an hors d'oeuvre *(pages 14-15)* can also be boiled for the same purpose. In fact, boiling—a quicker process than steaming—is preferable when cooking large amounts of vegetables and is the method of choice for such dense vegetables as beets or artichokes. Boiling does not preserve quite so many nutrients as steaming but, if properly done, guarantees the maximum retention of a vegetable's natural color.

Preparation of vegetables for boiling is as simple as for steaming: They need only be rinsed clean and trimmed as necessary. In the top demonstration on these pages, for instance, the artichokes are trimmed of their coarse outer leaves and sharp leaf tips; in the bottom demonstration, a cauliflower is broken up into florets to speed cooking.

For the finest flavor, the vegetables should be cooked in large quantities of lightly salted boiling water, allowing 4 to 5 quarts [4 to 5 liters] of water for each pound [½ kg.] of vegetables. Some vegetables—artichokes, red cabbage and salsify—contain tannins that cause their flesh to discolor when it is exposed to air. To keep these vegetables from discoloring, acidulate their cooking water by adding 1 tablespoon [15 ml.] of lemon juice to each quart [1 liter]; or if the vegetables are white, cook them in a *blanc* ("white" in French): Add 1 tablespoon each of flour, vegetable oil and lemon juice to each quart of water. In all cases, cook the vegetables as briefly as possible. They should emerge tender enough to be pierced with a knife point, but still firm enough to offer a bit of resistance.

Once cooked and drained, the vegetables can be served warm, at room temperature or chilled, and the presentation may be as simple or as elaborate as you wish. The artichokes here are relieved of their prickly centers (their "chokes") and served at room temperature with a sharp vinaigrette sauce *(recipe, page 91)*. The cauliflower is re-formed into its original shape, then served with a pungent *salsa verde*, or green sauce *(recipe, page 93)*.

Artichokes Hollowed to Hold a Dressing

1 **Topping the artichokes.** Wash artichokes to remove grit from between their leaves. Hold each one firmly in one hand and, with the other hand, snap off the stem. Break off any damaged outer leaves. With a sharp knife, cut off the top quarter or so of each artichoke and discard it. Rub the cut surfaces with lemon to prevent discoloration.

2 **Trimming the leaves.** With the knife, trim the base of each artichoke fla so that it can stand upright. Use kitchen scissors to snip off the sharp tips of the outer leaves; rub the edges of the leaves with lemon.

A Molded Dome of Cauliflower

1 **Cooking.** With a sharp knife, cut the leaves and stem from a cauliflower. Divide the cauliflower into florets about 1½ inches [4 cm.] in diameter. Drop the florets into boiling salted water; boil them for about 12 minutes, until a knife pierces them easily. Drain the florets and run cold water over them to arrest their cooking.

2 **Shaping the cauliflower.** Press a layer of florets, stems in, onto the sides and bottom of a bowl. Pack the center of the bowl with more florets, stems up. Place a plate and a 1-pound [½-kg.] weight or a can of food on the packed cauliflower. Let it stand for 15 minutes, then, holding the plate and weight in place, tip the bowl to drain off water.

3 **Cooking the artichokes.** Put the artichokes in a nonreactive pan of boiling, acidulated water. Cover, reduce the heat to a simmer and cook the artichokes, turning them at 10-minute intervals, until the tip of a knife can easily pierce their bases—20 to 40 minutes. Drain them upside down on a towel.

4 **Removing the choke.** Serve the artichokes whole, accompanied by sauce. Or for a more formal presentation, remove their chokes and fill the centers with sauce. To expose each choke, twist out the central cone of tender leaves; reserve it. With a spoon, scoop out the choke; discard it.

5 **Serving.** Arrange the artichokes on a platter with the separated cones of leaves. Make a vinaigrette sauce. Pour sauce into the center of each artichoke. To eat an artichoke, the diner pulls off each leaf, dips its base in the sauce and scrapes off the flesh with his teeth; he then eats the bottom with knife and fork.

3 **Unmolding.** Refrigerate the weighted cauliflower for at least two hours. Then remove the weight and plate, invert a serving dish over the bowl, and invert bowl and dish together. Lift off the bowl and garnish the dish— watercress leaves are used here.

4 **Serving.** Whisk together olive oil, lemon juice, salt and cayenne pepper, and stir in chopped capers, parsley, watercress, black olives and peeled red pepper (page 10). Spoon sauce over the cauliflower; pass more separately.

Vegetable Containers for Savory Fillings

Among vegetable hors d'oeuvre, some of the most appealing are those formed by filling vegetable cases. The variations on the theme are many. Naturally hollow red or green peppers, cup-shaped artichoke bottoms or mushroom caps, and hollowed-out zucchini, onions, potatoes and fennel bulbs all may serve.

The cases may be prepared in any of a range of ways. Some vegetables, such as tomatoes and mushrooms, may be used uncooked, or they can be filled and baked *(pages 22-23)*. Denser vegetables such as onions or peppers must be parboiled before they are filled and baked. Or these vegetable containers can simply be parboiled or boiled—depending on the degree of crispness desired—then assembled with their separately cooked fillings just before serving, as in the demonstrations at right.

Vegetable containers can be boiled according to the basic rules given on pages 16-17, but additional flavor may be introduced by means of the boiling liquid. Instead of using water, you can cook the containers in stock *(recipe, page 163)* or in an aromatic court bouillon, made by simmering together wine, vegetable oil and flavorings *(recipe, page 164)*.

Once prepared, the cases may be filled with any ingredients that strike your fancy—meats, seafood or, for lightness and color, other prepared vegetables. In the upper demonstration here, artichoke bottoms are filled with a colorful medley of chopped parboiled peas, turnips and carrots, bound together with mayonnaise *(recipe, page 161)*; a seafood salad would be an appropriate substitution. In the bottom demonstration, peppers serve as vases for an arrangement of asparagus spears, broccoli florets, Belgian endive and snow peas, all cooked in a court bouillon and garnished with a mayonnaise flecked with more red pepper.

Sculpting Artichoke Bottoms

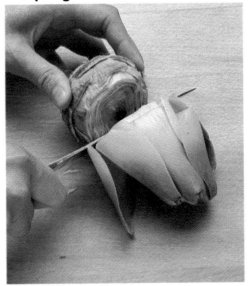 

1 Snapping off leaves. Break off the stem end of an artichoke, then bend back each outer leaf until its tough upper part breaks away from the fleshy base. Discard the leaves. When you reach the yellow-green inner leaves, cut off and discard the top two thirds of the artichoke.

2 Turning the bottom. Peel the tough, green exterior of the artichoke bottom, starting at the stem end and paring in a spiral. You will be left with the pale green bottom, capped by a rim of fleshy leaf bases. To prevent discoloring, moisten the artichoke bottom with lemon juice.

Ready-made Cases from Peppers

1 Preparing vegetables. Slice the stem ends from sweet red peppers; seed and derib the peppers *(page 14)*. Divide broccoli into florets with stems about 4 inches [10 cm.] long. Trim asparagus spears into 6-inch [15-cm.] lengths and pare the skin from the stalks. String snow peas.

2 Parboiling. In a court bouillon, parboil each vegetable separately; when just tender, transfer it to an ice-filled dish. Snow peas will take about 30 seconds, asparagus two minutes, broccoli and red peppers about three minutes. Pack ice into the peppers to keep them from collapsing.

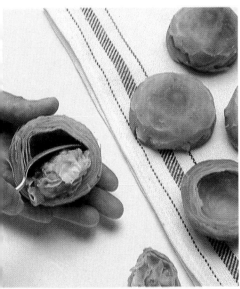

3 **Removing the choke.** Cook artichoke bottoms in a simmering *blanc* (page 16), until they are tender—20 to 40 minutes. Drain them upside down on a kitchen towel, then carefully pry out their chokes with a spoon (above).

4 **Preparing the filling.** Parboil separately, in salted water, equal amounts of peas, diced carrots and turnips, and green beans cut into ½-inch [1-cm.] pieces. Allow three to five minutes for each vegetable, depending on its size and age. Drain and cool. Place the vegetables in a large bowl and stir mayonnaise (page 11) into them.

5 **Serving.** Toss the vegetables together with the dressing and season the vegetable filling to taste with salt and freshly ground black pepper. Heap a large spoonful of filling in the center of each artichoke bottom. Garnish, if you like, with parsley or chervil.

3 **Moistening the vegetables.** Place a little of the vegetable cooking liquid in a small bowl and set the bowl in ice to cool the liquid. When the vegetables and liquid are cool, remove them from the ice and transfer them to a deep dish. Spoon the liquid over the vegetables to flavor them.

4 **Serving.** Flavor mayonnaise with red pepper that has been broiled, peeled, seeded, deribbed and chopped (page 10). Drain the vegetables. Spoon a little mayonnaise into each pepper. Stand the broccoli florets, asparagus spears and snow peas in the pepper cases. Here, uncooked leaves of Belgian endive are included in the assembly; chicory leaves provide a garnish for the plate. Pass additional mayonnaise separately.

Packages Wrapped in Edible Leaves

With only a little effort, individual cabbage, Swiss chard, spinach, lettuce or grapevine leaves can be made flexible enough to wrap around a stuffing. The first step in preparing the leaves is to remove tough parts that would resist rolling—stems and, for Swiss chard and cabbage, the thick central ribs. Most fresh leaves should then be briefly immersed in boiling water so that they become supple enough to roll without cracking. Vine leaves preserved in brine need to be well rinsed in cold water to remove the brine, but because they have been blanched before preserving, they do not require the boiling-water treatment.

Although boiling water will soften the leaves, further moist cooking is needed to blend their flavor with those of the stuffing. Fill the softened leaves with a partly cooked stuffing that will complete its cooking wrapped in the leaves. The fresh vine leaves used here enclose a stuffing of half-cooked rice, pine nuts and dried currants *(recipe, page 98)*. The rice will swell as it continues to cook, but the leaves are supple enough to hold it without bursting. You can, of course, vary the stuffing and use a meat-based one instead *(recipes, pages 97-98)*.

The leaf parcels cannot be boiled: The agitation would cause them to unroll and disgorge their stuffing. Instead, they are packed tightly into a pot and weighted down with a plate. They start their cooking moistened with oil and completely immersed in liquid—in this demonstration, veal stock *(recipe, page 163)*. By the end of cooking, the stuffing will have absorbed the liquid; the wrapping and stuffing will be tender and the stuffing imbued with the sharp flavor of the leaves.

1 Preparing vine leaves. Make a V-shaped incision in the base of each vine leaf to cut off the stem and the first ¼ inch [6 mm.] of the thick veins that branch from it. Pile the leaves in a deep bowl and pour boiling water over them. Let them stand for about five minutes to soften. Drain the leaves in a colander.

2 Preparing filling. Sauté chopped onions in olive oil for about five minutes until soft. Stir in white rice and cook gently for two or three minutes, until the rice turns opaque. Add dry ingredients— here, pine nuts, currants and parsley— and enough water to cover them. Simmer about 10 minutes, until the rice is dry. Mix in tomato sauce *(page 7)*.

4 Arranging the rolls. Line the bottom of a deep, heavy pot with leaves to prevent sticking. Arrange a layer of leaf parcels on top. To keep the parcels from unrolling, position them with their flaps underneath. Fill the pot with layers of leaves alternating with layers of rolls, ending with a layer of leaves. Moisten the leaves with oil.

5 Cooking the rolls. To prevent the parcels from floating in the braising liquid and unrolling, fit an inverted plate into the pot. Fill the pot up to the plate with veal stock or water containing a few drops of lemon juice. Cover; bring to a boil over medium heat, then reduce the heat. Simmer gently for 45 minutes to one hour.

3 **Stuffing the leaves.** Lay a leaf on a work surface, glossy side down. Place a spoonful of stuffing close to the base of the leaf. Fold the lowest pair of leaf sections over the filling *(above, left)*, then fold in the middle sections *(center)*. Starting at the fold, roll the leaf around the filling toward its top *(right)*, making a neat parcel. Stuff more leaves in the same way, but reserve enough unstuffed leaves to make three or four flat layers in the pot.

6 **Serving the rolls.** When nearly all of the braising liquid has been absorbed and the parcels are easily pierced with a knife tip, drain them and arrange them on a platter *(left)*. Include two or three rolls in each serving *(above)*; accompany them, if you like, with a velouté sauce enriched with egg yolks and lemon juice *(recipe, page 163)*.

Baking to Blend Flavors

Baking gives stuffed vegetables appealing textural contrasts: The assemblies emerge from the dry heat of the oven crisp and golden on top, yet tender and moist within.

Containers made from quick-cooking vegetables such as tomatoes or mushrooms *(top demonstration at right)* require the least preliminary preparation. They need only be cleaned, trimmed and hollowed out as necessary, then given a light coating of oil or butter to prevent them from burning during their brief sojourn in the oven.

Because their cooking time is short, vegetable cases of this type should be filled either with stuffings that require no cooking at all—soft cheeses mixed with herbs, for instance—or with precooked mixtures. Stuffings that contain meat or fish are usually sautéed beforehand to cook the ingredients. Mushroom stuffing—the mixture of mushrooms, aromatic vegetables and seasonings called *duxelles (Step 2, top; recipe, page 164)*—is cooked to rid the mushrooms of excess fluid and bring out their flavor.

Once stuffed, quick-cooking vegetable containers are topped with ingredients that will crisp and brown to a gratin finish. Bread crumbs and grated cheese are both suitable.

Vegetable cases that need relatively long periods of cooking—hollowed-out onions, peppers or fennel bulbs *(bottom demonstration)*—require somewhat different preparation to prevent drying. In most instances, the vegetables are parboiled *(pages 16-17)* before baking to soften them somewhat, thus reducing the baking time. These containers can be filled with either uncooked or cooked stuffings. Once stuffed and arranged in their baking dish, the vegetables should be masked with liquid—cream, perhaps, or the tomato sauce shown here—to keep them moist as they bake.

Bread crumbs or grated cheese sprinkled on top of the vegetable assemblies will provide a crisp finish, but to keep these coatings from drying out during their relatively long baking time, you should either sprinkle oil or melted butter over them or, in the case of bread crumbs, sauté the crumbs in butter before adding them to the dish.

Mushroom Caps Stuffed and Gratinéed

1 **Coating mushrooms.** Wipe large mushrooms clean. Pull off, chop and reserve the stems. Place the caps in a large bowl, pour on vegetable oil and, with your hands, gently turn the caps in the oil to coat them completely. Arrange the coated mushroom caps close together in a gratin dish.

2 **Making duxelles.** Sauté chopped onions in butter until they are soft— approximately five minutes. Add the mushroom stems and stir them over high heat for 10 minutes, until they look dry. Add salt, pepper, chopped parsley and lemon juice and cook for two more minutes, until the juice evaporates.

Fennel Stalks Topped with Tomato

1 **Separating fennel stalks.** Cut the green upper stems and feathery leaves from fennel bulbs. Cut a slice from the bottom of each bulb to release its stalks so that you can separate them. Pull the bulb apart into stalks. Reserve the fennel hearts for the stuffing.

2 **Removing strings.** The three or four largest stalks from each bulb have coarse fibers on their outer surfaces. To remove the fibers, cut into the top of the stalk with a small knife. Grasp a few fibers firmly between the blade and your thumb and pull them toward the stalk base. Repeat to remove all fibers.

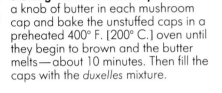

3 **Stuffing the mushroom caps.** Place a knob of butter in each mushroom cap and bake the unstuffed caps in a preheated 400° F. [200° C.] oven until they begin to brown and the butter melts—about 10 minutes. Then fill the caps with the *duxelles* mixture.

4 **Serving.** Prepare bread crumbs from stale bread, or dry fresh bread crumbs in a 425° F. [220° C.] oven for 10 minutes. Sprinkle the crumbs on each stuffed mushroom cap *(inset)*. Put the gratin dish back in the oven for five minutes—or under a hot broiler for two minutes—until the crumbs are crisp and brown *(right)*.

3 **Stuffing the fennel.** Parboil the fennel stalks for five minutes in salted water to soften them slightly; drain the stalks on a towel. Allow about 1 cup [¼ liter] of stuffing for six stalks; in this case, 24 stalks are stuffed with a mixture of 3 cups [¾ liter] of fresh bread crumbs, 9 tablespoons [135 ml.] of butter, three eggs, the chopped fennel hearts, parsley and coriander. When the stalks cool, fill each one and press the edges together around the stuffing. Arrange the stalks close together in a buttered gratin dish.

4 **Serving the fennel.** Coat the stuffed fennel with tomato sauce *(page 7)*. Sprinkle the top with grated firm cheese— Parmesan, Cheddar or Gruyère, for example—or with bread crumbs sautéed in plenty of butter. Bake in a 375° F. [190° C.] oven for 50 minutes to one hour, until the sauce has thickened and the top of the assembly has browned. Serve immediately.

Deep Frying for Textural Contrast

Deep frying keeps any kind of vegetable juicy and succulent while endowing it with a crunchy crust. The vegetables themselves must be cut small: In the high heat deep frying demands, large pieces would scorch on the surfaces before the interiors could cook through. Cut the vegetables into slices or chunks no thicker than ½ inch [1 cm.], or into even thinner julienne. If cut into slices or chunks, dense vegetables such as carrots and turnips should be parboiled almost to tenderness before frying to ensure that they cook completely without burning: This preliminary is unnecessary if dense vegetables are cut into quick-cooking julienne *(top demonstration)*.

However they are cut, almost all vegetables must be given a protective coating before frying to keep their surfaces from burning and drying. The exceptions are potatoes, which are protected by their own starch, and leaves such as spinach, which spend only seconds in the oil.

If you use a batter coating, make it thin so that the hors d'oeuvre remains delicate. Japanese tempura batter is chosen here for the julienned vegetables and snow peas that accompany them. It is kept lumpy by chilling, which prevents the flour from absorbing liquid evenly; this gives the vegetables an appealing lacy surface. Alternatively, you could coat the vegetables with layers of flour, beaten egg and either cornmeal or—as with the eggplant slices in the bottom demonstration at right—bread crumbs flavored with cheese.

For the deep-frying medium, use a mild-flavored vegetable oil such as peanut oil. You can also use lard, although its flavor does not please all tastes. The oil must be preheated to the correct temperature—375° F. [190° C.]—and that temperature must be scrupulously maintained: If the oil is too cool, the coating will absorb it and become soggy; if it is too hot, the coating will scorch. Monitor the oil temperature with a deep-frying thermometer. To keep from lowering the temperature during cooking, fry only a few vegetable pieces at a time.

Crisp Morsels with Lacy Batter Coatings

1 **Preparing vegetables.** Pull off the strings of snow peas. Peel carrots, and julienne them by slicing them lengthwise into strips ⅓ inch [1 cm.] thick. Slice unpeeled zucchini into julienne of the same thickness.

2 **Mixing batter.** In a bowl set in a larger, ice-filled bowl, beat eggs briefly. Stir in ice water, then add flour. Stir the ingredients only long enough to moisten the flour: The batter should be lumpy.

Eggplant Fans with Crunchy Crusts

1 **Slicing the eggplant.** Cut unpeeled eggplant into cross sections ½ inch [1 cm.] thick. To form fans, slice through the peel on one edge of each cross section, angling the cuts *(above)*. Salt the slices on both sides to draw out their bitter juices and let them drain for 30 minutes in a colander.

2 **Coating with flour.** Mix fine bread crumbs and freshly grated Parmesan cheese in a shallow bowl. Place flour in another bowl. Rinse the drained eggplant slices and pat them dry with paper towels. Turn each slice of eggplant in the flour to coat both sides; gently shake off excess flour.

3 **Deep frying.** In a deep, heavy pan, heat a layer of vegetable oil at least 3 inches [8 cm.] deep to a temperature of 375° F. [190° C.]. Working in small batches, drop the whole snow peas and julienned vegetables into the prepared batter; using tongs, transfer the vegetables to the hot oil. Let them fry for about a minute, until the batter coating puffs and begins to turn golden. Turn the vegetables over and let them cook to the same stage on the other side; this will take about a minute. Transfer the vegetables to a rack covered with paper towels to drain.

4 **Serving.** When all of the snow peas and julienned vegetables have been cooked, fry rinsed and well-dried spinach leaves in the oil for about 15 seconds. Drain the leaves on the paper towels. Use the spinach leaves to garnish each serving of vegetables, and pass lemon wedges separately.

3 **Adding flavor.** Beat eggs with chopped herbs—here, basil and oregano. Lift each eggplant slice by its uncut edge, splaying the sections apart, and dip the slice into the egg. Sprinkle bread-crumb mixture on one side of each slice; drop the slice into the mixture to coat its other side. Let the slices dry on a rack for 10 to 15 minutes.

4 **Cooking.** Fry the slices for two minutes, turning them once, in deep oil heated to a temperature of 375° F. [190° C.]. Drain the slices on paper towels. Serve them with lemon wedges or, if you like, tomato sauce.

2

Poultry and Meat
A Light Touch
with Hearty Fare

How to bone a chicken breast
Marinades that add zest
Preliminary preparations for organ meats
A sausage founded on chicken
Puréed bases for a multi-layered mousse

Tender sweetbreads with velouté and brandy are spooned into the hollow of a miniature molded rice ring. To make the ring, the cook need only pack freshly boiled hot rice—flecked here with chopped parsley and chives—into small buttered molds; the rice is sticky enough to retain the shape of the mold when it is turned out.

Meats are usually considered the foodstuffs for main courses but, if handled with discretion, any meat or fowl can produce a tempting hors d'oeuvre. The secret is to be certain that the portions are small and the presentations imaginative.

In many instances, the simplest and sparest treatment is the most appropriate. Whole slices of poultry or meat, for instance, can be offered as a first course, as long as the slices are thin and the garnishes uncloying. A range of delicious hors d'oeuvre is made simply by marinating poultry or meat, before or after cooking, in ingredients that endow it with bright, sharp flavors. The marinade may consist of a mixture of wine, aromatic vegetables and herbs *(pages 28-29)*; or, for additional sharpness, you could use a blend of lemon or orange juice and such flavorings as ginger and soy sauce *(page 31)*. When the meat or poultry is served, the marinade can become a light sauce for it. For another effect, meat slices can be pounded paper-thin so that they are flexible, then wrapped around vegetables or fruit and sautéed to a golden finish; the result is tidy, individual first-course packages.

More elaborate presentations are best suited to delicate organ meats such as brains or sweetbreads *(pages 32-35)*. These fine-textured foods are handsomely complemented by smooth, rich sauces. Because of their richness, such hors d'oeuvre must be served in extremely small portions. To keep the dishes from daunting the diners, arrange the hors d'oeuvre in dainty single servings, using small gratin dishes, miniature rings of rice *(opposite)* or the various pastry and bread cases that are demonstrated on pages 76-77, 82-83 and 88.

Meat that is finely chopped or puréed rather than sliced forms the basis for another group of appealing hors d'oeuvre. Among them are the white sausages traditionally served during the Christmas season in France; these are made by filling sausage casings with mixtures of mild-flavored chicken, almonds, seasonings and cream, then gently poaching the assemblies in milk and water *(pages 36-37)*. And puréed meats provide yet another traditional group of first-course dishes: When the meats are mixed with flavorings, butter or cream and, in some cases, gelatinous stock, they form velvety mousses that can be spread on slices of toast and garnished, or served as molded presentations *(pages 38-41)*.

Marinated Fowl in Wafer-thin Slices

Of the meats used for hors d'oeuvre, poultry is perhaps the most natural choice because of its mild flavor. The most attractive presentations are those based on boned, trimmed poultry breasts.

Duck, turkey and chicken all are suitable candidates, and preliminaries are the same for all. Chicken and turkey breasts sometimes are sold separately from the rest of the bird, but you can buy any whole bird and remove the breast yourself. To do so, lay the bird on its back and use a long, sharp knife to sever the legs and wings. Slide the knife into the cavity of the bird and slice through the rib cage and flesh on either side of the backbone. You then will be able to pull breast and back apart and cut through the shoulder blades that join them, thus freeing the breast section.

The legs, wings and back of a bird cut up this way can be reserved for other uses; the breast section will be left with a breastbone in the center and ribs on each side, all attached at one end by cartilage to collarbones and the wishbone. All of these can be removed as demonstrated in Steps 1 through 4 at right.

You can either cook the delicate boned meat immediately or, for additional flavor, marinate it beforehand. The marinade should include acidic ingredients, such as lemon juice or white wine, which help tenderize the meat. It will also need extra liquid such as stock, and oil and flavorings. Powerful seasonings should be avoided, lest the flavors of the marinade eclipse the taste of the meat.

Poaching in liquid is the cooking method that best preserves the juiciness of breast meat. You can use stock as a medium or, if you have marinated the bird, the marinade. To preserve tenderness, the cooking must be gentle—the liquid should barely simmer—and brief.

The breast, sliced thin, may be served either warm or cool. A spoonful of marinade makes a good accompaniment to the meat in either case. Alternatively, you could serve warm slices with béarnaise sauce *(recipe, page 162)* and cool ones with mayonnaise *(recipe, page 161)*.

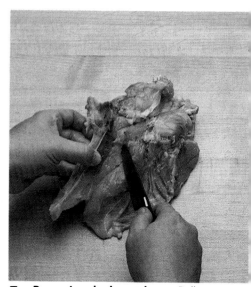

1 Removing the breastbone. Pull the skin and fat from a poultry breast—here, that of a 6-pound [3-kg.] capon. Slit open the membrane covering the breastbone. Make shallow cuts all around the bone to expose its edges. To free the bone, slice under the edges and cut through the cartilage that connects it to the collarbones.

5 Marinating the meat. In a nonreactive pan, boil 4 cups [1 liter] of dry vermouth until it is reduced by half—about 15 minutes. In another pan, sauté equal amounts of chopped shallots, leeks and scallions in olive oil with a few tarragon leaves until the vegetables are just limp. Add the vegetables and 1 cup [¼ liter] of chicken stock *(recipe, page 163)* to the reduced wine. Arrange the breast meat in a nonreactive baking dish, ladle the marinade over it and season it. Cover the dish with foil or plastic wrap and set it aside for at least two hours.

6 Poaching the meat. Pour the marinade into a nonreactive saucepan, set it over low heat and bring it to a simmer. Poach each section of breast meat separately in the marinade, using tongs to turn it. The two larger fillets will require about four minutes of cooking on each side to firm them, the two smaller fillets about two minutes on each side. Strain the cooking liquid and reserve it. Cool the meat to room temperature; you may either slice and serve the meat immediately *(Steps 7 and 8)*, or refrigerate the meat and bring it to room temperature before serving it.

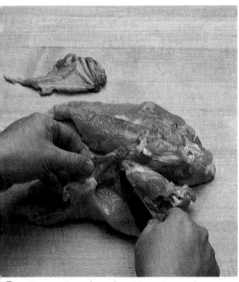

2 **Removing the ribs.** Slice through the cartilage that connects the rib cage to the collarbones on one side of the breast. Lift the exposed end of the rib cage with one hand, slicing under the bones to free them completely. Repeat on the other side of the breast.

3 **Removing collarbones.** The breast halves will remain attached at one end by the collarbones. Starting at the outer end of each bone, cut through the flesh that covers it, following the contours carefully. When the collarbone structure is attached only at the center, lift it up and slice it free.

4 **Removing the wishbone.** Feel the wishbone beneath the flesh and carefully cut away the flesh to expose it. Then lift the wishbone and cut it free. Separate the breast halves by cutting them apart, and trim away any extra fat or membrane from each. Detach the small loose fillet of meat along the inside of each breast half.

7 **Slicing.** For serving, cut each breast piece horizontally into long slices about 1/8 inch [3 mm.] thick. Steady the meat with your finger tips as you slice it.

8 **Serving.** Arrange slices of meat attractively on each serving plate. Garnish them with fresh parsley, watercress or—as here—tarragon and strips of broiled, peeled red pepper (page 10). Moisten each serving with the reserved cooking liquid.

Surprising Adaptations of Main-Course Meats

Veal Roulades with Tender Cores of Leek

Rich meats such as beef and veal are traditionally regarded as main-course fare, but they can also be presented as hors d'oeuvre. The portions of meat should be small, and any accompanying ingredients should be light. Both of these requirements are filled by small versions of the stuffed meat rolls known as roulades, or by marinated meat that is cooked, then served in paper-thin strips.

For rolls, the meat should be cut from a boneless piece consisting of only one muscle; the resulting slices will be free of connective membranes that could part during rolling and cooking. Veal roulades—demonstrated at right—can be made from loin roasts, bottom round or top round, cut across the grain. Appropriate beef cuts are bottom round and top round. Partially freeze the meat to firm it and make it easy to slice thin. After cutting, pound it lightly to break down meat fibers; this will give the slices the flexibility needed for rolling and will also minimize shrinkage during cooking.

Fillings for meat rolls should never be assertive or heavy. Parboiled aromatic vegetables such as celeriac or Jerusalem artichoke strips, fennel stalks, celery or leeks—used here—are good choices.

Once assembled, the rolls are briefly sautéed to give them a brown finish. Any sauce served with the rolls should be delicate. In this demonstration, the sauce is simply cream combined with leeks that have been chopped and sautéed. Fresh tomato sauce—enriched, if desired, with sour cream—and béarnaise sauce are other suitable options (recipes, page 162).

Meat to be served in slices without a filling can come from almost any boneless cut; flank steak is used in the demonstration opposite. A preliminary marinade will tenderize the meat and lend interesting flavor.

To preserve juiciness, the meat should be cooked in one piece—it can be either broiled or sautéed—and it should be left rare. Minimal cooking is particularly important for flank steak, which becomes tough when well done. After cooking, the meat can be sliced thin and, like the roulades, given only the lightest of garnishes—a little reserved marinade, perhaps, and sliced vegetables or fruit.

1 **Preparing leeks.** Cut off the base and all but about 3 inches [8 cm.] of the green tops from 10 leeks. Make two lengthwise cuts from the top of each leek. Rinse the leeks thoroughly in cold water. Reserve two leeks; parboil the rest until tender—five to 10 minutes. Plunge the parboiled leeks into cold water to stop the cooking, then drain them.

2 **Slicing veal scallops.** Freeze a thick veal steak—here a 1-pound [½-kg.] piece of round—for 30 minutes to firm it. Trim any fibrous connective tissue from the chilled steak. Keeping the meat firmly flattened with the finger tips of one hand, cut the steak horizontally into eight slices ¼ inch [6 mm.] thick.

5 **Browning the rolls.** In a skillet over medium heat, sauté the veal rolls in olive oil and butter. Turn the rolls with tongs so that they brown evenly. They will be browned and cooked through in about five minutes. Remove the skillet from the heat. Chop the raw leeks and measure their volume; set aside half this amount of heavy cream.

6 **Serving.** In a skillet, sauté the chopped leeks in butter until soft; add the cream and cook for about five minutes more so that the leeks can absorb the cream. To serve, ladle some leek sauce onto each plate. Then remove the strings from a veal roll and place the roll on the sauce. Garnish, if you like, with a basil leaf.

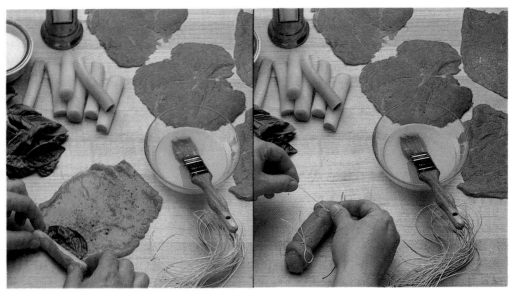

3 **Pounding the meat.** Cut each meat slice in half. Place one piece of the meat at a time between two sheets of wax paper or parchment paper and lightly pound it with a veal pounder or mallet to flatten it.

4 **Stuffing and rolling.** Cut the parboiled leeks slightly shorter than the width of the flattened meat slices. Brush each slice with melted butter and sprinkle on salt and pepper. Then place a fresh basil leaf near one end of the slice, lay a leek on top of the basil (above, left) and roll the meat to enclose the leek. Tuck in the edges of the slice as you roll, to form a neat, compact package. Tie a string around each end of the roll, using simple knots that will be easy to undo later (right).

A Citrus Counterpoint for Flank Steak

1 **Searing.** Steep a flank steak for two hours in marinade—here, ginger, hot chili, orange peel, garlic, soy sauce, oil, vinegar and orange juice. Drain the meat and dry it; reserve the marinade. In a skillet, brown the meat in hot oil on both sides; a steak 1 inch [2½ cm.] thick will take four or five minutes in all.

2 **Slicing the meat.** Let the meat cool. Peel the skin and white pith from three or four oranges and cut them into slices ¼ inch [6 mm.] thick. Hold the thick end of the steak firmly with one hand and cut across the grain to make slices ¼ inch thick (above), keeping the knife blade at a slight angle over the meat.

3 **Serving.** Lay a bed of watercress on a large platter. Arrange alternating rows of meat slices and orange slices on the watercress, letting the rows overlap slightly. Strain the marinade and spoon a little over each row of meat slices before serving.

Brains in a Golden Gratin

Because they are both light and delectably rich, brains make excellent hors d'oeuvre. Careful preliminary treatment will ensure that they retain their pale color and creamy texture. The options for presentation are numerous.

Beef, lamb and calf's brains all are appropriate for hors d'oeuvre, but calf's brains are commonly considered to have the best flavor. The brains that you buy should be pale pink, plump and evenly formed; a calf's brain weighs about ½ pound [¼ kg.] and will serve two people. Brains, like all organ meats, are highly perishable; cook them as soon as possible after you purchase them. Raw brains will keep for only two days in the refrigerator.

Before cooking, blood flecks and bits of surface membrane should be removed from the brains: The blood would affect the flavor and muddy the pale color of the meat, and the surface membrane might contract during cooking and distort the shape of the brains. Soaking the brains in cold water *(Step 2)* facilitates both tasks.

After the brains have been soaked and cleaned, they are ready for cooking. To firm the meat without damaging its texture, poach the brains very gently. The poaching liquid should contain acidic ingredients, which will help preserve the paleness of the flesh; in this demonstration, the poaching medium is a court bouillon flavored with vinegar.

Once cooked, brains can be garnished and served as you please. You might cool and slice them, dress them with vinaigrette sauce *(recipe, page 160)* and serve them as a salad. Or make the brains part of a hot assembly: Combine brain slices with mild-flavored vegetables, coat the ingredients with a sauce and bake them briefly to form golden-surfaced gratins. Here, for instance, brains are assembled with tomatoes and a flavored white sauce *(recipe, page 162);* the cooking vessels are small gratin dishes, which make tidy individual servings.

1 Draining excess liquid. Plunge tomatoes in boiling water to loosen the skins. Peel, halve and seed the tomatoes; cut them into chunks. Lay them on a piece of cheesecloth or muslin and salt them lightly to draw out their moisture. Gather the cheesecloth into a bag; tie it around the neck with string and hang it from a tap over a sink. Let the tomatoes drain while you clean and poach the brains.

5 Filling gratin dishes. Melt butter in a shallow pan. Add the drained tomatoes and stew them over low heat for one to two minutes, tossing them gently to keep them intact. Arrange the sliced brains in one layer in individual gratin dishes or large scallop shells. Place the tomato pieces in the spaces between the brains.

6 Flavoring a white sauce. Season *duxelles (page 22)* to taste with salt, pepper, nutmeg, chopped fresh parsley and strained fresh lemon juice; with a wooden spoon, stir the *duxelles* into a basic white sauce *(page 6)*. Stir in a little cream to thin the mixture.

2 **Cleaning brains.** Soak calf's brains in cold acidulated water *(page 16)* for at least an hour. Pull off any pieces of surface membrane *(above)*. If any blood remains on the brains, soak them in fresh cold water for another 30 minutes to remove all traces.

3 **Poaching in court bouillon.** Make a vinegar court bouillon *(recipe, page 164)*. Bring the court bouillon to a gentle simmer and poach the brains, with the pan lid ajar, for 15 to 20 minutes. Lift the brains out of the court bouillon with a large slotted spoon.

4 **Slicing the brains.** If you do not use the brains at once, cover them with a towel soaked in the court bouillon so that they remain moist and white. Cut the brains across the grain into slices ½ inch [1 cm.] thick.

7 **Coating the brains and tomatoes.** Generously ladle the mushroom-flavored sauce over the brains and tomatoes in each gratin dish. Grate some cheese—preferably Parmesan or Gruyère—and sprinkle it over the sauce. If you like, you can sauté bread crumbs in butter and scatter these over each of the gratins along with, or instead of, the grated cheese.

8 **Baking and serving.** Set the gratin dishes on a baking sheet and place them in a preheated 475° F. [250° C.] oven for five to eight minutes—or until the contents are warmed all the way through and the top of the sauce is lightly browned. Remove the gratins from the oven. Protecting your hands with a towel or hot pad, place each hot gratin dish on a plate and serve.

Sauced Sweetbreads in Rings of Rice

Like brains, sweetbreads make a first course that is distinctively rich and light. And, if properly prepared, sweetbreads lend themselves to many presentations.

Sweetbreads are the thymus glands of calves and lambs. If possible, choose veal sweetbreads, a designation that means they come from very young calves: They have the finest flavor. All sweetbreads are sold in two-lobed pairs, which should weigh between ¾ and 1¼ pounds [350 and 600 g.]. Like brains, sweetbreads should be cooked as soon as possible after they are purchased; do not keep them longer than two days.

Preliminary preparations for sweetbreads are similar to those for brains. If the butcher has not already done so, you must remove all traces of blood and surface membrane from the meat. To do this, soak the sweetbreads in acidulated water to preserve their whiteness, then parboil them (Step 1) in fresh acidulated water, after which you will be able to peel off the membrane. The peeled sweetbreads

should be weighted (Step 3) to compress their rather loose-textured flesh so that it can be easily cut into thin slices.

Prepared sweetbreads are suitable for poaching, braising, broiling or sautéing (recipes, pages 114-116), and they may be combined with cooked vegetables, with scrambled eggs, or with sauces ranging from velouté to tomato. In the demonstration at right and below, the meat is braised with shallots and mushrooms in veal stock (pages 8-9) enlivened with brandy (recipe, page 163); after cooking, the flavored stock can be turned into a rich sauce for the meat.

Thinly sliced and covered with sauce, the sweetbreads may be simply presented on a platter. But to make pretty individual servings—always desirable in a first course—provide containers for the meat and sauce. Use individual gratin dishes, as shown on pages 32-33, or, as here, rings of rice, formed by packing hot rice into small, ring-shaped molds, then carefully turning them out.

1 **Soaking sweetbreads.** Soak sweetbreads in cold acidulated water (page 16) for at least an hour to remove any blood. To firm them, place them in a pan of fresh cold acidulated water, bring them slowly to a simmer and cook gently for about two minutes. Drain the sweetbreads, and run cold water over them to stop the cooking.

5 **Basting the sweetbreads.** Bring the stock to a boil, reduce the heat and cover the pan. Simmer gently for 30 minutes, basting the sweetbreads with the pan liquid every 10 minutes or so. Add more stock as needed to keep the liquid from evaporating completely.

6 **Thickening the liquid.** Remove the sweetbreads with a slotted spoon and set them aside. The cooking liquid will be syrupy; to thicken it, as here, stir in knobs of beurre manié—about 1 tablespoon [15 ml.] of softened butter mashed with 1½ tablespoons [22 ml.] of flour. Continue cooking and stirring until the liquid thickens.

7 **Slicing the sweetbreads.** Cut each sweetbread lobe crosswise into thin slices. Return the slices to the pan with the thickened cooking liquid and keep them warm over very low heat. Boil unprocessed long-grain rice until it is tender. Let the cooked rice cool for 10 minutes, then stir in equal amounts of chopped fresh parsley and chives.

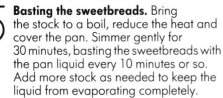

2 **Removing the membrane.** Peel the surface membrane and attached fat and gristle from each sweetbread lobe. Do not delve too deeply or you will break the lobes apart. Place the peeled sweetbreads in a bowl lined with a clean, dry towel.

3 **Weighting sweetbreads.** Cover the sweetbreads with another clean, dry towel and place a second bowl, slightly smaller in diameter than the first, on top of them. Place bricks or an equivalent weight—a 3-pound [1½-kg.] food can, for instance—in the second bowl. Refrigerate the weighted sweetbreads for about two hours.

4 **Cooking the sweetbreads.** In a large pan, sauté chopped shallots in butter until limp; add sliced mushrooms and cook until softened. Lay the sweetbreads on the bed of vegetables *(above)* and pour in brandy. Cook over high heat until the brandy evaporates; add veal stock. Season to taste with salt and pepper.

8 **Serving with molded rice.** While the rice is still hot, pack it firmly into small, buttered ring molds with a spoon *(left)*. Keep each filled mold warm in a shallow pan containing about ¼ inch [6 mm.] of hot water. Unmold each rice ring in the center of an individual serving plate. Spoon the sweetbreads into the center of each ring and serve garnished with parsley *(above)*.

Sausages with a Subtle Stuffing

Pleasantly rustic hors d'oeuvre are made by chopping meat or poultry, combining it with fat and flavorings, and stuffing the mixture into casings. Gentle poaching blends the flavors of the ingredients; brief broiling gives the sausages an appetizing finish.

The stuffing mixture for first-course sausages should be mild in flavor. In the demonstration at right the sausages include chopped roasted chicken, bread simmered in milk, onions stewed in veal stock, almond-scented cream, pork fat and egg yolks *(recipe, page 108)*. The pale color of the mixture earns the sausages their French name—*boudins blancs*, literally, "white sausages."

Natural casings—the cleaned intestines of cows, sheep or pigs—are best for homemade sausages. Beef casings make large sausages, lamb casings small sausages. Pork casings, normally used for *boudins blancs*, yield the medium-sized sausages shown here.

Your butcher will supply you with natural casings preserved by brining or dry-salting. Before use, they must be soaked to soften them and to remove the salt, and then rinsed *(box, opposite)*.

The only equipment you need to fill the casings is a pastry bag fitted with a wide tip. The stuffing mixture is squeezed gently from the bag into the casing; it should be packed fairly loosely since it will expand during cooking. The tied sausages should be pricked to prevent bursting, and then poached gently in water or, as here, a blend of milk and water.

Boudins blancs are generally poached as soon as they are formed, left to cool and firm up, and—just before serving—quickly broiled to warm them through and make the skin crisp and palatable. For an especially refined version of the dish, you can slit and peel off the skin after poaching and chilling the sausages. Then, to protect the sausages, roll them in bread crumbs, and baste them with butter during broiling. Without skins, the sausages will be very fragile; handle them with great care.

1 Simmering onions. Put quartered onions in a pan with a bouquet garni, and coriander seeds and cloves tied in cheesecloth or muslin. Add enough veal stock *(pages 8-9)*, with a little of its fat, barely to cover the onions. Simmer the onions, covered, for 30 to 40 minutes—or until they have absorbed the stock. Chop the onions fine.

2 Cooking bread in milk. Slice the crusts off stale bread. Crumble it into a pan and add enough milk almost to cover it. Simmer the mixture, stirring, until it becomes a smooth, firm paste *(above)*—10 to 15 minutes. To prevent sticking, stir frequently at first and then continuously toward the end of cooking.

5 Filling the casing. Fit a wide tip into a pastry bag. Half-fill the bag with the stuffing. Work about a yard [1 meter] of cleaned sausage casing over the tip of the bag, leaving about 3 inches [8 cm.] hanging free. Hold the pastry bag closed at the top and squeeze it gently as you ease off the casing so that the casing fills evenly.

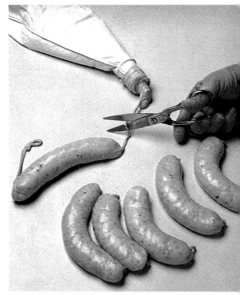

6 Separating the sausages. When you have stuffed enough casing to make a loosely filled sausage 5 to 6 inches [13 to 15 cm.] long, slide off a further 3 inches [8 cm.] of empty casing and cut it with scissors. Knot the spare skin each end of the sausage. Continue making sausages until the stuffing mixture has been used up.

3 **Flavoring cream.** Plunge whole almonds into boiling water. Drain them and pinch off their skins. Pound the almonds to a paste in a mortar or grind them in a food processor, adding a little water to keep the oil from separating out. Bring a pan of heavy cream to a boil. Turn off the heat, add the almonds and steep them for 15 minutes.

4 **Preparing the stuffing.** Skin a roasted chicken breast and chop it fine; dice pork fat. Put the chicken and fat in a bowl with the cooked onions, the bread-and-milk mixture, egg yolks, herbs and seasonings. Hold a sieve over the bowl, tip in the almond cream and press the cream through with a pestle. Mix all of the ingredients thoroughly.

Cleaning Sausage Casings

Rinsing with water. Soak sausage casings in several changes of tepid water for at least two hours, with a splash of lemon juice or vinegar to remove any trace of odor. To clean the casing, attach one end to a funnel and pour cold water through it from a pitcher; or attach the casing to a cold tap and run water through it.

7 **Pricking the sausages.** Trim the knotted ends of the sausages neatly. Prick each sausage all over at 1-inch [2½-cm.] intervals with a trussing needle to allow the steam to escape during poaching and prevent the delicate skin of the sausage from bursting.

8 **Poaching the sausages.** Mix two parts of water and one part of milk in a pan; add salt. Put the sausages into the pan. Set the pan over low heat and bring it just to the simmering point. Cover the pan, reduce the heat and poach the sausages very gently for 40 minutes—or until firm. Lift them out with a slotted spoon (above).

9 **Browning the sausages.** Chill the sausages until you are almost ready to serve them. Place them on a baking sheet. Brush them all over with melted butter and place them under a broiler; turn them occasionally so that they brown evenly. Use two forks to transfer the browned sausages to serving plates (above).

A Smooth Mousse of Chicken Livers

Savory meat mousses—purées that are stiffened, enriched and flavored in various ways *(recipes, pages 109-111)*—provide one of the most versatile elements in hors d'oeuvre cookery. Among them, mousses based on duck, chicken or rabbit livers are the richest in flavor. These easily made purées can lend distinction to either hot or cold assemblies; the technique of forming the purées is essentially the same in either case.

The livers—chicken livers are used in the demonstration here—need minimal preparation. They are first trimmed of any remnants of blood vessels and any green bile stains. Then the livers are briefly sautéed; they should be rare and still moist and flavorful. For extra flavor they can be sautéed with herbs, spices and aromatic vegetables such as the onions and shallots used here; a splash of Cognac added at the end of cooking will give sparkle. The cooked livers will be soft enough to purée through a sieve; they can then be enriched and served warm, at room temperature or cold.

If you plan to serve the mousse warm or at room temperature, the enrichment should be softened butter, which will give the mixture body. The mousse can then be spread on toast or used to fill mushroom caps or small pastry containers. In this demonstration, the purée is spread on toast, then topped with sautéed mushrooms and hollandaise sauce *(recipe, page 162)* and briefly broiled.

If you are planning to serve a cold hors d'oeuvre, the liver purée should be enriched with a mixture of butter and whipped cream: Butter used alone would harden too much during the chilling and spoil the velvety texture of the mousse. The mousse should be refrigerated for at least an hour before serving. Chilled mousse is typically served on a bed of lettuce, accompanied by rectangles of toast. It may also be used as a stuffing for a hollowed-out vegetable container such as a tomato or an artichoke bottom.

1 **Preparing chicken livers.** With a small paring knife, trim off any sections of chicken liver that are stained green—a discoloration caused by proximity to the gall bladder. Cut out and discard the white membrane on each liver, and cut each liver in half.

2 **Sautéing onions.** In a frying pan set over low heat, sauté finely chopped onions in melted butter until they are soft—about five minutes. Raise the heat, add the chicken livers and season with dried mixed herbs—thyme, savory and marjoram were used here—salt and freshly ground pepper.

5 **Enriching the purée.** If you plan to serve the purée warm, as here, add more chunks of softened butter *(above, left)*; gently stir the butter into the livers until it is thoroughly incorporated and the mixture forms a smooth purée *(right)*. If you prefer to serve the purée cold, whip heavy cream until it forms very soft peaks, add it to the livers instead of more butter, and refrigerate until firm.

3 **Cooking the livers.** Sauté the livers for a minute or two, turning them with a wooden spoon *(above, left),* until they are gray on the outside. (If you cut one open, it will still be pink and juicy inside.) If you like, a few seconds before the end of cooking, pour a splash of Cognac into the pan *(right);* then tilt the pan and hold a match to the liquid contents to ignite the alcohol. Roll the pan from side to side until the flames die.

4 **Puréeing the livers.** Transfer the livers and onions to a sturdy, wire sieve set over a large mixing bowl; add chunks of softened butter. With a pestle, press the livers and butter together through the sieve *(above).* Scrape any purée that clings to the mesh of the sieve into the bowl.

6 **Serving the purée.** Press plastic wrap onto the purée and set it aside in a cool place while you toast crustless rectangles of dark rye bread, sauté mushroom caps, prepare hollandaise sauce and chop parsley. Spread purée on the toast *(left),* lay two or three mushrooms on top, spoon on hollandaise sauce and garnish with parsley. Warm the toast rectangles under a broiler *(above)* for one minute and serve immediately.

A Trio of Mousses in a Single Dish

When puréed meats and vegetables are mixed with gelatinous stock *(pages 8-9)* and chilled enough for the stock to set, they can be molded to produce a mousse that features appealing contrasts of color and flavor *(recipe, page 111)*. The technique is not difficult; it requires only careful timing in the preparation of the various purées.

The meats and vegetables chosen for the purées can be varied at will. Among the appropriate meats are chicken, veal, ham, brains and sweetbreads. Vegetables should offer color contrasts: Choose green sorrel, spinach, watercress or peas for one layer; red tomatoes or peppers, white cauliflower or yellow corn can provide other layers.

For each layer of mousse, the basic ingredient is puréed with stock—this eases the puréeing—then mixed with more stock and lightened with whipped cream. Meat purées, once they have been enriched with stock, are quite thick and

can simply be folded together with the cream, then allowed to set. Vegetable purées, however, become very liquid after the addition of stock and would be difficult to combine with the thicker cream. In order to thicken them, vegetable purées are partly set by chilling over ice before they are combined with cream and allowed to set fully.

Because each layer of mousse must set firm before it is able to support the succeeding one, make the mousses in the order you plan to layer them; while one layer is setting, the next can be prepared. A meat-based mousse is customarily chosen for the bottom layer because it is heavier than a vegetable mousse; the meat mousse layer should therefore be formed first.

A glass mold that displays a mousse's rainbow of color is the best choice for a dish of this type. You can choose a large mold, as in this demonstration, or small individual molds.

1 **Puréeing chicken.** Using either a mortar and pestle or a food processor, purée skinned, boned and cooked chicken a handful at a time; as you work gradually add veal stock to make a moist pulp. Season with nutmeg, salt and pepper. If you use a mortar and pestle, pass the puréed meat through a food mill fitted with a fine disk.

5 **Puréeing the sorrel.** Set a sturdy sieve over a bowl. Because sorrel reacts chemically with most metals, choose a sieve with plastic or stainless-steel mesh. With a wooden spoon or pestle, press the sorrel through the sieve; then stir more veal stock into the purée. Season with salt and pepper.

6 **Thickening the sorrel purée.** Set the bowl of sorrel purée in a larger bowl of cracked ice. With a wooden spoon, stir the purée continuously until it thickens—about three minutes. Then fold in lightly whipped cream.

7 **Layering sorrel mousse.** When the chicken mousse has become firm, remove the serving dish from the refrigerator and pour the sorrel mousse on top of it. Spread out and smooth the mousse with a spatula. Return the dish to the refrigerator.

2 **Adding stock and cream.** Whip heavy cream until it forms very soft peaks. Add more veal stock to the chicken purée and stir well with a wooden spoon *(above).* Then fold in the lightly whipped cream.

3 **Molding the mousse.** Pour the chicken mousse into a deep glass serving dish, large enough to hold all of the mousses. With a spatula, smooth the surface of the mousse to make it as level as possible. Refrigerate the dish while you prepare the next mousse.

4 **Cooking the sorrel.** Parboil stemmed, washed sorrel leaves for a few seconds in boiling water, then drain them. Cook them gently in butter in a nonreactive pan, stirring occasionally, until they are very soft— about 20 minutes. Stir in veal stock and cook for five minutes, or until the liquid reduces by half.

8 **Making tomato mousse.** Sauté chopped onion until soft; add white wine and boil the mixture until nearly dry. Add prepared tomatoes *(page 32, Step 1)* and seasonings; simmer for 30 minutes. Add stock and boil to reduce by half. Sieve the mixture, add stock, thicken over ice and add cream *(Steps 5 and 6).*

9 **Layering tomato mousse.** Take the serving dish from the refrigerator and pour the tomato mousse to about ¼ inch [6 mm.] from the rim. Smooth the surface of the mousse and chill the dish until the mousse sets.

10 **Glazing and serving.** Spoon tepid veal stock evenly over the top of the triple mousse to coat it. Chill the dish in the refrigerator for one to two hours to set the glaze. Serve in spoonfuls.

3

Fish and Shellfish

Imaginative Presentations for Delicate Foods

In the cuisines of Asia, Latin America and Europe, fish and shellfish have long provided classic first courses, and with good reason: Delicate in texture and mild in flavor, these foods tempt the appetite but do not sate it. Fish and shellfish hors d'oeuvre, pleasing in their many manifestations, prepare the diner for other pleasures to come.

In Japan, the presentation of perfectly cut and garnished morsels of uncooked fish has been developed into a fine art. The elegant preparations that are used to compose Japanese fish assemblies are known collectively as *sashimi* when the emphasis is primarily on the fish and as *sushi* when the fish is complemented by vinegar-flavored rice *(opposite; demonstrations, pages 46-51)*. Scandinavian cooks make an hors d'oeuvre called *gravlax* by marinating uncooked salmon in salt and herbs to firm its flesh and enhance its flavor *(pages 52-53)*. In Mediterranean and Latin American countries, a first course might well be *seviche* or *escabeche,* formed by steeping raw or cooked fish in highly seasoned acidic marinades that give the flesh an aromatic tang. And the cooks of France and the United States offer a range of delectable assemblies, from stuffed clams and oysters *(pages 56-57)* to airy, cream-enriched mousselines of puréed fish *(pages 60-61)*.

The cardinal rule in preparing any of these dishes is that the basic ingredients be impeccably fresh. Mollusks and such shellfish as lobster and crab spoil with remarkable rapidity and should be bought live. Fish should be as recently caught as possible. If you start out with a whole fish and cut it up yourself *(pages 44-45)*, choose one that has clear, bulging eyes, bright red gills and shiny, tightly clinging scales. Whether it is purchased whole, filleted or sliced into steaks, truly fresh fish has a sweet rather than fishy odor, and its flesh springs back when it is lightly pressed with a finger tip.

Those who choose to prepare dishes of uncooked fish—whether the fish is marinated or not—should be aware that the flesh may contain parasites that can cause painful intestinal disorders. The parasites, undetectable to the untrained eye, can be destroyed by freezing or cooking the fish. Because freezing damages both the texture and flavor of the flesh, however, the very cautious cook would be well advised to offer only cooked-fish hors d'oeuvre.

A black lacquer dish frames an assortment of Japanese *sushi*—morsels of uncooked fish and shellfish on rice—and garnishes. Included here are shrimp, salmon roe, tuna, flounder and rockfish *sushi*, garnished with *nori*, or seaweed, lemon pieces, a carved aspidistra leaf and pickled ginger.

Steps to Perfect Fish Fillets

For perfectly fresh and perfectly shaped boneless pieces of fish, it is best to buy whole fish just before you plan to use them, then—immediately, to preserve freshness—clean and cut up the fish yourself. Basic cleaning rules are the same for all fish. The cutting techniques demonstrated here are those used in Japan to create pristine fillets for *sashimi* and *sushi (pages 46-51)*, but they will serve for any hors d'oeuvre presentation.

Any fish must first be scaled—if it has noticeable scales—then gutted. To scale the fish, scrape a short, rigid knife blade in short strokes against the scales; rinse the fish and wipe it clean. To gut the fish, remove its head, gills and the fins closest to the head, then slit open the visceral cavity and pull out and discard its contents. For the sake of cleanliness, you should wash any work surface touched by the viscera.

The method of dividing up a fish depends on whether the specimen at hand is a flatfish, such as a sole or flounder, or a roundfish, such as a trout or rockfish. A flatfish body consists of two broad, thin sheets of flesh that sandwich the backbone and attached rib bones. To make four neat pieces, use a sharp, flexible knife to divide each broad flesh sheet in two along the backbone, slice free the pair of fillets and skin them *(right, top)*.

The body of a roundfish consists of two thick flesh strips placed side by side with a backbone and ribs running down the center of the body between them. Each flesh strip can be removed in one piece and skinned, then divided lengthwise, if you wish, into two narrow fillets *(right, bottom)*. After skinning, the flesh of any fish to be served uncooked should be moved to a clean work surface; the skin may contain bacteria. Any blood veins should be cut away, and any tiny bones that remain should be pulled out.

If you plan to serve the fish raw, the thin flesh on each fillet that bordered the visceral cavity should be trimmed and discarded: It may contain live bacteria.

Boning and Filleting a Flatfish

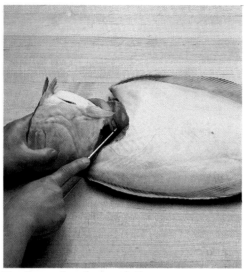

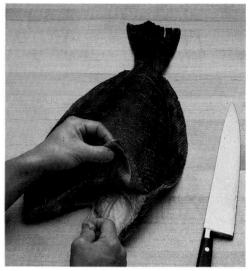

1 Removing the head. Place a flounder with its dark side up on a work surface. Insert a knife into the head behind the eyes and cut in a V shape across the head, around the gills, then down behind the pelvic fin. Turn the fish over and repeat the V-shaped cut on its underside; pull the head away.

2 Gutting the fish. Turn the fish on its belly, with the cavity left by removing the head facing you. Slit the fish along one side just deep enough to expose the visceral cavity. Lift the flap of skin above the cavity; pull out the guts and discard them. Wash the work surface, then turn the fish around again so that its tail is facing you.

Dividing a Roundfish

1 Removing the head. Lay a scaled, rinsed roundfish—here, a rockfish—on its side and grasp its head. Starting at the top of the head, cut around the outside of the gill opening and the fins on the sides and base of the belly. Turn the fish over, repeat the cut and remove the head. Slit the belly to its vent; scrape out and discard the viscera.

2 Slicing. Wash the work surface, then slit the fish from the vent to the tail. Slit open the fish down the length of its back to free the edge of the top fillet. Steady the fish with one hand and, holding the knife parallel to the work surface, slide the blade between the backbone and the flesh near the tail to create a passage through the fish.

3 **Cutting the first fillet.** Cut down the backbone of the fish from the head end to the tail. Slit open both edges of the fish inside the fins and cut across the fish above the tail. Insert the knife at a shallow angle in the center slit above the ribs on one side of the tail end. Lifting the fillet, slice over the ribs to one side slit. Cut the fillet free at the head end.

4 **Completing the filleting.** Turn the fish so that the head end faces you. Insert the knife blade above the backbone at the head end and slice toward the side slit to free the second fillet in the same manner as the first. Turn the fish over and, using the same technique, remove the remaining two fillets.

5 **Skinning.** Lay each fillet with its skin side down and separate ½ inch [1 cm.] of flesh from the skin at the tail end. Pressing down on this skin, insert the knife beneath the flesh and cut the fillet from the skin. Make a diagonal cut across the head end to remove any traces of viscera. Discard this flesh; reserve other trimmings for stock (pages 8-9).

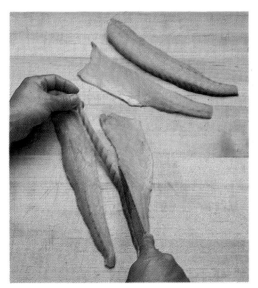

3 **Freeing a fillet.** Join the fingers and thumb of one hand in the passage created at the tail and lift the end of the fish. Insert the knife in the gap and slice down the fish along the backbone just above the ribs to free the top fillet. Detach the fillet at the tail. Turn the fish over and, using the same technique, free the second fillet.

4 **Trimming.** Lay each fillet with its skin side down on the work surface. Slicing at a slight angle from the thick edge of each fillet toward the thinner, belly edge, trim the flesh that surrounded the visceral cavity and any ribs still attached. Discard these pieces. Skin the fillets (Step 5, above). Reserve the trimmings for later use in fish stock.

5 **Removing veins.** To remove the veins and cartilage that run along the center of each fillet and to divide the fillet, cut through the fillet lengthwise along one side of the red center strip. Then cut down the other side of the red strip, pulling it away from the fillet as you cut. Discard the strips.

Sashimi: An Artful Offering of Uncooked Seafood

As examples of light, exquisitely presented hors d'oeuvre, few preparations can match the *sashimi* of Japan, made by cutting raw, boneless fish into dainty pieces, artfully garnishing them, then serving them with condiments that provide a sharp contrast to the mild flesh.

Most firm-fleshed fish—tuna, flounder and mackerel are favorites—can be used for *sashimi*, so long as the fish is absolutely fresh. Japanese cooks stipulate that the fish be refrigerated the moment it is caught and that it be served within 12 hours of leaving the water. To maintain freshness, they leave the skin on the fish until just before serving and touch the fish as little as possible during preparation to avoid warming it. If you wish to make *sashimi*, buy fillets from a reliable fishmonger, or fillet whole fish yourself *(pages 44-45);* in either case,

keep the fish refrigerated except when cutting or serving it.

To divide fillets into the popular *sashimi* shapes shown here, you will need a razor-sharp knife; Japanese cooks hone their knives frequently during the cutting process. The blade may be held at different angles, but the cutting motion remains the same. To keep from crushing the flesh, insert the broad end of the blade first and draw the blade lightly across the flesh; lift the blade at the broad end as you complete the slice.

Of several *sashimi* shapes, the most versatile are paper-thin slices shaved from the side of a fillet. If the slices are laid in an overlapping row, they will adhere and can be formed into a rosette *(opposite, top)*. Or the slices can be wrapped into bundles *(opposite, center)*. Easier-to-produce shapes are rectangles made by

dividing a fillet into cross sections *(opposite, bottom left)*.

Traditional *sashimi* garnishes are sold at Asian markets. For shaping bundles, Japanese chefs use *nori*, dried sheets of seaweed; to enhance the flavor of the *nori*, pass each sheet repeatedly across a medium flame for about one minute before using it. An attractive vegetable garnish is *daikon*, a large white radish that is cut into feathery shreds *(opposite, bottom right);* cucumber and carrot can be treated the same way.

The two condiments usually served with *sashimi* are soy sauce and fiery *wasabi* paste. *Wasabi* is a horseradish-like root grown in Japan. It is sold both as a paste or as a powder at Asian markets. The paste needs no preparation; to prepare the powder, mix it with water and let the mixture rest for 10 minutes.

Serving sashimi. The *sashimi* arrangement above includes fish in three forms: flounder wrapped with cucumber in seaweed, rectangles of flounder and a tuna rosette. Accompaniments are a molded cone of *wasabi* paste, parsley sprigs, a puffy mass of shredded *daikon*, a green leaf, and a lemon slice whose peel has been partly sliced off, then decoratively curled under. To eat the *sashimi*, each diner mixes *wasabi* paste with soy sauce to taste, then lifts a piece of fish with chopsticks and dips it in the sauce.

Coiling a Rosette

1 **Slicing.** Trim a fillet into a rectangle. With the knife at an acute angle to the flesh, cut paper-thin slices across the grain; lay them in an overlapping row.

2 **Rolling.** With the tip of the knife, lift one end of the strip of slices. Use your free hand to roll the strip up tighter on one edge than on the other.

3 **Shaping.** Set the roll with its looser side up. Open the edges of the roll with your fingers, pulling the outside layers farther out than the central ones.

Fish and Cucumber Rolled in Seaweed

1 **Slicing.** Cut strips of seeded cucumber the width of the *nori*. Cut slices from part of a fish fillet *(Step 1, above)* and lay them across the *nori*.

2 **Rolling.** Lay the cucumber strips across the slices of fish and tightly roll the *nori* around the fish. Trim the edges of the bundle; seal them with water.

3 **Cutting.** To prevent the *nori* from sticking to the knife, dampen the blade with cold water. Neatly cut the rolled bundle into cross sections.

The Simplest Shaping

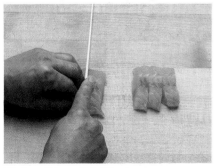

Slicing. Trim a fish fillet into a rectangle. Slicing straight down, cut the rectangle across the grain into strips.

A Crisp Radish Garnish

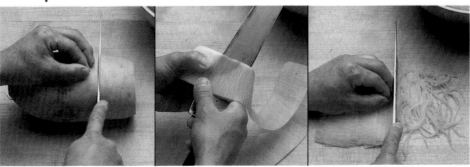

Shredding. Cut a 2-inch [5-cm.] cross section from a *daikon* radish *(above, left)*; peel it and bevel its edges. Cut around the section in one motion, producing a paper-thin strip *(center)*. Cut the strips into lengths, stack them, slice them into shreds *(right)* and crisp them in ice water.

Sushi: An Accent of Tangy Rice

Forming a Parcel by Hand

The ingredients and the cutting and garnishing techniques that produce *sashimi (pages 46-47)* are among those employed in the assembly of another classic Japanese preparation—*sushi*. To make it, vinegar-flavored rice (*sushi* means "vinegared rice") is molded into small shapes that are embellished with a range of meat, fish or vegetable pieces and garnished with various condiments.

The flavored rice *(recipe, page 165)* is simple to make, but attention must be paid to certain details of preparation to ensure that the rice remains properly tender and fluffy. Use raw, unprocessed short-grain rice for *sushi*. Before cooking, rinse the rice thoroughly to wash off surface starch, which would make the cooked rice gummy. Cook and season the rice as demonstrated in Steps 1 to 3 at right, using mild-flavored rice vinegar.

Among the methods of molding the rice, three are shown on this and the following pages. The rice can be molded by hand into small finger shapes, which form suitable platforms for other ingredients *(below)*. Or, with a false-bottomed mold, the rice can be compacted around a filling *(pages 50-51)*. Wooden *sushi* molds are sold at Asian markets. Or you can substitute a false-bottomed tart pan, using a plate slightly smaller than the pan for compressing the rice. A third way of shaping rice is to roll it up with a filling inside a sheet of seaweed. For neat shapes, roll the ingredients with the aid of a flexible bamboo mat *(page 50)*—also sold at Asian markets—or an undyed, flexible straw place mat.

Toppings, fillings and garnishes for *sushi* must be of the same impeccable freshness and must be treated with the same care as those for *sashimi*. Fish should be cut into small, neat pieces; if you use shrimp, cook them and flatten them into tidy shapes, as demonstrated in the box opposite. Suitable garnishes include *wasabi* paste, pickled ginger and soy sauce for dipping, as well as nontoxic leaves such as aspidistra.

1 **Cooking the rice.** Rinse rice until the water runs clear. Drain the rice in a sieve for 20 minutes. In a heavy pan, combine the rice with water, cover the pan, set it over medium heat and bring the water to a boil. If the rice foams over, lift the lid for a second. When the rice boils, lower the heat and simmer it, covered, for eight to 10 minutes.

5 **Pressing ingredients.** Press the wad of rice onto the fish slice, using your forefinger to shape the rice so that it is roughly the length of the fish. Then invert the bundle so that the rice is resting against your palm.

6 **Shaping sushi.** Holding the *sushi* in your palm, use the thumb and forefinger of your other hand to press the sides of the rice, aligning them with the edges of the fish slice. Set the shaped rice and fish aside while you fix another bundle.

7 **Wrapping with nori.** When you have finished forming bundles, cut a sheet of *nori* in half and toast it *(page 46)*. From the half sheet of toasted *nori*, cut two long, thin strips. Wrap one of the strips around each *sushi* bundle. Seal the ends of the strip with a little vinegared water.

2 **Flavoring the rice.** Take the pan off the heat, remove its lid and cover it with a towel. Replace the lid and let the rice stand for 15 minutes. Combine rice vinegar, sugar and salt in a bowl. Empty the rice into a large, shallow dish. Spread the rice, sprinkling it with vinegar dressing as you lightly toss the grains with a flat wooden spatula or paddle.

3 **Cooling the rice.** Continue tossing the rice for about 15 minutes to cool it, using horizontal strokes to keep the grains separate and to prevent them from being mashed. A helper can accelerate the cooling process by using a fan or a piece of cardboard to fan the rice while you toss it. Put the cooled rice into another bowl.

4 **Assembling sushi.** Cut rectangular slices ⅛ inch [3 mm.] thick from a fillet of fish—here, rockfish. Moisten your hands with water flavored with a little vinegar. With one hand squeeze about 1½ tablespoons [22 ml.] of rice into an egg shape. With your other hand, pick up a fish slice. Use your finger to dab *wasabi* paste on the fish.

Straightening and Butterflying Shrimp

1 **Straightening shrimp.** Rinse shrimp and run a skewer lengthwise through each one, starting from the tail end. Bring water and salt to a boil in a large pan. Drop in the shrimp and cook them until the water returns to a boil and the shrimp are pink—about two minutes. Remove them from the pan and plunge them into cold water.

2 **Peeling shrimp.** Drain the cooked, skewered shrimp in a colander. Pull out the skewers. Holding a shrimp by its tail, run your thumb along the underside to separate the shell from the flesh. Peel the shell and attached legs from each shrimp, leaving the tail intact.

3 **Butterflying shrimp.** With a sharp knife, slit open the top of each shrimp. Spread the shrimp open and rinse the flesh in a bowl of cold water. With your fingers, pick out any vein running down the center of the slit. Press the shrimp open and flat; let them drain on paper towels.

Rice and Seafood Pressed in a Mold

1 **Cutting.** Slice two crosswise strips 1 inch [2½ cm.] wide from a flounder fillet *(pages 44-45)*. Lay butterflied shrimp *(box, page 49)* cut sides up and, slicing horizontally, open their flaps of flesh. Flatten out each flap. Cut off the tails. Salt the seafood; let it stand for two minutes. Rinse and dry it. Transfer it to a bowl of rice vinegar.

2 **Layering.** Rinse a wooden *sushi* mold with cold water. Cut an aspidistra leaf or wax paper to fit the mold and lay it, waxy side up, in the bottom. Remove the fish and shrimp from the vinegar and dry them. Lay the slices of fish on the leaf. Trim a shrimp to fit snugly beside the fish, and press the pieces into the mold.

3 **Adding rice.** Moisten your hands with vinegared water and distribute about 2 tablespoons [30 ml.] of vinegared rice *(pages 48-49)* over the fish and shrimp. Dampen the inside of the mold lid and press it onto the rice for about 15 seconds to compact the rice. Cut toasted *nori (page 46)* to fit the mold and lay it on the rice.

A Mat for Wrapping

1 **Layering.** Prepare vinegared rice and *wasabi* paste. Cut a cucumber strip the length of a half sheet of *nori*. Cut tuna into rectangles ½ inch [1 cm.] thick, ½ inch wide and 3 inches [8 cm.] long. Lay the *nori* across a bamboo mat, 1½ inches [4 cm.] from the edge. Distribute about 2 tablespoons [30 ml.] of vinegared rice over the *nori*.

2 **Filling.** Spread the rice layer, leaving a 1-inch [2½-cm.] border along the far edge of the *nori* and a ½-inch [1-cm.] border along either side. With your finger, dab a strip of *wasabi* paste *(page 46)* down the center of the rice. Lay the tuna strips end to end over the *wasabi*. Lay the cucumber strip beside the tuna.

3 **Rolling.** Steady the filling with your fingers and lift the edge of the mat with your thumbs so that the *nori* rolls around the filling. Drape the edge of the mat over the roll. Squeeze the roll into a rectangular shape. Uncover it and seal the flap of *nori* with vinegared water. Transfer the roll to a work surface; slice 1-inch [2½-cm.] pieces crosswise.

4 **Adding the final layer.** Dampen your fingers and palms with vinegared water and press a layer of rice onto the *nori*. Dampen the lid of the mold again and place it on the rice. Press down the mold lid for about 30 seconds.

5 **Starting to free the sushi.** Press down on the mold lid with your thumbs and pull the sides of the mold straight up with your finger tips. Lift the mold off and set it aside. Tilt the lid up carefully so that the block of *sushi* comes away from the base of the mold. Set the lid upside down with the block of leaf-covered *sushi* on top.

6 **Finishing.** Slide a dampened knife blade between the lid and the rice to separate them. Using the flat of a knife or spatula, transfer the block of *sushi* to the work surface. Peel off the aspidistra leaf. Slice even cross sections of molded *sushi*, dampening the knife before cutting each slice.

A Seaweed Cylinder for Roe

1 **Forming a container.** Make vinegared rice and *wasabi* paste. Place salmon roe in a small bowl; cut a lemon slice in eighths. Dampen your hands and shape a tablespoon [15 ml.] of vinegared rice into an oval. Cut a strip of *nori* 1½ inches [4 cm.] wide and wrap it around the rice. Seal the flap of *nori* with vinegared water.

2 **Filling the container.** Dab a small amount of *wasabi* paste on top of the rice. Place a lemon piece on the rice. Spoon about 1 teaspoon [5 ml.] of salmon roe onto the rice.

Scoring a Leaf

Carving. Cut the central rib from an aspidistra leaf. Cut the base from the leaf so that the remainder is 6 inches [15 cm.] long. Fold the leaf lengthwise along its center, waxy surface in. Trim the outer edges so that they are symmetrically and identically curved. Following the curve, score lengthwise slices through the leaf; unfold it.

Salmon Transformed by Salt and Dill

Layered with a dry marinade of salt, sugar, herbs and spices, fillets of raw fish gradually acquire a firm yet tender texture as the salt and sugar draw out their juices. At the same time, the flavors of the seasonings are absorbed by the fish. After a few days' marinating, the fish need only be sliced thin to make a delicious cold hors d'oeuvre.

Gravlax, the traditional Swedish dish shown at right *(recipe, page 121)*, consists of salmon flavored with chopped dill and a mixture of white and black peppercorns in addition to the salt and sugar. You can substitute fresh fennel for the dill, vary the proportions of the pepper to suit your taste, or add a few whole allspice for a more aromatic result.

The dish's name comes from *gravad lax*, or "buried salmon," which may describe how, in times past, the fish was kept cool under a covering of earth while it marinated. Nowadays a refrigerator is a more convenient storage place, and a covering of plastic wrap or aluminum foil prevents the surface of the fish from drying. A weighted board or platter—you can use kitchen weights or 1-pound [½-kg.] food cans—compresses the wrapped fish and accelerates the marinating procedure. Periodically, the fish must be unwrapped, turned over and reweighted so that the salt and seasonings penetrate evenly. Any liquid that has been drawn from the fish should be discarded when the fish is turned.

The treatment will take two to three days, depending on the size of the piece of fish. However, if you prefer the fish to be strongly seasoned, it can be marinated for as long as five days.

1 Removing the upper fillet. Lay a piece of salmon—here, a tail section—on its side. With a long, flexible knife, cut a deep slit along one side of the fish, just above the rib bones. Then, keeping the edge of the knife against the fish's rib bones and backbone, gradually cut and lift away the upper fillet.

2 Removing the bones. Insert the blade of the knife horizontally under the ribs and backbone and carefully peel the bones up and away from the lower fillet. Cut the fillet free at the tail end and discard the bones and tail.

6 Weighting. Cover the salmon with plastic wrap or foil to make an airtight seal. Place a board, as here, or another platter on top of the fish and weight it. Refrigerate the fish for two or three days. Unwrap the fish every 12 hours. Drain liquid and turn the fillets, then reseal and weight them again.

7 Scraping off the marinade. Before serving, unwrap the fish and place it on a kitchen towel to drain. Separate the fillets and place them on paper towels. Scrape off the dry marinade with a knife. Wipe the fish clean with a paper towel. Pick out any tiny bones that remain in the fillets.

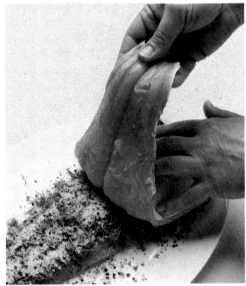

3 **Preparing the marinade.** Using a mortar and pestle, crack white and black peppercorns into small pieces; if you like, you can include a few whole allspice. Stir coarse salt and superfine sugar into the crushed spice mixture.

4 **Coating the fish.** Place one of the salmon fillets skin side down on a platter. Coat the fish evenly with half of the dry marinade mixture. Cut fresh dill coarse and spread a generous layer on top.

5 **Layering the fish.** Distribute the remainder of the dry marinade on top of the dill. Place the second salmon fillet, skin side up, on top of the dry marinade.

 Serving the gravlax. Place each fillet, skin side down, on a carving board. Holding the knife blade almost horizontal, cut across the grain to divide the fillet into thin diagonal slices. Lift the slices off the skin and arrange them on a platter with lemon slices; serve, if you like, with a mustard-and-dill sauce.

Infusing Fragrance with Marinades

When fish is steeped in a wet marinade—an acidic liquid, often mixed with oil, herbs and spices—its flesh develops an aromatic tang. Any firm-fleshed fish lends itself to this treatment: Herring and bass are used here; trout, flounder, sole and red snapper are other good choices. The way the fish is prepared depends on whether the fish will be cooked before it is marinated and on the intensity of flavor you desire.

If the fish will not be cooked before it is marinated, trim it into pieces thin enough to absorb the marinade thoroughly and evenly: The acid in the liquid will turn the flesh firm, white and opaque, as if it was cooked. To achieve the necessary thinness, you can either butterfly it, as shown in the top demonstration, or cut it into fillets or chunks.

Small fish are sometimes sautéed before marination to give them a crisp, brown surface *(bottom demonstration)*. They may simply be cleaned, boned and left whole, or they too can be cut into fillets or chunks.

Marinades range from the straightforward to the complex. If you marinate raw fish, the liquid must be very acidic, for it is the acid that firms the flesh. The marinade used here for the herring consists of lemon juice alone; lime or grapefruit juice may be substituted, and you could augment any of these ingredients with a little oil, aromatic vegetables or herbs. For cooked fish, extreme acidity is not required. Use a marinade with a more complex and assertive taste: Citrus juice or vinegar combined with a generous amount of oil, herbs and aromatics produces a delicious marinade, especially if it is cooked to reduce it and intensify the flavors *(Step 2, bottom; recipe, page 124)*.

The vessel used for marinating the fish should be made of a nonreactive material such as glass: The acid in the marinade will acquire an off taste if the dish is aluminum. If the fish is raw, marinate it in the refrigerator for at least five hours. Serve cooked fish warm after it has been marinated briefly at room temperature or, for stronger flavor, after several hours of refrigeration.

To garnish either sort of dish, choose crisp, sliced vegetables or citrus fruits. Both complement marinated fish.

Butterflied Herrings in Lemon Juice

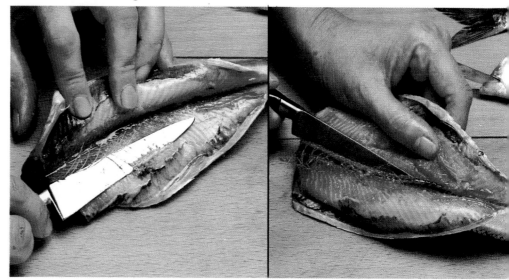

1 **Preparing the fish.** Scale, wash and dry small fish—here, herring. Gut them *(pages 44-45)* and cut off their fins and heads. Spread open each fish and, starting near the backbone, slide a knife blade under the ribs *(above, left)*. Cut the ribs from the flesh on each side. To free the backbone, make a shallow cut along each side of it *(right)*. With your fingers, remove the backbone and attached ribs and any remaining viscera or bones.

Sautéed Sea Bass Bathed in Flavored Vinegar

1 **Boning.** Clean and gut small fish— here, sea bass. Insert a knife into the body cavity and between ribs and flesh at the head end; push the blade to the backbone. Slicing at an angle, separate the ribs and backbone from the fish. Use scissors to free the separated bone structure at the head and tail ends.

2 **Cooking the marinade.** In a nonreactive pan, combine julienned carrots, peppers, onions and ginger with peppercorns, a bay leaf, mace, salt and water. Cover the pan and simmer the contents for 30 minutes. Add olive oil and vinegar and simmer the contents for a minute longer.

2 **Marinating.** Skin the herring and lay them in a shallow dish. Pour in just enough lemon juice to form a shallow layer in the bottom of the dish. Cover and refrigerate the fish. After two or three hours, turn them over; marinate for two or three hours more.

3 **Garnishing.** When the fish is opaque *(inset)*, transfer it to a platter and garnish it. Here, salt anchovies—filleted, soaked for 30 minutes in water to soften them and remove excess salt, then rinsed and patted dry—form a lattice. Strew capers, sliced scallions and broiled, peeled, diced peppers *(page 10)* on top. Moisten the fish with olive oil *(above)*.

3 **Sautéing.** Lightly flour the fish to prevent their delicate skins from disintegrating when they are cooked. Heat oil in a heavy skillet, then sauté the fish over medium heat until they are lightly browned and their flesh is opaque—about one minute on each side. Transfer the fish to a deep dish.

4 **Marinating the fish.** Arrange the fish in a single layer and ladle in the hot marinade. Include the vegetables, as here, or strain them out if you wish. Serve the fish as soon as the fish and marinade cool to room temperature. For more flavor, cool the fish, then marinate them in the refrigerator for at least two hours.

5 **Serving the fish.** Place each fish on a plate and arrange the vegetables on top. Spoon a little of the marinade over each fish. Garnish each plate, if you like, with lemon and lime slices and strips of lemon and lime peel that have been blanched for five minutes in boiling water and drained.

Mollusks Baked in their Shells

The shells of bivalves such as clams, oysters and mussels can serve as dishes in which to cook and present the shellfish. A buttery coating mounded over each one bastes the flesh and prevents drying as you heat the shellfish through in an oven or under a broiler.

Before you cook them, bivalves must be inspected for freshness and cleaned. Clams *(top demonstration)*, oysters *(bottom demonstration)* and mussels should all be alive, as indicated by closed shells. Any shells that are open and do not close in response to a sharp tap should be discarded. Clam shells should be scrubbed clean before they are cooked. Mussels should be scrubbed and the barnacles scraped from their shells. You must also pull out or cut off the beard, a cluster of strands that protrudes from each mussel shell. Oysters should be scrubbed with a stiff brush under cold running water to remove the mud that clings to the crevices in their shells.

Clams and mussels usually are opened by steaming, a process that also cooks them. Although plain water will serve for the steaming, the bivalves will taste richer if cooked with a mixture of aromatic vegetables, herbs such as parsley, tarragon or fennel, water and a little white wine that has been simmered for 15 minutes to concentrate its flavor.

Oysters, on the other hand, are opened raw: Prolonged exposure to heat would toughen them. Open the shells by inserting a stout knife through the hinge and severing the muscle *(Step 1, bottom)*.

The buttery topping used to protect bivalves' flesh during baking or broiling generally plays a major flavoring role as well. Here, the clams are covered with a garlicky butter typically used for preparing snails *(recipe, page 128)*. The oysters are coated with a mixture based on spinach, bread and butter *(recipe, page 128)*.

Because the bases of bivalve shells are rounded, they will not remain stable in a gratin dish without support. To steady the shells, put a bed of coarse sea salt or kosher salt in the dish (inexpensive, inedible rock salt would also serve, but its gray color is less appealing).

Moistening Clams with Garlic Butter

1 **Making snail butter.** Fillet salt anchovies, soak them, rinse them and pat them dry. Pound the fillets to a paste in a mortar with peeled whole cloves of garlic. Pound in softened butter. Season the butter and, if you like, add cayenne pepper, chopped parsley, lemon juice and *pastis*—anise-flavored liqueur.

2 **Preparing clams.** In a covered pot set over high heat, steam clams with a precooked mixture of herbs, vegetables and wine for three minutes, shaking the pot occasionally. When the shells open, remove the clams and cool them. Twist the empty half of each shell from the half with the clam; discard the empty half.

Topping Oysters with Herbs and Vegetables

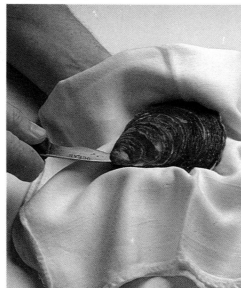

1 **Opening an oyster.** In a cloth-covered hand, hold a cleaned oyster, flatter side up. Insert an oyster knife in the hinge. Twist the tip, opening the shell; slide the blade against the upper shell to sever the oyster. Discard that shell. Slice the oyster from the lower shell.

2 **Cooking a coating.** In a skillet set over low heat, mix butter with chopped parsley, scallions and celery and parboiled, chopped spinach. As the butter melts, stir in bread crumbs. Stirring, cook the mixture for 10 minutes, until it coheres.

3 **Stuffing the clams.** Hold a clam in its half shell between your thumb and forefingers. Use a teaspoon to spread the snail butter over each clam and to the edge of the shell, forming a smooth, even coating. Spread coarse salt in a shallow ovenproof dish. Arrange the coated clams on the salt.

4 **Baking the clams.** If you want to give the coating more body and a crisp surface, sprinkle bread crumbs evenly over the top of the snail butter. Place the dish in a preheated 400° F. [200° C.] oven and bake the clams for five to eight minutes, until the crumbs brown and the butter bubbles. Serve the clams at once.

3 **Coating the oysters.** Spread coarse salt in the bottom of a shallow ovenproof dish. Spoon coating into each half shell until the oyster is thickly covered. Using the hollow side of a spoon, smooth the surface of the coating to give it a neat dome shape. Arrange the oysters on the bed of salt.

4 **Cooking the oysters.** Place the dish in a preheated 400° F. [200° C.] oven and bake the oysters for five to 10 minutes, until the tops brown. If the coating has still not browned after 10 minutes, place the oysters under a preheated broiler for a few seconds. Alternatively, cook the oysters under a preheated broiler for three to five minutes, or until they brown. Serve them piping hot.

Alternative Techniques for Frogs' Legs

The tender white flesh of frogs' legs—the only part of the animal plump enough to be worth eating—has a delicate, faintly sweet taste that makes them a felicitous choice for hors d'oeuvre. The legs lend themselves to piquant flavorings and require only brief cooking. Baking and sautéing are the best methods for preserving their delicate texture *(recipes, pages 126-127)*. Similar guidelines for preparation apply in both cases.

Always sold as pairs and stripped of their tough skins, frogs' legs are available at specialty markets. Fresh legs often are sold between April and October; frozen legs are sold the year round.

In order to enhance their taste, you can marinate the legs for an hour before cooking. If you wish to keep the flavor mild and uncomplicated, use milk and water; to add contrasting tastes, you can use olive oil and fresh herbs such as chives or tarragon.

Before frogs' legs are baked or sautéed, they need a coating that prevents the flesh from drying out. Butter and bread crumbs serve that purpose for baking. For frying, you can coat each pair with flour or—for extra richness—flour and beaten egg. Both types of coating provide a crisp surface for the tender legs.

Frogs' legs benefit from association with sharp, clear-tasting ingredients. The bread-crumb mixture used on the baked assembly at right is enlivened with garlic, shallots and parsley. The sautéed frogs' legs below are garnished after cooking with a *persillade*—a mixture of chopped garlic and parsley—and a sprinkling of lemon juice.

When serving the frogs' legs, allow three to six pairs for each diner, depending on the size of the legs. No knives and forks are necessary: These crisp morsels are best enjoyed when they are eaten with the fingers.

A Gratin of Buttery Crumbs

1 **Mixing crumbs and herbs.** Chop shallots and parsley fine. Make bread crumbs from dry, day-old bread and sieve the crumbs. Chop a garlic clove. Mix the ingredients in a shallow dish.

Sautéed Legs with a Parsley Finish

1 **Sautéing frogs' legs.** Season rinsed and dried frogs' legs with salt and pepper; dredge them with flour. In a small bowl, lightly beat one or more eggs—enough to coat the number of frogs' legs you are cooking. Cover the bottom of a large sauté pan with oil and heat over medium heat. Dip each pair of legs in the egg and place them in the pan.

2 **Turning the frogs' legs.** To ensure that the frogs' legs cook evenly, arrange them in a single layer in the pan. Do not crowd them lest they stick to one another. Sauté them until their undersides have colored—about five minutes—then carefully turn each pair over with a fork or spatula.

3 **Garnishing.** Chop parsley and garlic—allow about 1 tablespoon [15 ml.] of chopped parsley for each garlic clove—and mix them. Sauté the frogs' legs for another two or three minutes, until golden brown all over. Scatter the *persillade* over the legs, add a little lemon juice and serve at once.

2 **Buttering frogs' legs.** Melt butter in a small, heavy saucepan; pour it into a shallow dish and let it cool. Rinse the frogs' legs and dry them thoroughly. Salt and pepper the legs, then turn them in the butter to coat them on all sides.

3 **Coating with crumbs.** One pair at a time, lift the frogs' legs out of the butter and put them in the dish of bread crumbs. Sprinkle the crumb mixture onto the frogs' legs and then transfer them to a buttered shallow baking dish—a gratin dish is used here.

4 **Moistening.** Fill up any spaces between the frogs' legs with the bread-crumb mixture, and sprinkle the remaining crumbs over the frogs' legs. Spoon melted butter over the surface.

5 **Serving the frogs' legs.** Put the dish in a preheated 400° F. [200° C.] oven and bake for 15 to 20 minutes, or until the bread-crumb topping is crisp and brown. Serve the legs at once, directly from the baking dish.

Mousseline: The Sublime Stuffing

When bound with egg white and enriched with cream, the puréed raw flesh of fish is transformed into a delicate mixture known as mousseline *(recipe, page 164)*. The mousseline can be poached in molds or even spooned directly into simmering water to produce the feathery dumplings known as quenelles. Or, as demonstrated here, it can be used as a stuffing for hors d'oeuvre.

Any well-flavored lean fish, such as pike or whiting, is a suitable base for a mousseline. If you use a fattier fish such as salmon, chosen here for its color, combine it with twice its weight of lean white fish—sole, for instance—to prevent the mousseline from becoming heavy.

The proportions of the flesh, egg white and cream must be carefully gauged. Too much egg white will produce a rubbery mixture; too little will keep the mousseline from binding. Weigh the flesh for best results: ½ pound [¼ kg.] of flesh to one egg white and 1 cup [¼ liter] of cream is a reliable ratio.

To purée the fish and incorporate the egg white, you can use a pestle and mortar, but a food processor will make light work of the chore. In either case, the mixture must be sieved to eliminate all traces of fiber and bone.

The purée absorbs cream only with difficulty, especially at room temperature. Chill the purée to firm it so that it will take as much cream as possible, and add the cream a little at a time. The mixture will be stiff at first, but once you have added about half of the cream it will be looser; to lighten the mousseline, whip the rest of the cream and fold it in.

For variety, the mousseline can be augmented with other ingredients. Here, for instance, a mousseline is mixed with pieces of sole and shrimp, green peppercorns and chopped truffles. Pistachios and scallops are apt alternatives.

In its role as a stuffing, a mousseline can be used in rolled-up fish fillets, in a fillet-lined mold or, for an unexpected presentation, in sausage casings. The beef casings used in this instance are prepared in the same way as the pork casings on pages 36-37, and the sausages are made by the same technique. The mousseline sausages are then poached in water and served with a sauce.

1 **Preparing the fish.** Skin sole and salmon fillets. Cut out any red veins on the sole *(page 45, Step 5, bottom)*. Cut the fillets into chunks. Weigh out the required amounts of salmon and sole so that you can determine proportionate quantities of egg whites and cream. Dice additional sole and refrigerate it.

2 **Puréeing the fish.** Put the fish chunks into the chilled bowl of a food processor fitted with a steel blade, and grind the fish with salt, pepper, cayenne pepper and nutmeg. Add the egg whites and grind again. Press the purée through a fine drum sieve a spoonful at a time. Scrape the purée off the bottom and put it in a metal bowl.

4 **Adding whipped cream.** Whip the remaining cream until it barely holds a peak, and add it to the chilled purée mixture. Working over a bowl of ice, stir in the whipped cream with a wooden spoon until the mixture becomes fine and smooth. Cover with plastic wrap and return the bowls to the refrigerator.

5 **Adding garnishes.** While the purée chills, sauté the diced sole in butter until just firm—about two minutes. Parboil shrimp *(box, page 49)*, shell them and cut them into small pieces. When they are cold, mix the sole and shrimp with the fish purée; stir in green peppercorns and, if you wish to use them, chopped truffles.

3 **Beating in cream.** To keep it moist, press plastic wrap onto the purée. Set the metal bowl inside an ice-filled bowl and refrigerate for one hour. Remove the bowls from the refrigerator, replenish the ice if necessary, and beat half of the measured heavy cream into the purée ¼ cup [50 ml.] at a time, refrigerating it for 15 minutes after each addition.

6 **Filling the casing.** Put mousseline into a pastry bag fitted with a large plain tip and slip a length of beef casing over the tip, leaving 3 inches [8 cm.] free. Squeeze the stuffing into the casing to make a sausage of the desired length. Pull off another 3 inches of empty casing and cut it off. Knot both ends of the casing and trim it close to the knots.

7 **Serving the sausages.** Prick the sausages all over with a trussing needle and put them in a pan of cold salted water. Partially cover the pan and heat the water slowly to just below the simmering point. Maintain this temperature and poach the sausages for 20 minutes to firm them. Remove them from the pan and cut them into diagonal slices. Serve the slices, accompanied by a white butter sauce *(page 7),* on heated plates.

4

Eggs
A Range of
Transmutations

The right method for poaching
Molding a savory custard
Layering custard with leaves
Egg whites aerated for a soufflé

Eggs are particularly useful in hors d'oeuvre, not only because their mild flavor combines pleasingly with almost any other food, but also because of the remarkable range of effects they can engender. Consider just the poaching possibilities. For a hot first course, a poached egg may be displayed on a base of toast, in a cooked vegetable case such as an artichoke bottom *(pages 18-19)* or in a tiny tartlet shell *(pages 76-77)*, and garnished with any vegetable, seafood, cheese or meat the cook desires, then swathed in sauces ranging from tomato to hollandaise *(recipes, page 162)*. For a delicious cold hors d'oeuvre, poached eggs may be chilled and molded in glittering aspic *(opposite)*.

For an equally diverse range of presentations, eggs can be beaten and combined with other ingredients before cooking. For instance, mixed with milk or cream and cooked in the gentle, even heat of a water bath, they will slowly thicken into custard. Exquisitely smooth and savory custards are produced by enriching the basic egg mixture with puréed ingredients such as chicken livers *(pages 66-67)*, ham or roast duck, or with grated cheeses ranging from Cheddar to Parmesan. Alternatively, the custard mixture can be used to bind solid ingredients together, creating an assembly with varied textures and colors as in the vegetable pudding demonstrated on pages 68-69, which is formed by layering leafy vegetables and sliced leeks with an herb-flecked custard.

Perhaps the most spectacular use of eggs is in soufflés *(pages 70-71)*, which, contrary to popular myth, are simple to prepare and easy to cook. A soufflé is made by folding beaten egg whites into a thick, flavorsome base, then baking the mixture. The lightest soufflés have as their base puréed starchy vegetables such as potatoes or squash; most soufflés, however, are founded on a thick white sauce that is merely flavored with chopped or puréed vegetables, shellfish, fish, meats or cheeses. The beaten egg whites added to the base incorporate hundreds of tiny bubbles; the heat of baking causes the air in these bubbles to expand, puffing the ingredients until the soufflé has a high, golden dome and—in the classic French presentation—a creamy interior. Because of this soft center, a soufflé will collapse as soon as you spoon into it for serving; if you choose individual molds for baking, you will be able to present miniature whole soufflés in pristine form.

Encased in a shimmering aspic coat made from gelatinous veal stock, poached eggs rest on a nest of slivered lettuce leaves. Blanched leaves of fresh tarragon embedded in the aspic provide the decoration for each egg *(pages 64-65)*.

A Cloak of Sparkling Aspic

Among the myriad ways of presenting poached eggs, perhaps the most elegant is in individual molds of clear amber aspic. The jewel-like results belie the simplicity of the ingredients and preparation: Besides the eggs, the dish requires only a clear, gelatinous stock made from veal or chicken or both *(pages 8-9)*.

Newly laid eggs are best for poaching, both because of their fresh flavor and because they have cohesive whites and will retain a compact shape when cooked. Test the age of an egg by placing it in a bowl of cold water: A fresh egg will lie flat on the bottom of the bowl because it contains little air; older eggs contain enough air to make them buoyant, and their broad ends will tilt upward.

To prevent eggs from toughening as they cook, the poaching must be as gentle as possible. Slip the eggs into water that has been first brought to a boil, then removed from the heat. Poach them for three or four minutes, until their whites are set but their yolks are still soft. Cook the eggs in small batches, bringing the water to a boil again for each batch: In an overcrowded pan, the water temperature would fall and keep the eggs from cooking properly.

To ensure that the eggs will be completely surrounded by the aspic, their molds should be coated lightly with liquid stock before the eggs are put in place. If you like, add a few decorations to this preliminary aspic coating. A pattern of tarragon leaves is shown here; you could also use strips of sweet red pepper, or slivers of cooked ham or black olives.

Once the eggs have been slipped into their molds and covered with the remaining stock, they should be refrigerated for three hours to set the jelly. A brisk shake will be enough to unmold them *(Step 8)*. Serve the eggs on a bed of chopped aspic, on top of a sorrel or tomato mousse *(pages 40-41)*, or—as in this demonstration—on lettuce chiffonade.

1 **Poaching the eggs.** Bring water to a boil in a large, heavy pan; turn off the heat. Carefully crack each egg and break it open just at the water's surface so that the white and yolk slip gently into the water; put no more than four eggs into the pan at one time. Cover the pan and let the eggs cook for about three minutes.

2 **Testing the yolk.** When the egg white appears firm and opaque, lift out an egg with a slotted spatula; the yolk should still be soft to the touch. To arrest the cooking, transfer the poached eggs to a shallow dish of cold water.

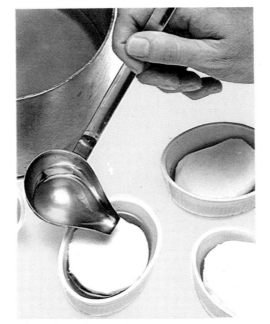

6 **Filling the molds.** Ladle stock over each egg, filling the mold to its rim. To set the aspic, return the filled molds to the refrigerator for at least three hours.

7 **Cutting chiffonade.** Separate lettuce leaves—romaine, here. Wash the leaves in cold water, dry them with paper towels and stack them. Roll the stack into a cylinder and slice it into cross sections at ¼- to ½-inch [6 mm.- to 1-cm.] intervals to form strips. Arrange the strips on a serving dish.

3 **Trimming the eggs.** With the spatula, lift the eggs from the cold water and place them on a towel that has been dampened to prevent the eggs from sticking. With a small, sharp knife, trim the edges of each egg to give it a neat shape that will fit the mold.

4 **Preparing the molds.** Melt jellied stock; let it cool to room temperature. Ladle a layer of stock into small molds. Refrigerate the molds for 15 minutes to set the jelly. Blanch fresh tarragon to soften it. Pinch off the leaves and dry them. Dip the leaves into the stock and arrange them in the molds. Pour a little stock over the leaves.

5 **Molding the eggs.** Refrigerate the molds for five minutes to firm the aspic and secure the leaf decoration. Then carefully lift each egg by hand and place it, yolk side down, in a mold.

8 **Serving.** Run a knife tip around the inside of each mold. Hold the mold in one hand and cover it with the other. Invert the mold and lift it so that the egg drops into your palm *(above)*. Slip each egg onto the serving dish. Garnish individual servings, if you like, with additional chopped aspic *(right)*.

Savory Custard Enhanced by Meat

Eggs combined with milk and puréed or finely grated flavorings yield delicate, smooth-textured custards firm enough to unmold. Success with dishes of this type depends on close attention to the proportions of ingredients and on careful, gentle cooking.

Egg yolk and egg white both thicken as they cook, but the white sets more quickly and firmly than the yolk, ensuring that the custard holds its shape when unmolded. The proportion of egg white in the custard mixture is critical: Too little would lead to collapse, and too much would give the custard a coarse, rubbery texture. The quantity of egg yolk is less important: Extra yolks can be added to enrich the custard. For a delicate, trembling custard, use two whole eggs and two or three yolks for every 2 cups [½ liter] of milk. To flavor the custard base, use grated cheese or puréed meats such as the marrow and chicken livers shown here (recipe, page 134).

Slow, even heat during cooking is essential for a smooth texture: Excessive heat would produce bubbles in the custard and make it watery. To control the heat, use a water bath. Set the dish of custard mixture on a wire rack in a large, ovenproof pot, partly fill the pot with warm water, and either put the water bath, uncovered, in a moderate oven, or cover it and set it over very low heat on top of the stove. Do not let the water approach a boil; if it begins to simmer, reduce the heat and, in the case of an oven, open the door for a minute.

To allow it to settle and firm up a little, leave the cooked custard in its dish for 10 to 15 minutes before unmolding it. It will be easier to turn out if it is cooked in a lightly buttered dish, whose bottom is lined with buttered parchment or wax paper (box, right). An unmolded custard needs no embellishment, but you can serve it, if you like, with a sauce such as tomato purée.

1 Pounding flavorings. Trim chicken livers (page 38). Extract the marrow from a section of marrowbone: Ease the blade of a small knife around the edge of the marrow to loosen it, then pry it out. Rub a mortar with a cut garlic clove, put in the livers and marrow and pound them to a paste; or purée the ingredients in a food processor.

2 Adding eggs and milk. Put the puréed chicken livers and marrow in a bowl. Whisk in whole eggs and egg yolks, and season the mixture with salt and pepper. Pour in cold milk and, if you have any, a spoonful or two of degreased juices from a beef or veal roast. Whisk the mixture until all the ingredients are thoroughly blended.

A Neat Technique for Lining a Mold

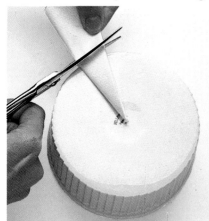

1 Folding and cutting paper. Fold a square of parchment or wax paper diagonally to make a triangle. Fold the triangle in half repeatedly, until the closed tip forms a narrow point. Lay the triangle on an inverted mold with the point in the center; cut off the paper that extends beyond the mold.

2 Fitting in the paper. With your fingers, lightly butter the inside of the mold. Open out the paper and press it into the bottom of the mold. Smear the upper surface of the paper with butter so that the paper can be removed at the end of cooking without pulling away the surface of the custard.

3 **Filling the mold.** Butter a mold, then line the bottom with buttered parchment or wax paper *(box, opposite)*. Pour the custard mixture through a fine-meshed sieve into a clean bowl. Transfer the mixture to the mold, leaving a 1-inch [2½-cm.] space at the top of the mold to allow the custard to puff during cooking.

4 **Cooking the custard.** Place the mold on a wire rack set in a large pot. Pour enough warm water into the pot to come two thirds of the way up the sides of the mold. Put the pot in a preheated 325° F. [160° C.] oven and cook for about one and one quarter hours, or until a metal knife inserted into the center of the custard comes out clean.

5 **Unmolding the custard.** Remove the cooked custard from the water bath and let it cool for about 10 minutes. To unmold the custard, place an inverted plate on the mold and turn the plate and mold over so that the custard is resting on the plate. Lift off the mold.

6 **Serving the custard.** Peel the paper off the top of the custard and serve. In this instance, a ring of tomato sauce *(page 7)* is spooned around the custard and the rest of the sauce is passed separately in a sauceboat. Garnish each serving with a twist of lemon peel or a sprig of parsley.

Leafy Greens for Textural Interest

If custard is layered with an assortment of leaf vegetables or thinly sliced cooked meats, it will fuse the diverse ingredients into a savory baked pudding that has an appealing range of textures. In the demonstration on these pages, Swiss chard, spinach, sorrel and leeks are combined with an herb-flavored custard in a mold that is lined with cabbage leaves *(recipe, page 92)*, yielding a light and refreshing hors d'oeuvre.

To make the cabbage leaves supple enough to line the cooking vessel and wrap around the filling, the outer parts of their ribs are shaved off. With the exception of the sorrel, which has a fragile texture, all of the vegetables are briefly parboiled to soften them before they are layered with the custard mixture. The parboiled vegetables must be thoroughly drained and patted as dry as possible with paper towels to keep the custard from becoming watery.

If you prefer a more luxurious dish, you can stew the leeks in butter and gently sauté the leaf vegetables in butter after parboiling. The cooking will bring out the vegetables' flavor and, at the same time, help to dry them. You could also enrich the custard that binds the leaves by incorporating extra egg yolks into it and substituting cream for the milk. These opulent custard-puddings are best served without sauce. Less rich versions of the pudding, however, might benefit from a creamy sauce: a hollandaise, a tomato sauce with extra cream or a velouté made with egg and lemon juice *(pages 6-10)*, for example.

1 Preparing vegetables. Remove the stems from spinach leaves and slice sorrel leaves into fine shreds. To remove the stalks from Swiss chard, make a V-shaped incision at the base of each leaf, following the contour of the stalk; discard the stalks. Cut off the root bases and fibrous tops of leeks. To rid them of grit, make two vertical cuts in the green part of each leek and rinse the leek well in cold water. Slice the leeks into rounds.

5 Layering ingredients. Line a baking dish with the cabbage leaves. Let each leaf overhang the dish to fold over the assembled pudding. Fill the dish with layers of the dried Swiss chard, spinach, sorrel and leeks, alternating the vegetables with the custard mixture. Fold the cabbage leaves over the filling, and cover it with more cabbage leaves and a sheet of foil.

2 **Softening cabbage.** Core a cabbage, separate the leaves and shave off the rib at the base of each leaf. Wash the leaves and stack them in a pan. Pour enough boiling water over the leaves to cover them, add salt and set the pan over high heat. Boil the leaves, uncovered, for four minutes; drain them and dry them with paper towels.

3 **Parboiling vegetables.** Lower the Swiss chard leaves into a large pan of boiling salted water—flavored with a bouquet garni, if you like. After four minutes, lift out and dry the chard. Parboil the spinach for two minutes; remove and dry it. Cook the leeks for eight to 10 minutes in just enough lightly salted boiling water to cover them.

4 **Blending the custard.** In a bowl, combine milk, eggs and egg yolks, salt, pepper, a little chopped onion, and some finely chopped parsley, chives and tarragon. With a fork, beat the eggs and then stir all the ingredients together until they are well mixed.

6 **Serving the dish.** Set the custard on a rack in a water bath; cook it in a preheated 425° F. [220° C.] oven for one and one quarter hours, until it feels firm to the touch. Take it out of the oven and let it stand for 15 minutes. Remove the foil and turn the custard out onto a plate (above). Cut into wedges (right).

Baking Individual Soufflés

The dramatically puffed surface and the creamy interior that characterize a perfect soufflé result from careful mixing of the ingredients and equal care in the application of heat. Among the ingredients, the starting point is the so-called base, a smooth, saucelike mixture that provides the soufflé's body. The base is enriched with egg yolks, and beaten egg whites are folded in to incorporate air. In a hot oven, the moisture in the blend turns to steam and the bubbles of air that are trapped in the whites expand, causing the soufflé to puff up.

Most soufflé bases are made from the same ingredients used for a velouté or white sauce (*pages 8-9 and 6*), but with a larger proportion of flour and butter to the liquid. The resulting thick paste may be flavored with puréed fish, chicken or vegetables; asparagus is used in the demonstration at right (*recipe, page 136*). A starchy vegetable purée can also be used on its own as a base, although the soufflé will be particularly fragile. Four egg yolks and five egg whites are enough to enrich and raise 2 cups [½ liter] of any soufflé base.

Whisk the egg whites just before using them; if left to stand, they would subside and become watery. The whites should be at room temperature: Cold whites do not rise well. Although you can use any large bowl for whisking, an unlined copper bowl is best, because the metal and egg whites react together to create a more stable foam. Whatever the type of bowl, be sure it is scrupulously clean: Even a trace of grease will prevent the whites from mounting fully.

In order to keep its structure intact, the airy mass of egg white must be combined with the soufflé base as gently as possible. Some of the egg white is stirred carefully into the base to thin it and ease mixing, then this mixture is folded into the beaten whites by hand.

The individual soufflés demonstrated here are baked at a high temperature for 12 to 15 minutes, depending on the degree of doneness desired (*Step 9*). Larger soufflés, which need longer cooking periods, require a slightly lower oven temperature to ensure that the outer edges of the soufflés do not dry out before the centers are cooked.

1 Parboiling asparagus. Cut the tips off asparagus spears. Peel the stalks (*page 14*) and slice them into ½-inch [1-cm.] lengths. Bring a pan of salted water to a boil over high heat. Add the tips, parboil them for two minutes, then remove them with a skimmer and drain them. Parboil the stalks for eight minutes.

2 Enriching asparagus. Melt butter in a skillet over medium heat. Remove the asparagus stalks from their cooking water, let them drain and put them in the skillet. Toss them in the butter for two or three minutes. Remove the stalks. Add the asparagus tips, toss them briefly in the butter and take them out.

6 Adding egg yolks. Separate eggs; add an extra white to the egg whites. Beat the whites until they form firm, moist peaks. Quickly add the yolks to the soufflé base and whisk the mixture until the ingredients are evenly blended. Season the base with salt, pepper and, if you like, a little nutmeg.

7 Incorporating whites. Using the whisk, immediately transfer about a third of the whites to the soufflé base; stir them in to lighten it. Then add the base to the remaining whites and—with a rubber spatula—fold the ingredients gently. The mixture should be streaky: Overmixing will deflate the whites.

3 **Sieving asparagus.** In a food mill or processor, purée the sautéed asparagus stalks. Set a drum sieve over a plate. To remove any fibers, push the puréed stalks through the sieve, using a flexible scraper. Reserve the purée and the sautéed tips separately.

4 **Preparing the soufflé base.** Make a thick white sauce (recipe, page 162). When the sauce is too thick to pour (above), remove it from the heat and allow it to cool slightly.

5 **Flavoring the soufflé base.** After about five minutes, add the asparagus purée to the soufflé base. Whisk the ingredients until they are evenly blended.

8 **Filling the molds.** Half-fill small buttered molds with the soufflé mixture. Add a few asparagus tips to each mold, and then cover them with a spoonful of the soufflé mixture. To give the soufflé an attractive cap, run your thumb around the edge of each filled mold. Put the molds on a baking tray.

9 **Baking the soufflés.** Set the tray in a preheated 400° F. [200° C.] oven for 12 minutes. The soufflés are ready when they are a deep golden brown and have risen well. Serve them immediately if you prefer soufflés with the insides still moist; bake them for three more minutes if you prefer drier soufflés.

5

Crepe, Pastry and Bread Cases

A Spectrum of Textures and Shapes

A velouté sauce *(pages 8-9)*, enriched with egg yolks and colored with saffron, is spooned over a crisp bread case *(page 82)* that encloses a mixture of diced roasted chicken and ham, cubes of parboiled and sautéed cucumber, and slivers of truffle. The filling ingredients were prepared separately, then warmed together in some of the sauce.

Of all the preparations used in hors d'oeuvre cookery, crepes, pastries and bread doughs offer the widest opportunities for graceful and inventive presentation. They can be shaped into many sorts of casings and wrappings and used to display—or conceal—a broad range of fillings.

The foundation for each of these preparations is formed by adding liquid to flour—the liquid activates a network of flour proteins called gluten, causing the ingredients to cohere—but the proportions of flour and liquid can be varied, and other ingredients can be included in the mixture. Crepes, for instance, are made from a creamy batter containing a high proportion of liquid as well as eggs and butter for richness. The batter can be flavored, if you like, with herbs or puréed vegetables. Frying turns it into thin, soft pancakes, flexible enough to wrap or fold around a filling *(pages 74-75)*.

Each of the pastries *(pages 76-83)* used for hors d'oeuvre presentations begins as a firm but malleable mass of dough containing much less liquid than crepe batter. Fat—usually butter—is incorporated in the dough in small, solid bits, which waterproof some of the flour, limiting gluten development and ensuring the flaky tenderness that distinguishes good pastry. The most basic pastry is short crust, for which the dough is simply rolled into a flat sheet for shaping and baking. A short-crust mixture can be repeatedly folded to make a sheet of many layers; when this sheet—now known as rough puff dough—is baked, the moisture in it steams, forcing the layers to puff apart. A sheet of dough rolled and folded around a sheet of butter expands even more dramatically, producing classic puff pastry. Any pastry can form large shells or small ones; any pastry can also be used as a wrapping.

When yeast is added to flour and water, it inflates the mixture into bread dough, which may be plain and rustic *(pages 84-85)* or enriched with butter and egg to form luxuriant brioches *(pages 86-88)*. Like pastry, bread dough can be shaped into shells or used as a wrapping.

Fillings for crepes, pastries and breads are practically interchangeable, although fillings that are to be wrapped must obviously be firmer and drier than those spooned into prepared shells. Combinations of sauces with seafoods, meats, vegetables or poultry all make delectable fillings; even leftovers may be put to elegant use.

Flexible Wrappers from a Thin Batter

Lightly blended and quickly fried, a batter composed of flour, eggs, milk, butter and seasonings *(recipe, page 167)* yields paper-thin crepes—light, flexible pancakes that make perfect wrappers for stuffings. These can easily be made in quantity, provided the batter is the right density and the pan is properly prepared.

The batter ingredients should be combined thoroughly but gently: If the batter is overbeaten it becomes elastic, and pancakes riddled with holes result. The consistency should be like that of cream.

As a general rule the batter can be used as soon as it is mixed. However, if you have to beat it briskly to eliminate lumps, let it rest for an hour to permit the gluten in the flour to relax.

Using the right kind of pan is critical. Pans are sold specifically for crepe making, but you can use any frying pan that shares similar characteristics. The pan should have shallow, sloping sides to facilitate turning the crepes. It should be made of a heavy metal—cast iron or carbon steel—that heats evenly and can be seasoned. (Seasoning ensures that the surface is slick and smooth so that the crepe batter does not stick.) To season a pan, pour in a layer of vegetable oil about ¼ inch [6 mm.] deep, set it over low heat until the oil smokes, then dry the pan.

Before cooking the crepes, preheat the pan—the batter must set at once—but do not let it smoke or the crepes will burn. A well-seasoned pan requires light buttering only before the first crepe is made.

The cooked crepes can be used immediately, if you wish. Or they can be stored in the refrigerator enclosed in plastic wrap for as long as two days.

Crepes can enfold a range of different fillings *(recipes, pages 140-143),* from the simple cheese-and-spinach mixture shown at right to mousseline *(box, opposite).* You can roll the crepes around the filling, stack them in layers, or shape them into half-moons or cornucopias.

Once they are stuffed, the crepes are cooked briefly if they need only be heated through, or for longer periods if necessary to cook the fillings. The cooking can be done in a buttered pan set over low heat or in the oven; if you choose the oven, cover the crepes with melted butter or sauce to prevent drying.

1 Mixing batter. Mix flour and salt in a large bowl. Make a well in the flour and break in eggs. Slowly pour milk into the center of the bowl; at the same time, working from the center of the bowl outward, whisk the eggs and the milk into the flour. Let the batter rest for 30 minutes. Then stir in melted butter.

2 Starting to cook a crepe. Warm a dab of butter in a heavy pan over medium heat; wipe off any excess. Allow two or three minutes for the pan to heat up, then lift it and ladle in just enough batter to coat the base thinly. The batter should sizzle as it touches the hot metal. As you pour, tilt and roll the pan to spread the batter evenly.

6 Reheating the crepes. Arrange the crepes flap side down in a buttered gratin dish. Spoon a little melted butter over the surface of the crepes, and sprinkle them with grated hard cheese such as Parmesan. Cook the crepes in a preheated 375° F. [190° C.] oven for 20 to 25 minutes until they brown lightly.

7 Garnishing. While the crepes reheat, prepare a garnish. Halve small peeled tomatoes and seed them, or use drained whole canned tomatoes. Stew the tomatoes in butter until they have softened. Remove the crepes from the oven and top each one with a warm tomato. Or garnish the crepes with tomato sauce *(pages 6-7).*

3 **Turning the crepe.** Cook the crepe until its underside is evenly colored and its edges are dry—about 20 seconds. Slip a narrow-bladed spatula under the crepe. With a quick movement, lift up the crepe and flip it over. Cook the underside until dry and lightly speckled—about 10 seconds.

4 **Stacking the crepes.** Slide the cooked crepe out of the pan onto a warmed plate. Before making a fresh crepe, take the pan off the heat for a few seconds so that it does not become too hot; stir the batter if it has separated. As you cook more crepes, stack them so that they remain moist.

5 **Stuffing.** Cradle each crepe— even-colored side down—in one hand. Spoon a stuffing—here, a mixture of ricotta and grated Parmesan cheese, egg, and chopped, cooked spinach *(recipe, page 164)*—down the center of the crepe to within ½ inch [1 cm.] of the ends. Fold both sides of the crepe over the stuffing, leaving the ends open.

Cones Packed with Mousseline

1 **Filling.** Make crepes, adding chopped fresh parsley and chives to the batter; cook them on one side only. Lay a crepe cooked side up and cut it in half. Spread mousseline *(pages 60-61)* on the half circle, fold it into a triangle and cover the upper surface with mousseline. Roll the triangle into a cone around the mousseline filling.

2 **Cooking.** Melt butter in a frying pan set over low heat. Place two or three cones in the pan and sauté them until they are golden, rolling them with a spatula so that they cook evenly. Each time you roll a crepe, press the spatula flat against the cone to give it a triangular shape. Drain the crepes on a rack covered with paper towels.

3 **Serving the crepes.** Make a white butter sauce *(pages 6-7)*. Place two of the rolled crepes on an individual serving dish and spoon some of the sauce over them. Serve immediately.

Short Crust: The Simplest Formula

Simple to make and wonderfully versatile, short-crust dough contains only flour, butter and enough water to promote gluten development in the flour (*recipe, page 166*). To produce pastry that is flaky and tender, the ingredients have to be kept at the right temperature and mixed in just the right way.

The butter for short crust must remain cold: Soft, warm butter will spread through the flour rather than remain in discrete, scattered pieces as it should. The result will be a sticky mass that will not cohere properly when water is added.

To prevent the butter from softening, work quickly when you mix it into the flour. You can use your finger tips to do the mixing, as shown here. Or, to avoid touching and possibly warming the butter, use a fork, two knives, or a food processor operated in short spurts.

When the butter is evenly distributed throughout the flour, bind the mixture with ice water. Begin with a little less water than a recipe specifies: Too much water will cause excessive gluten development and tough pastry. Add extra water drop by drop if necessary to make the dough cohere. And continue to work quickly, not only to keep the butter cold but also because overworking activates too much gluten. To firm the butter and relax the gluten, refrigerate the dough for at least an hour before rolling it out.

The rolled-out dough can be shaped in any number of ways. It can, for instance, be folded around a filling in a manner similar to that shown on pages 80-81. Or it can be molded in pans to make large or small open-faced tarts, as in this demonstration.

An open-faced tart can contain almost any filling, cooked or uncooked; but the shell should always be blind-baked—precooked without its contents—to keep the dough from absorbing liquid and becoming soggy. Line the empty shell with parchment paper, fill it with dried beans to brace the sides, then bake the shell to set the dough. If you plan to cook a filling in the shell, blind-bake it only partially; this takes about 10 minutes. If you intend to fill the shell with separately cooked ingredients, as in this demonstration, blind-bake the shell completely.

1 Mixing flour and butter. Sift flour and salt into a large mixing bowl. Cut chilled butter into pieces and scatter them over the flour. Using the tips of your fingers and thumbs, pick up a small amount of flour and butter and lightly rub it together. Continue until all of the butter is incorporated and the mixture resembles very coarse bread crumbs.

2 Adding water. Make a shallow well in the flour-and-butter mixture. Pour in a little ice water and stir it lightly with a fork in order to distribute the water evenly without overworking the dough. If the dough is still crumbly and dry, add a few more drops of water.

5 Blind baking. Place the pans on a baking sheet, press parchment paper into each one, and fill it with dried beans (*above*). Bake for 10 minutes in a preheated 400° F. [200° C.] oven. Remove the paper and beans, prick the pastry shells to prevent blistering, and bake about 10 minutes more, or until golden brown.

6 Preparing the filling. Parboil shrimp for two minutes, or until they turn pink; plunge them into cold water, then drain them in a colander. Peel, devein and halve the shrimp. Cut strips from a peeled red pepper (*page 10*). Use a melon baller to scoop balls from an avocado; place them in lemon juice to prevent discoloration.

3 **Finishing the dough.** Gather the mixture together with one hand; if it feels crumbly and dry, add drops of water until the dough coheres. Press the dough into a ball. Enclose it in plastic wrap, wax paper or foil, and chill it in the refrigerator for at least an hour.

4 **Lining tartlet pans.** Form the dough into a cylinder and divide the cylinder into even-sized portions. On a lightly floured surface, roll each of the dough pieces into a round ⅛ inch [3 mm.] thick; use the pan you have chosen—false-bottomed tartlet pans in this demonstration—as a template to ensure that the circle of dough is about 1 inch [2½ cm.] larger all around than the pan *(above, left)*. With a spatula, place dough on top of a tartlet pan. Press the dough against the sides and bottom of the pan, folding in the excess to reinforce the rim *(right)*.

7 **Assembling and serving.** Prepare rémoulade sauce *(recipe, page 161)* and spoon it into the cooled pastry shells *(left)*. Arrange halved shrimp in a pinwheel pattern on top of the rémoulade, place avocado balls in the center, and garnish with parsley and red-pepper strips. To unmold each tart, press the removable pan bottom up and out of the rim; slide the tart off the bottom onto a serving plate *(inset)*. Moisten the shrimp with lemon juice before serving.

Lightness from Repeated Folding

Pastry containers for savory fillings acquire special lightness when they are shaped from a dough that has been rolled and folded into a layered sheet. During baking, moisture in the dough turns to steam, puffing and separating the layers into fragile, buttery flakes. The amount of puffiness is determined by the ingredients in the dough, and also by the method used for folding and rolling it.

Of the several varieties of puff-pastry dough, the one shown here—known as rough puff dough *(recipe, page 166)*—is the easiest to make. The dough is basically a flour-and-butter short crust *(pages 76-77)*, containing more butter than usual. The butter in the dough should be left in relatively large pieces—about the size of beans—to ensure flakiness.

To form layers, the dough is repeatedly rolled into a strip and folded in four. Each rolling flattens the butter pieces, and each folding creates more layers of flattened butter interspersed with dough.

Because a rough puff dough receives so much handling, extra care should be taken to prevent the butter from softening. The dough must be chilled after every two repetitions of the rolling and folding. This firms the butter and also allows the gluten in the dough to relax so that rolling does not toughen the dough.

The method of shaping the dough into a shell differs slightly from that used for short crust. Pans or molds are unnecessary: Simply cut the dough sheet to form a base of the shape you desire, place the base on a baking sheet and set strips of dough along the edges. During baking, the strips will puff vertically to form a rim for the shell.

Rough puff shells should be partially blind-baked *(page 76)* to prevent sogginess, then filled and baked to doneness. Or they may be fully blind-baked and then filled. Rough puff shells need not be weighted during blind baking, since there is no danger of the rim's collapsing.

Virtually any filling is suitable for a rough puff shell. Here, peppers and tomatoes, stewed to a thick consistency and topped with anchovies, are used *(recipe, page 143);* you could add olives or sautéed eggplant or zucchini.

1 **Rolling and folding the dough.** Prepare and chill rough puff dough. The volume of butter can range from half that of the flour to an equal amount, depending on the richness you desire. Lightly flour a work surface. Roll the dough into a strip ¼ inch [6 mm.] thick and four times as long as it is wide *(above, left)*. Fold the ends to meet in the center, then fold the dough in half so that the folded edges meet *(right)*.

4 **Glazing the dough.** Dilute an egg yolk with water; use it to stick the dough strips along the edges of the rectangle. Prick the bottom of the shell with a fork to keep it from blistering. Paint the tops of the strips with the egg mixture *(above)*, but do not glaze the sides, or puffing will be inhibited. Draw the back of a fork over the border to pattern the glaze. Bake the case in a preheated 425° F. [220° C.] oven for 10 minutes.

5 **Preparing vegetables.** Peel, halve and seed tomatoes *(page 32, Step 1)*, then chop them coarse. Broil sweet peppers, then peel, halve and derib them *(page 10);* cut them into strips. Peel and chop fine two or three garlic cloves.

2 **Repeating the rolling and folding.** Give the dough a quarter turn so that one of its open sides is facing you. Roll it out again *(above, left)*. Fold the dough in four as before *(right)*, enclose it in plastic wrap and chill until it is quite firm—one to two hours in the refrigerator or 15 to 20 minutes in the freezer. Repeat Steps 1 and 2; for an even lighter pastry, repeat the sequence again.

3 **Cutting the dough.** Roll out the chilled dough to a thickness of about ⅛ inch [3 mm.]. Using a dough scraper or sharp knife, trim the dough into a rectangle. Cut a ¾-inch [2-cm.] strip from all four sides *(above)*. Then place the rectangle on a buttered baking sheet.

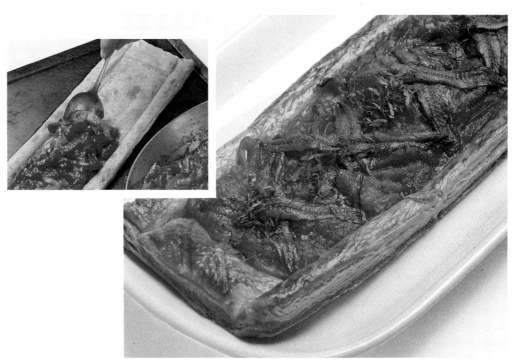

6 **Stewing the vegetables.** Heat a little oil in a pan and add the chopped tomatoes, the garlic and salt. Cook the tomatoes, uncovered, for about 20 minutes over a fairly high heat, stirring occasionally, until they have reduced to a thick pulp. Add the pepper strips and stew the mixture for 10 more minutes. Correct the seasoning; if you like, add a few drops of vinegar.

7 **Baking.** Fillet salt anchovies; soak them in water for 30 minutes, dry them and moisten them with olive oil. Spoon the vegetables onto the dough *(inset)*; arrange the anchovies on top. Bake in a preheated 375° F. [190° C.] oven for 20 to 30 minutes, until the pastry is golden. Transfer the tart to a platter, sprinkle it with parsley and serve it in cross sections.

An Aromatic Olive-Oil Pastry

Pastry dough made with olive oil *(recipe, page 166)* has a fragrance and supple texture quite different from butter dough. The oil can be used instead of butter for short-crust or, as here, for rough puff dough. The mixing method varies according to the way the dough is to be used.

Olive-oil dough for short crust is simple to prepare: The ingredients are mixed together with a fork. Because the oil cannot be kept in distinct chunks, however, the pastry will never attain the flakiness of butter short crust. An egg added to the mixture will contribute some crispness.

To help blend the oil and eggs, use warm water for binding, then knead the dough. The kneading makes the dough elastic, and a resting period is essential if you are to roll the dough out thin. Chilling is unnecessary because the dough contains no solid fat that is liable to melt.

The same ingredients form olive-oil dough for rough puff pastry, but the mixing method is slightly different: If the oil were added to the flour all at once, it would become so thoroughly mixed with the other ingredients that no layered structure would be possible. The basic dough is therefore made with only part of the olive oil required; the rest is brushed on the rolled-out dough. Repeated rolling, painting and folding create many layers of dough separated by oil.

The rough puff olive-oil dough can usually be rolled out and painted twice before handling makes it so elastic that it needs to be rested. If a second rolling cannot be managed, allow the dough to rest for about 30 minutes before continuing. In any case, resting periods between each pair of rollings and foldings are essential.

Like butter rough puff dough, olive-oil rough puff dough can be shaped without the aid of molds. Here, two sheets of dough form the base and lid of a pie containing layers of cabbage, rice, hard-boiled egg and leftover boiled beef *(recipe, page 145)*. Other leftovers can be put to attractive use in the same way.

To keep the pastry firm during baking, any filling must be fairly dry; holes cut in the pie lid will permit steam to escape. After the baking, the same holes allow melted butter to be funneled into the filling, moistening and enriching it.

1 **Kneading dough.** Thoroughly mix flour, salt, eggs, olive oil and a little water. Gather the resulting dough into a ball. Knead it briefly on a floured work surface until the ingredients have blended smoothly. Enclose the dough in plastic wrap or wax paper. Let it rest for one hour at room temperature.

2 **Painting the dough with oil.** Flour the work surface again. Roll out the dough into a long strip. With a pastry brush, paint two thirds of the length of the dough with olive oil. Do not paint too generously, or the oil will be squeezed out again when the dough is folded.

5 **Covering the base.** Stew chopped onion in butter until soft; combine it with cold cooked rice. Boil cabbage leaves for three minutes; drain and chop them and then sauté the pieces in butter. Hard-boil and quarter eggs. Chop cold boiled beef. Mound the rice mixture on the dough, leaving a 1-inch [2½-cm.] border. Make a trough in the rice; fill it with the cabbage.

6 **Completing the filling.** Line up the hard-boiled eggs on top of the cabbage. Distribute the beef on top of the eggs. Roll out the larger portion of dough into a roughly rectangular shape that is large enough to cover the filling and pie base.

3 **Folding the dough.** Lift the unpainted end of the strip and fold it over the central third of the piece of dough. Fold the remaining third on top to make a third layer. Give the dough a quarter turn so that the open ends are facing you.

4 **Shaping.** Once more, roll out the dough, paint and fold it. Let it rest for one hour. Repeat the sequence—including the resting period—twice. Oil a baking sheet. Divide the dough into two unequal portions; roll out the smaller piece into a rectangle. Transfer the rolled-out dough to the baking sheet.

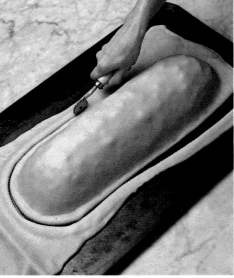

7 **Covering the pie.** Moisten the rim of the base with water or egg white. Drape the lid over the rolling pin and transfer it to the pie. Mold it against the filling and, with your fingers, press it firmly against the rim of the base. Trim the lid and base edges with a pastry wheel. For a pattern, indent the rim lightly with the back of a fork. Glaze the pie with egg yolk mixed with water.

8 **Baking and serving.** Using a small knife, cut holes in the pie top. Bake the pie at 425° F. [220° C.] for 35 minutes or, if the pie is thicker than 5 inches [13 cm.], at 400° F. [200° C.] for about an hour, reducing the heat to 350° F. [180° C.] if the pastry browns too much. When the pie is brown, slide it onto a platter. Funnel in hot melted butter (above). Serve in slices (inset).

Puff Pastry: The Finest of Casings

Individual, high-sided containers for fillings made with sauces can be as hearty as a simple bread case *(box, below)* or as light as a vol-au-vent—literally, "flight on the wind" *(right)*. The preparation of vol-au-vent is fairly demanding, but the results are incomparable: The cases are carefully built from layers of puff-pastry dough in such a way that when the dough expands during baking, it forms a hollow container with crisp, buttery sides. Vol-au-vent may be constructed from butter or olive-oil rough puff dough *(pages 78-81)*, but the lightest containers are fashioned from classic puff pastry.

This type of pastry is made by folding a sheet of dough around a sheet of butter, then repeatedly folding and rolling the package until hundreds of paper-thin layers of dough and butter have been formed. Like other pastry doughs, the basic dough for classic puff pastry *(recipe, page 167)* is based on flour, butter and ice water; but because of the extensive handling involved, part of the flour must be low-gluten cake flour to ensure tenderness. Also, classic puff-pastry dough in-

cludes a smaller amount of butter than other pastry doughs; ample butter is incorporated during folding.

Before the butter is enclosed in the dough, it must be kneaded to rid it of excess liquid, which could spoil the pastry. To remove liquid, place chilled butter on a floured surface and press and fold it with your hands for about five minutes. Some liquid will be absorbed by the flour; some will appear on the surface of the butter and can be wiped off. Chill the kneaded butter, then place it between sheets of parchment paper and roll it into a sheet about ¾ inch [2 cm.] thick.

The package of butter and dough is rolled out and folded four times. The dough must be refrigerated each time for ever-longer periods to keep it firm and tender; in all, the pastry-making process will take at least eight hours. Once it has been formed, however, classic puff-pastry dough is easily shaped, baked, hollowed out and used as an elegant container for creamy fillings, such as the sauced sweetbreads and ham demonstrated at right and below.

1 Enclosing butter. Place a sheet of kneaded butter on a larger square of puff-pastry dough that is ½ inch [1 cm.] thick; the sides of the butter should be placed at right angles to the corners of the dough. Fold the corners of the dough over the butter, overlapping them and leaving a ½-inch margin of dough all around the butter. Press the seams of the package gently together.

Cutting and Coloring Bread Cases

1 Cutting cases. Trim the crusts from a stale, unsliced loaf of white bread. Cut it into 2-inch [5-cm.] slices. Score the top of each slice ½ inch [1 cm.] in from the edges and to within ½ inch of the base. Insert the knife horizontally ½ inch above the base of a corner and swivel it *(above)*.

2 Hollowing the center. Withdraw the knife and insert it in the diagonally opposite bottom corner. Swivel the knife again to loosen the center section, and lever it out *(above)*. Shake out any loose crumbs of bread remaining in the case.

3 Baking the cases. Place the cases on a buttered baking sheet. Liberally coat their surfaces with melted butter. Bake the cases in a preheated 325° F. [160° C.] oven for one hour, until crisp and golden; turn them occasionally so that they color evenly.

2 **Rolling.** Roll the dough into a rectangle three times as long as it is wide; fold the rectangle into thirds, aligning the edges. Turn the dough so that the folded edges are at right angles to the rolling pin; roll it out, turn and fold again. Then cover and chill for one hour. Repeat the sequence twice more, doubling the chilling time after each repetition.

3 **Assembling.** Roll the chilled dough into a sheet ⅛ inch [3 mm.] thick; with a cookie cutter, stamp the dough into disks. Prick the center of each disk to prevent it from puffing, brush its edges with water and set the disks in stacks of three on a dampened baking sheet. Score a circular lid on the top disk of each stack before positioning it.

4 **Baking.** Glaze the top only of each case with beaten egg yolk mixed with water. Chill for 20 minutes. Then bake the cases in a preheated 400° F. [200° C.] oven for 30 minutes, turning the sheets at intervals for even browning. Cool the cases for 10 minutes; cut out each lid and remove the raw pastry inside. Dry the cases for 10 minutes in a preheated 300° F. [150° C.] oven.

5 **Preparing filling.** While the cases dry, make a veal velouté (pages 8-9); color it with spinach purée (page 10). Add pieces of cooked ham, slices of truffle if you have them, and pieces of pressed sweetbreads (pages 34-35) that have been poached in veal stock for 30 minutes and drained. Stir the mixture over low heat until it is hot.

6 **Enriching the sauce.** Mix egg yolks and heavy cream. Add a few spoonfuls of the sauce to the egg and cream to warm them. Take the pan off the heat and stir in the egg mixture. Return the pan to very low heat and stir until the sauce thickens. Remove the pan from the heat, let it cool two or three minutes, and stir in chunks of butter.

7 **Filling vol-au-vent cases.** Set the vol-au-vent cases on individual plates. Spoon the filling into and around each vol-au-vent. Pour more sauce over the filled cases, taking care not to drown the exterior of the pastry in liquid. Finish each presentation, if you like, with slivers of truffle and ham.

Yeast Dough to Enclose an Ample Filling

Yeast-bread dough, the source of a variety of appealingly rustic wrappings and containers for hors d'oeuvre, is not at all difficult to make: Success requires only an understanding of the properties of the basic ingredients—and patience.

The dough is composed of all-purpose flour, salt for flavor, water and the living organisms called yeast *(recipe, page 165)*. Yeast for baking is sold either as fresh compressed cakes or as dried granules. Either type must be softened in water or milk before use, and the liquid—like all ingredients used in doughmaking—must be tepid, not cool. Its ideal temperature is 100° F. [40° C.]. Measure the temperature with a yeast thermometer purchased at a kitchen-equipment shop or by sprinkling a drop of liquid on your wrist: The liquid should feel barely warm.

When flour, softened yeast and water are mixed together, several processes begin. The water activates the gluten in the flour so that the dough forms a coherent mass. And, feeding on sugars formed from the starch in the flour, the yeast cells grow and ferment, producing bubbles of carbon-dioxide gas that puff up—or raise—the dough. Kneading the dough until it is smooth and glossy *(Step 3)* strengthens the network of gluten strands; allowing the dough to rest undisturbed gives the carbon-dioxide bubbles time to develop, stretching the gluten network and endowing the dough with its necessary lightness. A typical rising lasts an hour and a half; for a finer-textured dough, punch the mass to expel large bubbles, then let it rise again.

The risen dough is pliable enough to be wrapped around a substantial quantity of savory ingredients; it can then be baked to form an hors d'oeuvre. No rigid rules govern the size or contents of filled breads of this type. You could enfold a filling in a disk of dough to make turnovers, for instance. Or you could sandwich the filling between two disks of dough and bake it in a piepan or cake pan, as in this demonstration.

Savory fillings may comprise meats, seafood, vegetables and cheese, alone or in simple combinations. The filling for the pie shown here is based on shredded escarole *(recipe, page 157)*; spinach and chard are appropriate substitutes.

1 Incorporating yeast. In a large mixing bowl, mix salt and flour. In a small bowl, mix yeast and a little tepid water; let the mixture stand for 10 minutes. Pour the softened yeast, with additional tepid water, into the center of the flour. Rotate the bowl with one hand, and with the other scoop and turn the flour and liquid together, working in from the sides of the bowl.

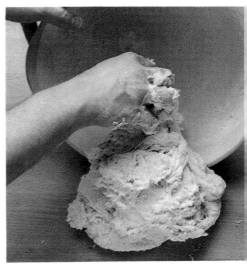

2 Turning out the dough. The dough will form a moist but not liquid mass. Work in a little more flour if the dough seems sticky or loose. Add a small amount of water if it seems stiff. Tip the bowl and push the dough out onto a work surface. Wash, dry and butter the bowl; set it aside.

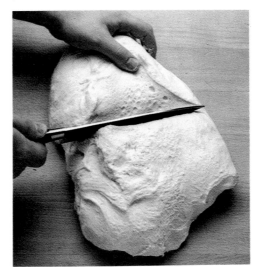

5 Dividing the dough. Punch your fist into the risen dough to expel large gas bubbles. Turn out the dough onto the work surface and slice it in half. Cover one portion with a damp cloth or plastic wrap to keep it from drying while you knead the other *(Step 3)* until it forms a flattened ball. Knead the reserved portion of dough in the same manner. Let both of the portions rest, covered, for 10 minutes.

6 Adding the filling. Lightly butter a round cake pan. Roll out one round of dough to make a disk slightly larger than the pan. Put the dough in the pan and press it into place; its edge should come halfway up the sides of the pan. Spoon the cooled filling onto the dough

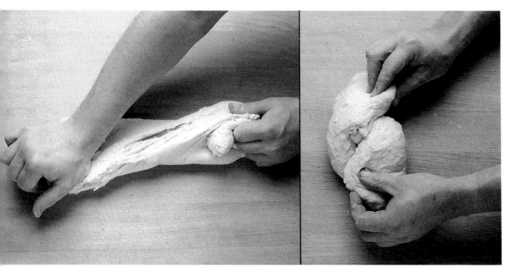

3 **Kneading.** Hold the dough with one hand and use the heel of the other hand to push part of the mass away from you *(above, left)*. (Work gently at first to avoid tearing the dough, which would damage the gluten mesh.) Next, fold the dough back on itself and give it a slight turn *(right)*. Repeatedly stroke, fold and turn the dough for 10 to 15 minutes. Pick up the dough occasionally and throw it back onto the work surface to strengthen the gluten. When the dough feels smooth and stretches easily, place it in the prepared bowl. Cover it with a damp cloth or plastic wrap and set it in a warm, draft-free place. After about one and one half hours, when the dough has doubled in bulk, press it with your finger. It is ready if the dent you make fills in slowly.

4 **Cooking the filling.** While the dough is rising, prepare the filling. Warm olive oil in a pan set over medium heat; add trimmed, shredded escarole leaves, reduce the heat and cook for three or four minutes. Add pine nuts, raisins, capers, black olives, chopped garlic, chopped parsley, and salt and pepper. Stir them together, remove the pan from the heat and let the mixture cool to room temperature.

7 **Making a rim of dough.** With a narrow spatula, spread the filling evenly over the dough. Using the tip of the spatula, turn the free edge of the dough inward over the filling to form a rim. Brush it with water to make it sticky.

8 **Enclosing the filling.** Roll out the second round of dough and, using the base of the pan as a guide, trim the dough into a neat circle. Place the circle on top of the filling. With your fingers, firmly press down the edges of the dough onto the dampened rim formed by the bottom layer of dough, sealing in the filling. Brush the surface with oil, then cover the dough with a damp cloth and let it rise for about 45 minutes.

9 **Baking and serving.** Brush the dough with a lightly beaten mixture of egg white and a little water to glaze it. For a decorative finish, lightly score the surface with a razor in a crisscross pattern. Bake the filled bread at 375° F. [190° C.] for 50 minutes, until it is golden brown. Turn the bread out onto a towel and then invert it onto a plate. Serve it warm, cut into wedges.

Endowing Dough with a Silken Texture

Among the wrappings and containers used for savory fillings, few are so luxuriant in flavor and silken in texture as rich egg-bread dough. Also known as brioche, this is a yeast dough enriched with copious amounts of butter and eggs (recipe, page 165). The dough is formed in a manner similar to that used for plain yeast bread (pages 84-85), but because of the butter and eggs it requires somewhat different handling, and the rising periods are extremely long.

The dough begins with a basic mixture of flour, yeast, and so many eggs that no other liquid is necessary; in fact, this dough is initially so moist that it must be kneaded with the aid of a dough scraper until it is elastic, at which point butter can be kneaded in.

The fine texture of a rich egg-bread dough is the result of three long risings. The first of these takes place, in the usual way, at room temperature. After the risen dough has been punched down, it is refrigerated for its second rising: This chilling slows the process so that the gluten network in the dough is stretched very gently. After this rising, the dough can be shaped, allowed its third and final rising, then baked.

How you shape the dough depends on the texture of the filling you plan to enclose in it. If you wish to use a liquid, stewlike filling, bake the dough in molds to form the hollow containers demonstrated on page 88. If you use a more cohesive filling, however, you can make the dough with a little extra flour—add ¼ cup [50 ml.] per pound of dough—so that it will be stiff enough to hold its shape when it is molded free-form. The strengthened dough may be rolled out into a sheet and used as a wrapper for fillings such as the mixture of seasoned meat, vegetables and grains demonstrated on pages 80-81. Or, as here, you can cut a sheet of dough into strips to coil around lean, spicy pork sausages such as Polish kielbasa or French cervelas (recipe, page 160). Dense fillings of this type should, of course, be precooked: They will not cook through in the time it takes to bake the brioche.

1 Mixing dough. Combine flour, sugar and salt in a large bowl, adding more flour than the recipe specifies if you plan to use the dough as a wrapper. Make a well in the flour and pour in yeast mixed with tepid water. Break eggs into the well; with your fingers, gradually stir the ingredients together to make a loose dough.

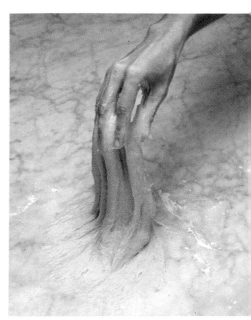

2 Kneading. Turn the dough out onto a work surface, preferably marble. Pull it up with one hand and slap it down. Knead this way until the dough is elastic and pulls away from your hand— about 10 minutes. The dough will spread; use a dough scraper to gather it in. If the dough is too loose to hold together, work in a little sifted flour.

6 Preparing the dough sheet. Coat the peeled sausage lightly with flour. On a floured surface, roll out the dough to a ½-inch [1-cm.] thickness and trim it into two strips, each about 10 inches [25 cm.] long and 2 inches [5 cm.] wide. Lightly brush the strips with cold water.

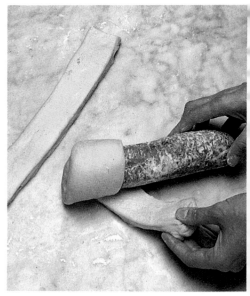

7 Wrapping. Place the tip of the sausage about 1 inch [2½ cm.] from one end of a dough strip, angling the sausage across it. Tuck the end of dough around the sausage and roll it in the dough, overlapping the edges. When you have coiled most of the first strip, press its end onto the second.

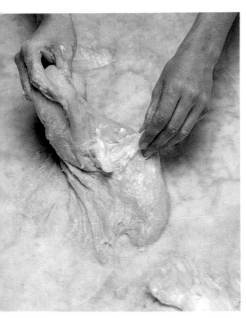

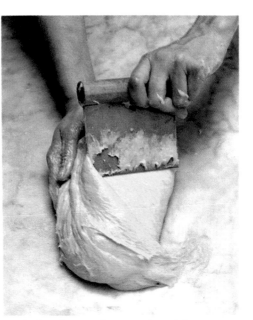

3 **Folding in butter.** Knead butter with the heel of your hand to soften it. Pull the dough slightly apart and tuck a small piece of butter into it. With the dough scraper, repeatedly lift and fold the dough to incorporate the butter. Add the remaining butter bit by bit in the same manner.

4 **Blending and rising.** Knead the dough with one hand, gathering it up with the scraper as it spreads. Continue until the ingredients are blended—two or three minutes. Put the dough in a bowl, cover, and leave at room temperature to rise for three to four hours, until trebled in bulk.

5 **Punching the dough.** Punch the dough several times with your fist. Cover the bowl with plastic wrap and refrigerate it for six to eight hours, until it has doubled in bulk. Meanwhile, prick a 1-pound [½-kg.] pork sausage and simmer it in salted water for 40 minutes. Drain, cool and peel it.

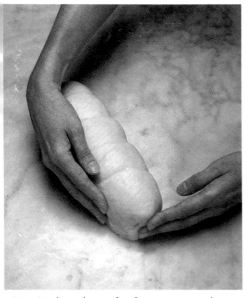

8 **Sealing the ends.** Continue to coil the dough until the sausage is covered. Gently press the open ends of the dough together to seal them. Place the brioche on a buttered baking sheet, positioning it so that the seam joining the two dough strips is underneath.

9 **Glazing the dough.** Brush the dough with lightly beaten egg. Cover the wrapped sausage with a bowl and let it rise for about two hours, until the dough has almost doubled in bulk. Brush the dough again with beaten egg.

10 **Baking and serving.** Bake the assembly in a preheated 425° F. [220° C.] oven for about 35 minutes, until the wrapping is brown. Remove it from the oven and cool it on a rack for about 10 minutes. Transfer it to a wooden board, slice the assembly into rounds and serve immediately.

Brioche Miniatures with Rounded Caps

Rich egg-bread dough *(pages 86-87)* can easily be formed into individual brioches, baked, and then hollowed out to hold a filling. Properly prepared, these containers display a topknot-like lid, which earns them their French name, *brioche à tête*, or "brioche with a head."

To shape the containers, you will need small molds about 3 inches [8 cm.] in diameter; use ramekins or the fluted brioche molds shown here. Fit a portion of dough into each mold and top it with a smaller ball of dough to form the lid. A glaze of beaten egg and cream gives the containers a shiny, golden brown finish.

Once baked and hollowed out, the individual brioches should be dried briefly in a 200° F. [100° C.] oven to help counter any tendency to sogginess after they are filled. As further insurance against sogginess, the fillings should be drier than those used for the less-susceptible vol-au-vent *(pages 82-83):* A moist but not soupy consistency is optimal. But the ingredients for the filling can be varied at will: Cooked vegetables, seafood or meats bound with heavy cream or with thick sauces such as velouté are all suitable.

1 **Shaping cases.** Shape rich egg-bread dough into a cylinder about 2 inches [5 cm.] in diameter. Cut off and reserve a third of the cylinder. Divide the rest into eight pieces; shape each into a ball and fit it into a brioche mold, pressing a hollow in the center.

2 **Forming topknots.** Shape the reserved dough into eight balls and fit each into the hollow of a molded brioche. Cover the molds with a towel and let the brioches rise to the mold rims—about 30 minutes. Brush each brioche with beaten egg and cream.

3 **Baking.** Bake the brioches in a preheated 400° F. [200° C.] oven for 10 minutes; reduce the heat to 375° F. [190° C.] and bake 10 minutes more. Cool and unmold. Cut off the topknots, hollow the brioche centers, and warm brioches and topknots in a low oven.

4 **Serving.** Soak dried wild mushrooms in water for 10 minutes; drain and chop them. Prepare equal amounts of chopped prosciutto, boiled ham, fresh mushrooms and shallots. Sauté the shallots in butter until soft. Add the other ingredients, season, and sauté five minutes more. Stir in veal velouté *(inset; demonstration, pages 8-9)*. Spoon filling into each brioche, cover with a topknot and serve *(right)*.

Anthology of Recipes

Drawing upon the cooking literature of more than 16 countries, the editors and consultants for this volume have selected 200 published recipes for the Anthology that follows. The selections range from the simple to the complex—from an easily made assembly of herring, sour cream and dill to a demanding presentation of poached and diced chicken, sweetbreads and mushrooms, coated with a rich sauce and served in puff pastry.

Many of the recipes were written by world-renowned exponents of the culinary art, but the Anthology also includes selections from rare and out-of-print books and from works that have never been published in English. Whatever the sources, the emphasis in these recipes is always on fresh, natural ingredients that blend harmoniously and on techniques that are practical for the home cook.

Since many early recipe writers did not specify amounts of ingredients, sizes of pans or even cooking times and temperatures, the missing information has been judiciously added. In some cases, clarifying introductory notes have also been supplied; they are printed in italics. Modern recipe terms have been substituted for archaic language; but to preserve the character of the original recipes and to create a true anthology, the authors' texts have been changed as little as possible. Some instructions have necessarily been expanded, but in any circumstance where the cooking directions still seem somewhat abrupt, the reader need only refer to the appropriate demonstrations in the front of the book to find the technique explained.

In keeping with the organization of the first half of the book, most of the recipes are categorized by technique and ingredients. Recipes for standard preparations—stocks, sauces and pastry dough among them—appear at the end of the Anthology. Unfamiliar cooking terms and uncommon ingredients are explained in the combined General Index and Glossary.

All ingredients are listed within each recipe in order of use, with both the customary U.S. measurements and the metric measurements provided. All quantities reflect the American practice of measuring such solid ingredients as flour by volume rather than by weight, as is done in Europe.

To make the quantities simpler to measure, many of the figures have been rounded off to correspond to the gradations on U.S. metric spoons and cups. (One cup, for example, equals 237 milliliters; however, wherever practicable in these recipes, the metric equivalent of 1 cup appears as a more readily measured 250 milliliters—¼ liter.) Similarly, the weight, temperature and linear metric equivalents have been rounded off slightly. Thus the American and metric figures do not exactly match, but using one set or the other will produce the same good results.

Vegetables

Cold Artichoke Bottoms with Salmon Mousse

The author suggests serving this dish with buttered pumpernickel bread. The technique of turning artichoke bottoms is demonstrated on pages 18-19.

	To serve 6	
6	very large artichoke bottoms or 12 medium-sized ones	6
½	lemon plus 1½ tbsp. [22½ ml.] fresh lemon juice	½
2 tbsp.	flour	30 ml.
4 cups	cold water	1 liter
	salt	
¾ cup	vinaigrette *(recipe, page 160)*, made with lemon juice	175 ml.
	paprika	
	large capers	
	fresh dill sprigs	
	ripe olives, preferably Mediterranean-style black olives, pitted	
	Salmon mousse	
1 lb.	salmon fillets, poached for 2 minutes, drained, skinned and flaked (about 2 cups [½ liter])	½ kg.
3 tbsp.	mayonnaise *(recipe, page 161)*	45 ml.
	freshly ground white pepper	
	cayenne pepper	
1 tbsp.	finely cut fresh dill	15 ml.
3 tbsp.	*crème fraîche* or whipped cream (optional)	45 ml.

Rub the artichoke bottoms with the cut side of the lemon half. In a large enameled saucepan, combine the flour, 1 tablespoon [15 ml.] of the lemon juice and the water. Bring the mixture to a boil; add a pinch of salt and the artichoke bottoms. Cook them for 20 to 30 minutes, or until tender. Drain and cool them, and dry them well on paper towels. As soon as they are cool enough to handle, remove the choke from each bottom with a spoon. Pour the lemon vinaigrette over the bottoms, cover, and marinate for two hours.

Purée the salmon in a blender or put it through the fine disk of a food grinder. Add the mayonnaise, salt, white pepper, a touch of cayenne, the remaining lemon juice and a few sprigs of dill. Chill the mixture for one hour. The mixture must be quite thick in order to stay on the artichoke bottoms—but if it seems too thick, thin it out with a little *crème fraîche* or whipped cream.

Drain the artichoke bottoms and dry them well on paper towels. Top each one with a dome of salmon mousse. Sprinkle the mousse lightly with paprika. Make a little circle of capers on each dome and top each one with two tiny sprigs of dill and an olive. Chill again and serve cold.

PERLA MEYERS
THE SEASONAL KITCHEN

Stuffed Artichokes

Carciofi Ripieni

The technique of turning and stuffing artichoke bottoms is demonstrated on pages 18-19. Cepes are edible wild mushrooms, available dried at specialty food stores.

	To serve 6	
⅓ cup	chopped ham, including the fat	75 ml.
1	small scallion, the green part discarded, the white part chopped	1
1	garlic clove, finely chopped	1
1 tbsp.	chopped celery leaves	15 ml.
1 tbsp.	chopped fresh parsley	15 ml.
1 tbsp.	dried cepes, soaked in warm water for 30 minutes, drained and finely chopped	15 ml.
1 cup	fresh bread crumbs	¼ liter
6	artichokes, the bottoms turned and the tender inner leaves reserved	6
	salt and pepper	

To make the stuffing, combine the ham, scallion, garlic, celery leaves, parsley, cepes and bread crumbs. Chop the tender leaves removed from the artichokes and mix them with the other stuffing ingredients. Season the mixture with salt and pepper.

Fill the cavities in the artichoke bottoms with the stuffing, and use any leftover stuffing to line a buttered baking dish large enough to hold the artichoke bottoms in a single layer. Set the stuffed artichokes in the dish and add enough water to the dish to cover them by 1 inch [2 cm.]. Cover the dish and bake in a preheated 350° F. [180° C.] oven for about one hour, or until the artichoke bottoms are tender.

PELLEGRINO ARTUSI
LA SCIENZA IN CUCINA E L'ARTE DI MANGIAR BENE

Small Artichokes in Marinade

Petits Artichauts à la Grecque

The technique of turning artichoke bottoms is demonstrated on pages 18-19. If very small artichokes are not available, larger artichokes may be used: Halve or quarter them and remove the chokes before cooking.

To serve 6 to 8

½ cup	strained fresh lemon juice	125 ml.
36	small artichokes	36
¼ cup	olive oil	50 ml.
1 tsp.	salt	5 ml.
8 to 10	peppercorns	8 to 10
8 to 10	coriander seeds	8 to 10
½ tsp.	fennel seeds	2 ml.
1	celery rib	1
1	sprig thyme	1
1	bay leaf	1

Fill a large nonreactive pan almost full of water and add ¼ cup [50 ml.] of the lemon juice. Bring the water to a boil. Trim the artichokes, turn their bottoms and plunge the bottoms into the water. Boil for five minutes, then drain the bottoms. Plunge them into cold water to stop the cooking, and drain them again. Put the artichoke bottoms into a nonreactive saucepan with 1 cup [¼ liter] of cold water, the remaining lemon juice, the olive oil and seasonings. Bring to a boil, reduce the heat, cover, and simmer for 35 to 40 minutes, or until the bottoms are tender. Cool them in the cooking liquid, then chill before serving.

PROSPER SALLES AND PROSPER MONTAGNÉ
LA GRANDE CUISINE

Artichokes Stuffed with Ham

To serve 6

6	medium-sized artichokes, trimmed	6
3	shallots, chopped	3
8 tbsp.	butter	120 ml.
2 cups	chopped ham	½ liter
1½ cups	fresh bread crumbs	375 ml.
2	garlic cloves, crushed to a paste	2
2 tbsp.	chopped fresh parsley	30 ml.
	salt and freshly ground black pepper	
1½ cups	white wine	375 ml.
1½ cups	meat stock *(recipe, page 163)*	375 ml.

Cook the artichokes in plenty of boiling salted water for 20 to 30 minutes—just until a leaf can be pulled out with a sharp tug. Drain them and cool them upside down on a rack. Discard the inside leaves and scoop out the hairy chokes with a teaspoon, scraping the cavity of each artichoke clean to form a hollow cup. Sauté the shallots in the butter until soft but not brown, and stir in the ham, bread crumbs, garlic, parsley and plenty of pepper. Taste for seasoning; salt may not be needed if the ham is salty. Spoon this mixture into the cavities of the partially cooked artichokes.

Set the artichokes in a deep casserole or baking dish, pour in the wine and stock, cover, and cook in a preheated 350° F. [180° C.] oven for 35 to 40 minutes, or until the artichokes are very tender. Baste them occasionally during cooking. Serve the artichokes in soup bowls, with the cooking liquid spooned over them.

ANNE WILLAN
ENTERTAINING

Stuffed Beets

Gefüllte Rote Rüben

To cook the beets, trim them carefully to avoid damaging the skin, wash them, and immerse them in rapidly boiling water to which 1 to 2 tablespoons [15 to 30 ml.] of vinegar have been added. Simmer for about one hour.

To serve 6 to 8

6 to 8	medium-sized beets, cooked and peeled	6 to 8
1	medium-sized onion, chopped	1
4 tbsp.	butter	60 ml.
1 lb.	ground meat, cooked until browned	½ kg.
½ cup	white rice, boiled for 20 minutes and drained	125 ml.
1	egg	1
	salt and pepper	
1 cup	sour cream	¼ liter

Use a teaspoon to scoop out the centers of the beets. Fry the onion in half of the butter until transparent, then mix it with the cooked meat and rice, the egg, salt and pepper. Fill the beets with the stuffing. Butter a baking dish, arrange the stuffed beets in it and bake them in a preheated 400° F. [200° C.] oven for eight to 10 minutes to heat the stuffing.

Remove the beets from the oven, pour the sour cream over them and return them to the oven for a few minutes.

KULINARISCHE GERICHTE

Avocado Mousse
Mousse d'Avocats

The author suggests placing a seafood salad inside the ring.

To serve 6

2 tbsp.	fresh lemon juice	30 ml.
4	ripe avocados, halved, pitted, peeled and mashed to a purée with a fork	4
2 tbsp.	unflavored powdered gelatin, softened in ¼ cup [50 ml.] cold water	30 ml.
1 cup	mayonnaise *(recipe, page 161)*	¼ liter
1	small garlic clove, finely chopped	1
	salt and freshly ground black pepper	
¼ tsp.	cayenne pepper	1 ml.
3 tbsp.	heavy cream, lightly whipped	45 ml.

Blend the lemon juice into the mashed avocados. Melt the gelatin mixture over low heat and stir it into the avocados. Add the mayonnaise, garlic, salt, black pepper and cayenne. When the avocado mixture is cool, fold in the whipped cream. Taste for seasoning. Pour the mixture into a lightly oiled 5-cup [1¼-liter] ring mold, cover it tightly with plastic wrap and chill it for at least two hours, or until set.

Not more than 30 minutes before serving, run a knife around the edge and unmold the mousse onto a serving dish.

ANNE WILLAN AND JANE GRIGSON (EDITORS)
THE OBSERVER FRENCH COOKERY SCHOOL

Salad of Green Beans with Raw Mushrooms
La Salade des Haricots Verts aux Champignons

To serve 4

2 cups	water	½ liter
2 or 3	sprigs fresh summer savory, or substitute 1 tsp. [5 ml.] dried savory	2 or 3
1½ lb.	green beans	¾ kg.
2 or 3	sprigs fresh rosemary, or substitute 1 tsp. [5 ml.] dried rosemary	2 or 3
4 tbsp.	unsalted butter	60 ml.
about ¼ cup	chopped fresh basil leaves, or substitute 2 tsp. [10 ml.] dried basil	about 50 ml.
2 tbsp.	tarragon white-wine vinegar	30 ml.
½ cup	fresh button mushrooms, thinly sliced	125 ml.
1 tbsp.	walnut oil	15 ml.
¼ cup	chopped fresh parsley	50 ml.

In a 2-quart [2-liter] saucepan, bring the water up to boiling with the summer savory. Then let it simmer, covered, for as long as it takes to wash and cut the beans. If they are small, merely top and tail them. If large, they may be snapped, chunked or frenched through a cutter. Drop the beans into the simmering water, adding a little more hot water, if necessary, just to cover them. Add the rosemary, then keep the water bubbling merrily, uncovered, so that the beans steam as the water gradually boils down, until the beans are just done but still nicely crisp—usually in 12 to 15 minutes.

Meanwhile, soften the butter in a mortar and work into it the basil leaves, plus 1 tablespoon [15 ml.] of the vinegar. Toss the mushrooms with the oil and remaining vinegar.

As soon as the beans are perfectly done, pour off the water (saving it for stock) and put the saucepan over low heat for two or three minutes to dry out the beans. Pick out and discard any remaining sprigs of rosemary or savory. Finally, pile the beans into a hot serving bowl and toss into them the basil butter, mushrooms and parsley. Serve at once.

ROY ANDRIES DE GROOT
THE AUBERGE OF THE FLOWERING HEARTH

Cabbage Leaves Stuffed with Garden Greens
Gâteau d'Herbage à l'Ancienne

The technique of making a vegetable cake is demonstrated on pages 68-69. If the water in the water bath starts to simmer, turn down the oven to 350° F. [180° C.].

To serve 4

1	bouquet garni	1
1½ cups	fresh spinach, stems removed	375 ml.
2	large leeks, white part only, sliced	2
½ cup	sorrel, stems removed	125 ml.
8	large green cabbage leaves, ribs removed	8
½ cup	Swiss chard, stems removed	125 ml.
1	egg	1
½ cup	skim milk	125 ml.
	salt and pepper	
½ tsp.	chopped fresh tarragon	2 ml.
½ tsp.	finely cut fresh chives	2 ml.
½ tsp.	chopped fresh parsley	2 ml.
⅓ cup	chopped onion	75 ml.

Using the same lightly salted boiling water, boil each vegetable separately with the bouquet garni. Boil the spinach for three minutes, the leeks for nine minutes, and the sorrel, cabbage and chard for four minutes each. Drain each vegetable in turn and pat the pieces dry with paper towels. Beat the egg lightly with a fork, and add the skim milk, a pinch each of the salt and pepper, and the chopped herbs and onion.

Line a buttered 6-inch [15-cm.] cake pan, about 2 inches

[5 cm.] deep, with the cabbage leaves, letting the leaves overhang the sides by a measure wide enough to allow the leaves to cover the cake completely. Arrange the cake in the pan in layers: first the leeks; next the spinach, sorrel and chard; and then a few spoonfuls of the egg-and-herb mixture. Repeat with layers of vegetables and egg-and-herb mixture until all of the ingredients are used up, ending with the egg-and-herb mixture. Fold the cabbage leaves over the top.

Cover the cake with foil and bake it in a water bath in a preheated 425° F. [220° C.] oven for one and one quarter hours. Before turning it out of the cake pan, let it rest at room temperature for 15 minutes so that it will settle a bit and keep its shape when sliced.

MICHEL GUÉRARD
MICHEL GUÉRARD'S CUISINE MINCEUR

Cauliflower in Salsa Verde

To serve 4

1	cauliflower, trimmed and divided into florets, boiled in salted water for 10 minutes, drained and refreshed	1
½ lb.	watercress leaves, 2 tbsp. [30 ml.] chopped	¼ kg.
½ to ⅔ cup	olive oil	125 to 150 ml.
¼ cup	fresh lemon juice	50 ml.
2 tbsp.	chopped fresh parsley	30 ml.
2 tbsp.	finely chopped ripe olives	30 ml.
2 tbsp.	chopped, broiled and peeled sweet red pepper	30 ml.
1 tsp.	salt	5 ml.
	cayenne pepper	

In a medium-sized round mixing bowl, arrange the cauliflower florets snugly with the flowers pressed against the sides of the bowl and the stems pointing into the center. Pack the center full of the remaining cauliflower. Put a plate on top of the cauliflower and weight it down. Let it stand for at least 15 minutes, then tip the bowl carefully without removing the plate and drain off any liquid. Place the bowl, weight and all, in the refrigerator for at least two hours.

To make the *salsa verde,* combine the chopped watercress, the olive oil, the lemon juice, parsley, olives, red pepper, salt and a pinch of cayenne pepper. Mix well and chill.

To serve, remove the weight and plate from the cauliflower. Place a serving plate over the bowl, turn the bowl over quickly and remove the bowl carefully. The florets will turn out in a dome shape and will hold together. Arrange the watercress around them. Spoon on some *salsa verde* and pass the rest at the table.

ELEANOR GRAVES
GREAT DINNERS FROM LIFE

Stuffed Celery

To serve 4

2 tbsp.	butter	30 ml.
1 ¼ cups	sliced fresh mushrooms	300 ml.
¼ cup	flour	50 ml.
1 cup	milk	¼ liter
	salt and pepper	
8	celery ribs, cut into 1-inch [2½-cm.] pieces, parboiled in salted water for 5 minutes and drained	8
½ cup	finely shredded Cheddar cheese	125 ml.

In a saucepan, melt the butter and cook the mushrooms over low heat until they are soft. Sprinkle them with the flour, stir in the milk, and season with salt and pepper. Stirring continuously, cook until the sauce thickens—about two minutes. Arrange the celery in a buttered gratin dish. Pour the mushroom sauce over the celery and sprinkle with the shredded cheese. Bake in a preheated 425° F. [220° C.] oven for 10 minutes, or until the top is lightly browned.

RUTH LOWINSKY
LOVELY FOOD

Chick-pea Salad with Tahini

Ensalada de Garbanzos con Tahine

The tahini called for in this recipe is a paste made from roasted or unroasted ground sesame seeds. It is obtainable in cans or jars where Middle Eastern foods are sold.

To serve 4

2 cups	dried chick-peas (about 1 lb. [½ kg.]), soaked in water overnight and drained	425 ml.
3 tbsp.	*tahini*	45 ml.
3 to 4 tbsp.	strained fresh lemon juice	45 to 60 ml.
4	garlic cloves, crushed to a paste	4
	salt	
1 tbsp.	chopped fresh parsley	15 ml.
½ cup	olive oil	125 ml.

Blanch the chick-peas for about 30 minutes in enough water to cover them. Then drain and cool them and remove as many skins as possible. Simmer the chick-peas in fresh water for two to three hours, or until they are tender. Then purée them in a food processor or blender. Separately beat together the *tahini,* 3 tablespoons [45 ml.] of lemon juice, the garlic and salt, and combine this mixture with the chick-peas until you have a smooth paste. Taste, and add more lemon juice if desired. To serve, mound the paste on a dish, garnish with parsley and sprinkle the top with oil.

EL MUNDO GASTRONÓMICO

Stuffed Swiss Chard or Vine Leaves
Les Farcettes

The techniques of preparing and stuffing leaves are shown on pages 20-21. Although specific types of cooked lean meat are listed here, any combination of an equivalent volume of leftover meats can be used.

To serve 5

8 tbsp.	butter	120 ml.
¼ cup	flour	50 ml.
1 cup	meat roasting juices, skimmed of fat, or substitute meat stock (recipe, page 163)	¼ liter
½ cup	heavy cream	125 ml.
	salt and pepper	
½ cup	julienned roast chicken breast	125 ml.
½ cup	julienned lean roast beef	125 ml.
½ cup	julienned lean roast leg of lamb	125 ml.
½ cup	julienned lean ham	125 ml.
10	Swiss chard leaves, ribs removed, or fresh grapevine leaves, steeped in boiling water for 5 minutes and drained	10
⅔ cup	freshly grated Gruyère cheese	150 ml.

In a saucepan, combine about 2 tablespoons [30 ml.] of the butter with the flour. Stirring constantly, cook the mixture until it is browned—about 10 minutes. Moisten with 5 to 6 tablespoons [75 to 90 ml.] of the meat juices and beat to make a smooth paste. Dilute the paste by gradually adding the cream, a little at a time; keep the sauce fairly thick. Season with salt and pepper, and simmer over low heat for five minutes. Stir in the chicken, beef, lamb and ham.

Divide the stuffing among the 10 chard or vine leaves, and fold the leaves over the stuffing to make small parcels. Place the parcels, seams downward, in a gratin dish just large enough to hold them. Pour in the rest of the meat juices. Cut the remaining butter into equal-sized pieces and dot the stuffed leaves with it. Sprinkle the leaves with the grated cheese and bake them in a preheated 350° F. [180° C.] oven for one hour. If the leaves brown too quickly, reduce the heat during the cooking time.

LUCIEN TENDRET
LA TABLE AU PAYS DE BRILLAT-SAVARIN

Winter or Christmas Caponata
Caponata d'Inverno o di Natale

To roast almonds, place blanched almonds on a baking sheet in a preheated 400° F. [200° C.] oven for 10 minutes, or until lightly browned.

This dish is a specialty of Catania in Sicily. There, *caponata* is usually served as a summer or autumn hors d'oeuvre based on eggplant.

To serve 6 to 8

2	bunches celery, cleaned, sliced and parboiled for 8 to 10 minutes	2
1¼ cups	green olives, pitted	300 ml.
3 tbsp.	capers, rinsed and drained	45 ml.
½ cup	olive oil	125 ml.
3 tbsp.	vinegar	45 ml.
2 tsp.	sugar	10 ml.
¾ cup	coarsely chopped roasted almonds	175 ml.
2 tbsp.	dry bread crumbs	30 ml.
½ cup	seedless raisins, soaked in warm water for 15 minutes and drained	125 ml.

In a nonreactive pan combine the celery with the olives, capers and oil. Mix well, then add the vinegar and sugar. Cook over medium heat until the vinegar evaporates. Remove the pan from the heat, and add most of the almonds. Mix in the bread crumbs and raisins. Let the *caponata* cool to room temperature. Stir the *caponata* well, place it on a serving dish and garnish with the remaining roasted almonds.

LUIGI VOLPICELLI AND SECONDINO FREDA (EDITORS)
L'ANTIARTUSI: 1000 RICETTE

Baked Eggplant with Cheese
Parmigiana di Melanzane

The recipe for this dish can be prepared *in bianco*, that is, without the tomato sauce.

To serve 4

2	medium-sized eggplants, cut lengthwise into slices about ¼ inch [6 mm.] thick	2
⅓ cup	oil	75 ml.
8	fresh basil leaves, chopped	8
⅔ cup	freshly grated Parmesan cheese	150 ml.
1¼ cups	tomato sauce (recipe, page 162)	300 ml.
1 lb.	mozzarella cheese, thinly sliced	½ kg.
1½ tbsp.	butter, cut into pieces	22½ ml.

Spread out the eggplant slices in a large dish or tray, sprinkle them generously with salt and let them drain for 30 minutes. Then rinse them and pat them dry with paper towels. Heat the oil and fry the eggplant slices, a few at a time, until they are brown—about six to eight minutes. Turn the slices frequently and take care that they do not burn. Drain them on paper towels.

Mix the chopped basil leaves with the grated cheese. Butter a deep 8-inch [20-cm.] cake pan and cover the bottom with a layer of eggplant slices. Pour on a little tomato sauce, then sprinkle with the grated-cheese-and-basil mixture, and place a few slices of mozzarella cheese here and there. Cover with a second layer of eggplant slices, then some tomato sauce, grated cheese and basil and a few slices of mozzarella, and continue filling the pan with the layers until all the ingredients are used up, finishing with a layer of sauce and mozzarella cheese. Dot the top with the pieces of butter. Bake the eggplant in a preheated 375° F. [190° C.] oven for about 20 minutes, or until the mozzarella is melted and the sauce bubbly. Serve in the pan.

FERNANDA GOSETTI
IN CUCINA CON FERNANDA GOSETTI

Spicy Baby Eggplant

Baigan Masaledar

The garam masala called for in this recipe is a mixture of such spices as black pepper, cardamom, cinnamon and cloves. Asafetida is a spice with a garlic-like flavor. Both are available at Indian grocery stores.

This recipe calls for tiny eggplants—as small as 2 to 3 inches [5 to 8 cm.] and weighing about 2 ounces [60 g.] each; they are available in both white and purple. In India they are a highly prized delicacy. This particular recipe reflects the typical flavoring of the Rajasthanis, and is very spicy.

	To serve 4	
8	tiny eggplants (about 1 lb. [½ kg.])	8
2 tsp.	ground coriander	10 ml.
1 tsp.	ground cumin	5 ml.
¼ to ½ tsp.	cayenne pepper	1 to 2 ml.
1½ tsp.	fresh lemon juice	7 ml.
½ tsp.	garam masala	2 ml.
1 tsp.	coarse salt	5 ml.
2 tbsp.	vegetable oil	30 ml.
½ tsp.	cumin seeds	2 ml.
⅛ tsp.	ground asafetida	½ ml.
	salt	

Cut off the eggplant stems, being careful not to cut the green skirtlike top. Quarter the eggplants from the stem end, cutting through the green part, to within ¾ inch [2 cm.] of the bottom. Put the eggplants in a bowl and add enough cold water to cover. Soak them for 15 minutes. (This will make the eggplants open up slightly like flower buds. Do not oversoak or they will open up too much.) Drain and pat them dry. Combine the coriander, cumin, cayenne, lemon juice, *garam masala* and salt, and use this mixture to stuff the eggplants,

making sure to distribute it evenly. Press gently to reshape the eggplants.

Heat the oil over medium-high heat in a large skillet. When the oil is very hot, add the cumin seeds. When the seeds turn dark brown, after about 10 seconds, add the asafetida and immediately follow with the eggplants. Stir for 10 to 15 seconds, then reduce the heat to low. Sprinkle on any reserved stuffing mixture, and fry, turning and tossing for three to five minutes, or until the oil coats the eggplants. Increase the heat to medium, and fry the eggplants until they are lightly browned. Sprinkle 2 to 3 tablespoons [30 to 45 ml.] of water over the eggplants, reduce the heat to very low, and cook, covered, for about 20 minutes, or until they are tender. Stir a few times, being very careful not to break the eggplants. Uncover, increase the heat to medium-low, and continue cooking for five to 10 minutes, or until all of the remaining moisture has evaporated and the eggplants look glazed. Season with salt, if necessary, and serve.

JULIE SAHNI
CLASSIC INDIAN COOKING

Corsican Stuffed Eggplant

Aubergines Farcies

The eggplants may be served covered with a spicy tomato sauce (recipe, page 162).

	To serve 12	
6	medium-sized eggplants, halved lengthwise	6
6	slices firm-textured white bread, crusts removed, soaked in milk and squeezed dry	6
3	garlic cloves, chopped	3
5	large fresh basil leaves, chopped	5
	salt and freshly ground pepper	
2	eggs	2
1 tbsp.	butter, softened	15 ml.
⅔ cup	freshly grated Parmesan cheese	150 ml.
½ cup	oil	125 ml.

Parboil the eggplant halves for eight to 10 minutes, removing them while they are still firm. Let them cool until tepid, then scoop out the pulp. Strain it through an old cloth—the weave will be looser—or a sieve. Chop the strained pulp and mix it with the bread, garlic and basil; season with salt and pepper. Beat in the eggs, one at a time, then the butter and finally the grated cheese.

Fill the 12 eggplant shells with the prepared stuffing, and fry them in the oil on both sides, beginning with the stuffing side down, until they are golden—about five minutes on each side.

MARIA NUNZIA FILIPPINI
LA CUISINE CORSE

Jewish-Style Eggplant Bits

Melanzana Alla Giudea

To serve 4

4	large eggplants, ends trimmed	4
2 tsp.	salt	10 ml.
1 tbsp.	oil	15 ml.
1 tbsp.	butter	15 ml.
4	garlic cloves, finely chopped	4

Slice the eggplants in half lengthwise and scrape out the pulp, leaving a shell ½ inch [1 cm.] thick. (Reserve the pulp for another use.) Cut the shells into 1-inch [2½-cm.] squares. Place the squares in a strainer or colander and sprinkle them with the salt. Place a heavy saucepan on top to crush the eggplant, and set it aside for one hour so that the bitter juices drain off.

Heat the oil and the butter in a skillet, add the eggplant squares and the garlic, cover, and cook until the squares are soft—15 minutes. Remove the lid and fry the squares 10 minutes to brown them on all sides. Drain them on a paper towel. Chill the eggplant squares for at least two hours before serving them.

JOAN NATHAN AND JUDY STACEY GOLDMAN
THE FLAVOR OF JERUSALEM

Egyptian-Style Eggplant

Auberginen auf Ägyptische Art

To serve 4

2	medium-sized eggplants, peeled and cut lengthwise into ½-inch [1-cm.] slices	2
½ cup	oil	125 ml.
1¾ cups	fresh bread crumbs	425 ml.
1	onion, finely chopped	1
4	slices bacon, chopped	4
3 tbsp.	finely chopped fresh parsley	45 ml.
1	garlic clove, crushed to a paste	1
	salt and pepper	

Brown the eggplant slices on both sides in the oil and drain them on paper towels. To make a topping, mix the bread crumbs, onion, bacon, parsley, garlic, and salt and pepper to taste. Spread the topping over the eggplant slices and lay the slices side by side in buttered gratin dishes or on buttered baking sheets. Bake in a preheated 350° F. [180° C.] oven for about 20 to 30 minutes, or until the topping is light gold.

THEODOR BÖTTIGER
DAS GRILL-BUCH

Pickled Eggplant

Caponata

This Sicilian appetizer will keep for weeks if it is stored in the refrigerator.

To serve 8 to 12

1½ cups	olive oil	375 ml.
4	medium-sized eggplants, peeled and cut into 1-inch [2½-cm.] cubes	4
4	large onions, thinly sliced	4
1 cup	drained, canned Italian-style plum tomatoes, puréed	¼ liter
4	celery ribs, strings peeled off, cut into ½-inch [1-cm.] dice	4
½ cup	capers, rinsed and drained	125 ml.
½ cup	finely chopped fresh parsley	125 ml.
16	ripe black olives, pitted and chopped	16
2 tbsp.	pine nuts	30 ml.
½ cup	red wine vinegar	125 ml.
¼ cup	sugar	50 ml.
½ tsp. each	salt and freshly ground pepper	2 ml. each
⅛ tsp.	dried red hot-pepper flakes	½ ml.
	lettuce leaves	

Heat 1 cup [¼ liter] of the oil in a large, heavy skillet. Over medium heat, cook as many of the eggplant pieces at a time as will fit in one layer in the skillet. Stir constantly, until the eggplant pieces are soft and browned—about 10 minutes; do not overcook. Put the cooked eggplant in a bowl and cook the remaining pieces in the same way; add them to the first lot.

Add the remaining oil to the skillet. Add the onions and cook, stirring constantly, for three to five minutes, or until the onions are soft. Then add the tomatoes and celery, and cook, stirring frequently, until the celery is soft—about five minutes. If necessary to prevent scorching, add a little water. Add the capers, parsley, olives, pine nuts and the fried eggplant pieces. Mix well. Remove the skillet from the heat.

Heat the vinegar and sugar in a small saucepan; stir until the sugar is dissolved. Pour the mixture over the vegetables. Season with salt, ground pepper and hot-pepper flakes. Return the skillet to the lowest possible heat. Simmer covered, stirring frequently, for about 20 minutes. If necessary to prevent scorching, add a little water, a tablespoonful at a time; the *caponata* should be soft but not soupy. Cool before serving on lettuce leaves.

NIKA HAZELTON
THE REGIONAL ITALIAN KITCHEN

Stuffed Escarole

Scarola Ripiena

To serve 4 to 6

3	garlic cloves, crushed to a paste	3
½ cup	olive oil	125 ml.
1 cup	fresh bread crumbs	¼ liter
1 tbsp.	capers, rinsed and drained	15 ml.
1 tbsp.	chopped fresh parsley	15 ml.
4	salt anchovies, soaked in water for 30 minutes, filleted and drained	4
12	ripe olives, halved and pitted	12
	salt and freshly ground black pepper	
4	heads escarole, trimmed, blanched for 3 minutes in boiling salted water and drained	4

In a skillet, sauté the garlic in 6 tablespoons [90 ml.] of the oil. Remove the garlic when it is golden. Add half of the bread crumbs, the capers, parsley, anchovies, olives, salt and pepper. Stir well and sauté for a few minutes. Stuff the escarole heads with this mixture, and close them firmly without squeezing too much. Arrange them in an oiled, shallow baking dish. Sprinkle with the remaining bread crumbs and oil. Cover and bake in a preheated 350° F. [180° C.] oven for 20 minutes. Uncover and bake for 10 minutes more. Serve cold.

FRANCO LAGATTOLLA
THE RECIPES THAT MADE A MILLION

Belgian Endive Cooked Like Asparagus

Chicons en Asperges

To serve 4

2 lb.	Belgian endive, bases trimmed	1 kg.
⅓ cup	strained fresh lemon juice	75 ml.
1 tsp.	sugar	5 ml.
	salt and pepper	
	stiff flour-and-water paste	
10 tbsp.	butter	150 ml.
4	sprigs fresh parsley, chopped	4
4	eggs, boiled for 9 minutes, cooled in cold water and shelled	4

Put the endive in a baking dish with a lid. Sprinkle it with the lemon juice, sugar, salt and pepper. Cover the dish. Use the paste to seal the lid. Bake the endive in a preheated 350° F. [180° C.] oven for one and one half hours. To serve, melt the butter, add the parsley and pour into a sauceboat. Let each person crush an egg on his plate, dilute it with butter sauce and then soak the endive in the mixture.

CÉLINE VENCE
ENCYCLOPÉDIE HACHETTE DE LA CUISINE RÉGIONALE

Baked Fresh Garlic

Ail Nouveau au Four

Use only freshly dug garlic bulbs—available from August through October. Serve the garlic on buttered toast.

To serve 6

	salt	
8	large garlic bulbs, stems and roots cut off	8
3 tbsp.	butter, cut into 8 pieces	45 ml.

Generously butter a gratin dish and sprinkle it with 1 teaspoon [5 ml.] of salt. Put the garlic into the dish. Into the top of each bulb, put three pinches of salt and a piece of butter. Pour in 1 cup [¼ liter] of water and bake in a preheated 400° F. [200° C.] oven for 50 minutes, or until tender, basting the garlic every 10 minutes; add more water if needed.

MICHEL OLIVER
MES RECETTES

Russian Stuffed Grapevine Leaves

Dolma

For an alternative sauce, mix 2 teaspoons [10 ml.] of ground cinnamon with 2 tablespoons [30 ml.] of confectioners' sugar and 1¼ cups [300 ml.] of buttermilk.

To serve 6 to 8

1 lb.	boneless lamb, ground	½ kg.
1½ cups	cooked white rice	375 ml.
1	onion, grated	1
1 tbsp.	finely cut fresh dill	15 ml.
	salt and pepper	
1 lb.	fresh grapevine leaves, trimmed	½ kg.
1 tbsp.	butter, melted	15 ml.
1 cup	meat stock (recipe, page 163)	¼ liter
1¼ cups	buttermilk, or 1 cup [¼ liter] sour cream diluted with ¼ cup [50 ml.] milk	300 ml.
1	garlic clove, finely chopped	1

Mix the ground meat with the rice, onion and dill. Season with salt and pepper. Spread the grapevine leaves on a table in overlapping pairs. Put a bit of stuffing on the wide end of each pair of leaves, fold the edges inward and roll the leaves into a sausage shape. Sprinkle the stuffed leaves with salt and arrange them in layers in a buttered, heavy skillet. Pour in the butter and the stock. Cover the skillet tightly and simmer over low heat for about one hour, or until the leaves are very tender. Mix the buttermilk or diluted sour cream with the garlic and a little salt, and serve separately.

F. SIEGEL (TRANSLATOR)
RUSSIAN COOKING

Stuffed Vine Leaves

Yalanci Dolma

The technique of stuffing vine leaves is shown on pages 20-21.

To serve 4

1	medium-sized onion, finely chopped	1
1 tbsp.	olive oil	15 ml.
½ cup	white rice	125 ml.
½ cup	dried currants, soaked in warm water for 15 minutes and drained	125 ml.
¼ cup	pine nuts	50 ml.
1 tbsp.	chopped fresh parsley	15 ml.
	ground allspice	
	ground cinnamon	
	salt and black pepper	
1 tbsp.	tomato sauce *(recipe, page 162)*	15 ml.
about 40	fresh grapevine or cabbage leaves, parboiled for 1 minute, refreshed in cold water and drained	about 40
3 tbsp.	strained fresh lemon juice	45 ml.

In a skillet, fry the onion in the olive oil until it becomes transparent. Wash and rinse the rice well and add it to the onion, and fry them both for a few minutes, stirring well; then add just enough water to cover the rice. Add the currants, pine nuts, parsley and a pinch each of allspice, cinnamon, salt and pepper. Cover and cook the mixture until the rice is dry—about 10 minutes. Stir in the tomato sauce.

Using about 20 of the leaves, put a tablespoonful [15 ml.] of the stuffing in the center of each leaf. Roll up each leaf into a little parcel and place it in a heavy pot. Pack the rolled parcels tightly, and between each layer place some more leaves. When all of the parcels are wedged into the pot, press an inverted saucer on top and cover them with water and the lemon juice to the level of the saucer. Set the lid on the pot and simmer the vine leaves for one hour. Drain the parcels and arrange them on a platter. Serve them lukewarm or refrigerate until chilled.

VENICE LAMB
THE HOME BOOK OF TURKISH COOKERY

Stuffed Grapevine Leaves

Misov Derevapatat

If you use preserved vine leaves, there is no need to parboil them, but rinse them thoroughly in cold water and dry them

with a cloth. The technique of stuffing and cooking vine leaves is demonstrated on pages 20-21.

To serve 4 to 6

1 lb.	boneless lamb shoulder, finely chopped	½ kg.
1⅓ cups	finely chopped onions	325 ml.
2 tbsp.	chopped fresh parsley	30 ml.
¼ cup	long-grain white rice	50 ml.
1 tsp.	salt	5 ml.
	black pepper	
5 tbsp.	puréed tomato	75 ml.
1½ tbsp.	fresh lemon juice	22½ ml.
16 to 18	fresh grapevine leaves, parboiled for 2 minutes	16 to 18

Mix the lamb, onions, parsley, rice, salt, pepper, puréed tomato and lemon juice. Roll the vine leaves around spoonfuls of the mixture to make small packages about 3 by ¾ inches [7 by 2 cm.]. Place the stuffed leaves in rows in a baking dish and cover them with water. Cover the dish and bake in a preheated 350° F. [180° C.] oven for one hour.

GEORGE MARDIKIAN
DINNER AT OMAR KHAYYAM'S

Baked Leeks

Überbackener Lauch

To serve 4

8	leeks, trimmed, dark green parts removed	8
½ cup	water	125 ml.
½ tsp.	salt	2 ml.
2 tbsp.	butter, melted	30 ml.
2 tbsp.	dry bread crumbs	30 ml.
½ cup	freshly grated cheese	125 ml.
½ tsp.	paprika	2 ml.

Slice the leeks in half lengthwise, wash them thoroughly, then cut them crosswise into 1-inch [2½-cm.] pieces. Bring the water to a boil with the salt, add the leeks, cover, and simmer for 10 minutes. Transfer the leeks with their cooking liquid to a shallow baking dish, pour on the melted butter and sprinkle with the bread crumbs. Mix the cheese and paprika together and sprinkle them over the leeks. Put the dish in a preheated 500° F. [250° C.] oven or slide it under a hot broiler. Cook the leeks for five minutes to brown the top.

ARNE KRÜGER AND ANNETTE WOLTER
KOCHEN HEUTE

A White Fricasey of Mushrooms

This recipe is from a book published anonymously in 1747, but generally attributed to Hannah Glasse.

To serve 4

1 lb.	button mushrooms	½ kg.
3 tbsp.	water	45 ml.
3 tbsp.	milk	45 ml.
	salt	
	grated nutmeg	
	ground mace	
1¼ cups	heavy cream	300 ml.
1 tbsp.	butter, mixed with 1 tbsp. [15 ml.] flour and kneaded to a paste	15 ml.

Put the mushrooms into a saucepan with the water and milk and a very little salt. Set them over high heat and let them boil up three times, removing the pan from the heat and letting them cool for a moment each time they boil.

Off the heat, grate in nutmeg; put in a little mace, the cream, and the butter-flour paste, shaking the saucepan well all the time. Put over gentle heat and cook, stirring. When fine and thick—about 10 minutes—dish it up.

THE ART OF COOKERY, MADE PLAIN AND EASY

Mushrooms in White Wine

Champignons en Ragoût à la Diplomate

To serve 6

7 tbsp.	butter, 2 tbsp. [30 ml.] cut into pieces	105 ml.
½ cup	dry white wine	125 ml.
½ cup	meat stock (recipe, page 163)	125 ml.
1 lb.	button mushrooms, stems and a few of the caps chopped	½ kg.
1 tbsp.	chopped fresh parsley	15 ml.
1 tbsp.	finely cut fresh chives	15 ml.
1 or 2	shallots, chopped	1 or 2
	salt and freshly ground pepper	
1	egg yolk, beaten	1
	cayenne pepper	
	grated nutmeg	
1 cup	croutons, made by sautéing bread cubes in butter	¼ liter

In a saucepan, heat 1 tablespoon [15 ml.] of the butter with the wine and stock. Add the chopped mushrooms, the parsley, chives, shallots, salt and pepper, and cook over high heat for two or three minutes. Remove the pan from the heat.

Whisk the butter pieces into the egg yolk, then whisk this combination into the mushroom mixture. Add pinches of cayenne pepper and nutmeg. Keep the mixture warm.

Using the remaining butter, sauté the whole mushroom caps over high heat for a few minutes, or until well browned.

Scatter the croutons in the bottom of a buttered gratin dish. Spread the chopped mushroom mixture over them and arrange the mushroom caps—rounded side up—on top. Bake in a preheated 450° F. [230° C.] oven for five to 10 minutes, or until heated through. Serve very hot.

G. PORTEVIN
CE QU'IL FAUT SAVOIR POUR MANGER LES BONS CHAMPIGNONS

Fried Stuffed Mushroom Caps

To serve 6

3 tbsp.	finely chopped shallots or scallions	45 ml.
¼ cup	finely chopped green pepper	50 ml.
½ to 1 cup	clam juice	125 to 250 ml.
1½ cups	shredded crab meat	375 ml.
½ cup	grated Parmesan cheese	125 ml.
3 tbsp.	strained fresh lemon juice	45 ml.
1½ cups	fresh bread crumbs	375 ml.
	salt and pepper	
24	fresh mushroom caps, 2 inches [5 cm.] wide	24
1 cup	flour	¼ liter
1	egg, lightly beaten	1
	oil for frying	
1	lemon, cut into 4 wedges	1
	béarnaise sauce (recipe, page 162)	

Put the shallots or scallions and green pepper in a small pot with enough clam juice to cover them. Cover the pot and cook for five minutes, until the vegetables are tender. Pour them into a bowl, and add the crab meat, cheese, lemon juice and ½ cup [125 ml.] of the bread crumbs. Season with salt and pepper; add a little clam juice if this stuffing seems dry.

Fill two similar-sized mushroom caps with the stuffing, press the caps together and scrape off any excess stuffing. Repeat with the rest of the caps. Place some flour in a dish, the egg in a second dish and the remaining bread crumbs in a third dish. Dip the stuffed caps in the flour and coat them well. Dip the caps in the egg, then into the crumbs. Chill the stuffed mushrooms for at least one hour to set the coating. (If desired, run a wooden pick through each pair of caps and remove it before serving.) Heat 1 inch [2½ cm.] of oil in a large skillet to 365° F. [185° C.]. Fry the stuffed mushrooms—turning them frequently so that all sides will be golden brown—for three to four minutes. Serve them hot, garnished with lemon wedges and béarnaise sauce.

THE GOOD COOKING SCHOOL
PENNY-WISE, PARTY-PERFECT DINNERS

Virginia's Chinese Mushrooms

The mushrooms called for in this recipe are available at Asian food markets and some specialty food shops.

To serve 6

2 oz.	dried Chinese (or dried Japanese *shiitake*) mushrooms, rinsed, soaked in 1 to 1½ cups [250 to 375 ml.] boiling water for 1 hour, drained, the liquid reserved and tough stems removed	60 g.
2 tsp.	soy sauce	10 ml.

Pour the reserved soaking liquid into a pot, add the stemmed mushrooms, cover and bring to a boil. Simmer for 15 minutes. Add the soy sauce, re-cover, and simmer for 15 minutes more. Let the mushrooms cool in their cooking liquid, then chill them for several hours or—preferably—overnight.

To serve, put one, two or three mushrooms on each plate, depending on their size. Spoon 2 tablespoons [30 ml.] of the cooking liquid over each mushroom. Accompany the mushrooms with soy sauce, which should be sprinkled over them quite liberally.

CAROL CUTLER
THE SIX-MINUTE SOUFFLÉ AND OTHER CULINARY DELIGHTS

Baked Mushrooms

Gebackene Pilze

To serve 4 to 6

1 lb.	fresh mushrooms, sliced	½ kg.
3 tbsp.	butter	45 ml.
	salt	
	pepper (optional)	
1 tsp.	flour	5 ml.
1 cup	sour cream	¼ liter
⅓ cup	freshly grated Gruyère or Parmesan cheese	75 ml.

Sauté the mushrooms in 2 tablespoons [30 ml.] of the butter for a few minutes, until they render their liquid. Season with a little salt, and pepper if desired. Sprinkle the mushrooms with the flour, cook for a few more minutes, then gradually stir in the sour cream. Bring the mixture to a boil and pour it into a gratin dish. Melt the remaining butter and pour it over the top; sprinkle with the grated cheese and bake the mushrooms in a preheated 400° F. [200° C.] oven for 12 to 15 minutes, or until the topping is bubbly and light gold.

KULINARISCHE GERICHTE

Okra with Tomatoes

Bamies me Saltsa, Latheres

To serve 4

1 lb.	small fresh okra, stem ends trimmed	½ kg.
	salt	
½ cup	vinegar	125 ml.
¾ cup	olive oil	175 ml.
2	medium-sized onions, coarsely chopped	2
3	medium-sized tomatoes, peeled, seeded and chopped, or canned tomatoes, drained and chopped	3
	pepper	

Place the okra in a dish, sprinkle with salt and the vinegar, and set it aside for 30 minutes (this is to prevent the okra from splitting while cooking). Wash the okra again and then dry it thoroughly.

Heat the olive oil in a large frying pan and add the chopped onions. Cook gently until the onions are tender. Add the okra and cook, tossing lightly, until it is slightly browned. Add the tomatoes, and season with salt and pepper. Cover the frying pan and simmer gently for about 45 minutes, or until the okra is tender. Serve cold.

CHRISSA PARADISSIS
THE BEST BOOK OF GREEK COOKERY

Onions Stuffed with Tuna

Cipolle Ripiene con Tonno

To serve 4

4	large onions, peeled and trimmed, parboiled for 1 minute and drained	4
½ lb.	skinned and boned tuna, cooked in boiling salted water for 10 minutes, flaked and finely chopped	¼ kg.
½ cup	fresh bread crumbs, soaked in milk and squeezed dry	125 ml.
2	eggs, beaten	2
⅓ cup	freshly grated Parmesan cheese	75 ml.
	salt and pepper	
½ cup	oil	125 ml.
¼ cup	dry bread crumbs	50 ml.

Cut the onions in half crosswise and scoop out the inner layers. Chop these layers and mix them with the tuna and the soaked bread crumbs. Chop the mixture very fine and combine it with the eggs, cheese, and salt and pepper.

Pour a drop of oil into each onion half, then fill the cavities with the tuna mixture. Pour the remaining oil into a wide ovenproof dish and arrange the stuffed onions side by side in the dish. Sprinkle the onions with the dry bread crumbs and bake them in a preheated 350° F. [180° C.] oven for 30 minutes, or until the stuffing is firm and the crumbs are golden brown.

EMANUELE ROSSI (EDITOR)
LA VERA CUCINIERA GENOVESE

Baked Stuffed Onions

Cipolle Farcite

Leftover roast meat can be used instead of ham.

	To serve 6	
6	large onions, unpeeled	6
¼ lb.	ham, chopped (about ½ cup [125 ml.])	125 g.
½ cup	dry bread crumbs	125 ml.
4 tbsp.	butter, 2 tbsp. [30 ml.] melted, 2 tbsp. cut into small pieces	60 ml.
2 tbsp.	heavy cream	30 ml.
2 tbsp.	chopped fresh marjoram leaves	30 ml.
	salt and pepper	
⅓ cup	freshly grated Parmesan cheese	75 ml.

Wrap each of the onions in foil and bake them in a preheated 375° F. [190° C.] oven for one to one and one half hours. When the onions are soft, remove the foil, peel the onions and scoop out the centers.

Chop the centers and mix them with the ham, bread crumbs, melted butter, cream, marjoram, salt and pepper. Fill the onions with the ham mixture. Put them in a buttered baking dish and sprinkle them with the grated cheese and the pieces of butter. Bake the onions at 400° F. [200° C.] until the topping is golden brown—about 15 minutes.

JANET ROSS AND MICHAEL WATERFIELD
LEAVES FROM OUR TUSCAN KITCHEN

Onion Layers Stuffed with Cheese

Oignons Farcis au Brocciu

The original version of this recipe called for brocciu, also known as broccio, a Corsican fresh curd cheese made from sheep's milk. Brocciu is not obtainable in America, but ricotta cheese is a suitable substitute. To prevent the onions from drying out, they can be moistened with cream or dotted with

butter; alternatively, cover the dish with foil and remove the foil five minutes before the end of baking to brown the onions.

	To serve 10	
5	large onions, tops and bases carefully trimmed off and skins removed	5
¼ cup	chopped fresh parsley	50 ml.
½ lb.	ham, finely diced	¼ kg.
1 lb.	ricotta cheese	½ kg.
1	egg, beaten	1
	salt and pepper	

Blanch the onions in plenty of boiling salted water. Remove them from the pan after about 15 minutes; they should still be relatively firm. Cool the onions, slice them in half vertically and separate the layers.

Mix the parsley and ham with the cheese, add the beaten egg and season with salt and pepper. Mix well and fold each onion layer around a spoonful of stuffing.

Oil a baking dish, fill it with the stuffed onion layers—placed seam downward—and bake them in a preheated 350° F. [180° C.] oven for 45 minutes.

CHRISTIANE SCHAPIRA
LA CUISINE CORSE

To Stew Green Peas the Jews' Way

This recipe is from a book published anonymously in 1747, but generally known to have been written by Hannah Glasse. A pipkin was a small metal or earthenware pot; for this dish, the modern cook should use a skillet or sauté pan.

	To serve 6	
4 lb.	green peas, shelled (about 4 cups [1 liter])	2 kg.
⅓ cup	oil	75 ml.
¼ cup	water	50 ml.
	grated nutmeg	
	ground mace	
	ground cloves	
	cayenne pepper	
	salt and pepper	
3 or 4	eggs	3 or 4

To the peas put in the oil and water, the spices, salt and pepper. Let all this stew in a broad, flat pipkin. When the peas are half-done—about 20 minutes—make two or three holes with a spoon. Into each of these holes break an egg, yolk and white. When the eggs are set, take another egg and beat it and throw it over the whole. When the mixture is cooked enough, as you will know by tasting it, and the egg is quite set, send the dish to the table.

THE ART OF COOKERY, MADE PLAIN AND EASY

Peppers Stuffed with Cheese

Poivrons Farcis à la Brousse

Although far from being the real French *brousse*, ricotta is the closest equivalent in the United States. Use the very best available brand. Also use true Parmigiano-Reggiano.

To serve 6

3	red peppers	3
3	green peppers	3
¼ cup	olive oil	50 ml.
1	large onion, finely chopped	1
	salt and coarsely ground black pepper	
¼ cup	chopped fresh parsley	50 ml.
2	garlic cloves, crushed	2
½ tsp.	finely crumbled dried oregano	2 ml.
3	small zucchini, coarsely grated	3
¼ cup	dry bread crumbs	50 ml.
1 lb.	*brousse* or ricotta cheese	½ kg.
½ cup	freshly grated Parmesan cheese	125 ml.
½ cup	freshly grated *banon* or other hard goat's cheese	125 ml.
1	egg	1
1 to 2 tbsp.	white vinegar	15 to 30 ml.

Cut and reserve a lid from the top of each of the peppers. Remove the stems and all of the seeds and ribs.

Heat half the olive oil in a skillet and add the onion. Season with salt and pepper, and sauté the onion until lightly browned. Add the parsley, garlic, oregano and zucchini, and more salt and pepper. Toss together and cook, covered, for about five minutes over medium heat to draw out the zucchini juices. When the juices are flooding the pan, raise the heat and allow the juices to evaporate. Remove the pan from the heat and allow the zucchini hash to cool.

Combine the bread crumbs, cheeses and egg, and mix into the cooled zucchini hash. Taste for seasoning.

Heat the remaining olive oil in a braising pot or a *sauteuse*. Stuff the peppers with the cheese mixture. Stand them in the pot, season, cover the peppers with their lids, and bake in a preheated 325° F. [160° C.] oven for about one hour, or until the peppers are tender. The time will vary with the vegetable. The red peppers may be done before the green. In this case, remove them first.

When the peppers are ready, remove them from the pan and allow them to cool. There will be a lot of cooking juices; reduce these by half and add the wine vinegar. Remove the lids to pour this sauce over the peppers, then cover them.

Serve the peppers warm or cold, as a first course.

MADELEINE M. KAMMAN
WHEN FRENCH WOMEN COOK

Spinach Gratin

To serve 4 or 5

4 tbsp.	butter, 2 tbsp. [30 ml.] melted	60 ml.
1 tbsp.	finely chopped onion	15 ml.
½ cup	white rice	125 ml.
1¼ cups	hot water	300 ml.
	salt and pepper	
½ cup	milk	125 ml.
2 tbsp.	dry bread crumbs	30 ml.
1 lb.	spinach, parboiled for 1 minute, drained, squeezed dry and coarsely chopped	½ kg.
4 tbsp.	freshly grated Parmesan cheese	60 ml.
½ tsp.	freshly grated nutmeg	2 ml.
1½ tbsp.	strained fresh lemon juice	22½ ml.
1	egg, beaten	1

Melt 2 tablespoons [30 ml.] of the butter in a pan. Add the onion, cover and simmer for one minute. Add the rice, increase the heat and stir for about one minute, or until the rice grains turn opaque white. Add the water, salt and pepper to the mixture; cover, reduce the heat and cook the mixture for 20 minutes.

Meanwhile, in a small bowl, stir the milk into the bread crumbs and put aside. Take a handful of the spinach at a time and pull the pieces apart while putting them in a mixing bowl. Add 2 tablespoons of the cheese, the nutmeg, lemon juice, and more salt and pepper.

Scrape the cooked rice from the pan into the spinach mixture. Add the softened bread crumbs, the egg, the melted butter and mix thoroughly.

Butter a 9-inch [23-cm.] pie dish and scoop the spinach-rice mixture into it. Smooth the top and sprinkle with the remaining cheese. Bake in a preheated 375° F. [190° C.] oven for 15 minutes. Serve hot directly from the pie dish.

CAROL CUTLER
THE SIX-MINUTE SOUFFLÉ AND OTHER CULINARY DELIGHTS

Spinach and Cheese Balls

Storzapreti à la Bastiaise

To serve 6

1½ lb.	spinach, trimmed and chopped, or Swiss chard, ribs removed and leaves chopped	¾ kg.
¾ lb.	*brocciu* cheese, mashed with a fork, or substitute ricotta cheese	350 g.
2	eggs, beaten	2
	salt and pepper	
	freshly grated nutmeg	
1 cup	freshly grated Parmesan cheese	¼ liter
¼ cup	flour	50 ml.
1 cup	meat roasting juices, degreased, or substitute meat stock *(recipe, page 163)*	¼ liter

Mix the spinach or chard with the *brocciu* cheese, the eggs, salt, pepper, a pinch of nutmeg and about half of the Parmesan cheese. Shape the mixture into 2-inch [5-cm.] balls.

Bring a pot of salted water to a boil over high heat. Roll the cheese balls in the flour to coat them lightly, then drop them into the boiling water. As each ball rises to the surface, remove it with a skimmer and transfer it to a buttered gratin dish. Pour the meat juices over the balls, sprinkle them with the rest of the Parmesan, and bake in a preheated 350° F. [180° C.] oven for 15 minutes, or until the cheese melts.

CHRISTIANE SCHAPIRA
LA CUISINE CORSE

Spinach Fritters

To serve 4

3	eggs, the yolks separated from the whites, and the whites stiffly beaten	3
2 tbsp.	milk (fresh, sour or buttermilk)	30 ml.
1 tsp.	salt	5 ml.
½ tsp.	freshly ground black pepper	2 ml.
2 tbsp.	finely chopped onion	30 ml.
1 tbsp.	finely chopped celery	15 ml.
1 tbsp.	flour	15 ml.
1 lb.	fresh spinach, stems removed, leaves washed, patted dry and finely chopped	½ kg.
	oil for deep frying	

In a bowl, combine the egg yolks with the milk, salt, pepper, onion, celery and flour. Fold in the beaten egg whites and the spinach, mixing well. Shape the mixture into eight 3-inch [8-cm.] fritters. Heat the oil in a deep pan to 375° F. [190° C.] and fry the fritters until they are brown and firm—about two or three minutes. Drain the fritters on paper towels.

JOAN NATHAN AND JUDY STACEY GOLDMAN
THE FLAVOR OF JERUSALEM

Spinach Pudding

Spinaziepudding

The technique of preparing brains for cooking is demonstrated on pages 32-33.

Spinach plus calf's brains plus anchovies equals one of the best inventions to come out of Holland.

To serve 4

2	eggs, the yolks separated from the whites, and the whites stiffly beaten	2
2 tbsp.	semolina	30 ml.
2 lb.	spinach, boiled for 3 minutes, drained, squeezed dry and finely chopped	1 kg.
	grated nutmeg	
	salt and pepper	
¼ cup	finely chopped onion	50 ml.
4 tbsp.	butter, 2 tbsp. [30 ml.] cut into small pieces	60 ml.
1	calf's brain, blanched in salted water for 5 minutes, membrane removed, and diced	1
3	salt anchovies, filleted, soaked in tepid water for 30 minutes, drained, patted dry and finely chopped	3
½ cup	grated Edam or Gouda cheese	125 ml.
2 cups	tomato sauce *(recipe, page 162)*	½ liter

Stir the egg yolks and semolina into the chopped spinach, and season the mixture with a pinch of nutmeg and with salt and pepper to taste.

In a skillet, sauté the onion in 2 tablespoons [30 ml.] of the butter for about five minutes, or until transparent. Add the brain and stir gently until combined. Remove the skillet from the heat, add the anchovies and fold in the egg whites.

Butter a 1-quart [1-liter] baking dish, and fill it alternately with the spinach and brain mixtures and dot the pieces of butter over the top. Cover the dish and stand it in a baking pan filled with enough hot water to come halfway up the sides of the dish. Cook the pudding in a preheated 350° F. [180° C.] oven for about 30 minutes, or until set. Unmold the pudding onto a warmed plate and sprinkle it with the cheese. Serve it with the tomato sauce.

LILO AUREDEN
DAS SCHMECKT SO GUT

Stuffed Squash Blossoms

Fiori di Zucca Ripieni

The flowers of zucchini or yellow summer squash, and of winter squashes such as Hubbard, buttercup and pumpkin are suitable for this recipe.

If you have any leftover meat, use it instead of the ham. Instead of oil, 4 tablespoons [60 ml.] of butter may be substituted for frying.

	To serve 4	
6 oz.	mozzarella cheese, finely diced (about 1½ cups [375 ml.])	175 g.
⅓ cup	finely chopped ham	75 ml.
½ cup	chopped fresh parsley	125 ml.
1	garlic clove, chopped	1
	salt and pepper	
12	squash blossoms, stems trimmed	12
2	eggs, beaten	2
	flour	
½ cup	dry bread crumbs	125 ml.
1 cup	oil	¼ liter
1¼ cups	tomato sauce (recipe, page 162)	300 ml.

Put the diced mozzarella and chopped ham into a small bowl with the parsley, garlic and a pinch of pepper. Mix well and season with salt to taste. Using a teaspoon, stuff the squash blossoms with the mixture. The amount you put in each will depend on the size of the flowers, but it is best to put just a little stuffing in each flower and then add more if necessary.

Season the beaten eggs with salt. Roll the blossoms in flour to coat them lightly, taking care to hold the petals tightly together at the top so that none of the stuffing escapes. Brush off any excess flour. Dip the blossoms in the eggs and then in the bread crumbs, pressing them onto the petals with your fingers to make sure the crumbs stick well. Heat the oil over medium heat until it is very hot, and in it fry the blossoms. As soon as they are golden brown on one side—three or four minutes—turn them over and brown the other side. Drain them on paper towels. Arrange the blossoms on a warmed serving dish and serve them with the tomato sauce.

FERNANDA GOSETTI
IN CUCINA CON FERNANDA GOSETTI

Romaine with Cheese Stuffing

Romaines Farcies au Brocciu

	To serve 8	
16	large romaine lettuce leaves, soaked for 15 minutes in water mixed with 2 tbsp. [30 ml.] vinegar, rinsed and well drained	16
1 lb.	*brocciu* cheese, or substitute ricotta or farmer cheese	½ kg.
3	eggs, beaten	3
¼ cup	chopped fresh parsley	50 ml.
1 tbsp.	olive oil	15 ml.
1	garlic clove, chopped	1
	salt and freshly ground pepper	

Combine the cheese, eggs and parsley, and season them with salt and pepper. Place a heaping spoonful of stuffing on each lettuce leaf, and wrap the leaf around the stuffing to make a parcel. Tie the parcels with thread and arrange them side by side in a shallow pan. Add water—the parcels should be three quarters covered—then pour in the oil; add the garlic and salt. Cover the pan, and simmer the contents over very low heat for 35 to 45 minutes, or until the parcels are tender. Remove and drain them, reserving the cooking liquid. To serve, place one lettuce parcel on each plate, remove the threads and pour on a little of the cooking liquid.

MARIA NUNZIA FILIPPINI
LA CUISINE CORSE

Stuffed Tomatoes

Pomidoro Ripieni

	To serve 12	
2 tbsp.	butter	30 ml.
2	onions, finely chopped	2
1 cup	chopped fresh parsley	¼ liter
2 cups	fresh bread crumbs, soaked in milk and squeezed dry	½ liter
⅔ cup	freshly grated Parmesan cheese	150 ml.
1	egg, beaten	1
	salt and pepper	
3 tbsp.	chopped fresh oregano	45 ml.
12	tomatoes	12
⅓ cup	oil	75 ml.
¼ cup	dry bread crumbs	50 ml.

Heat the butter gently in a pan, add the onions and parsley, and fry until the onions are soft. Put the contents of the pan in a large mortar, add the soaked bread crumbs and pound the mixture to a paste. To this paste, add the grated cheese, egg, salt and pepper, and oregano. Mix well.

Slice off the tops of the tomatoes and reserve them. Scoop out the seeds and juice, and stuff the cavities with the onion mixture. Replace the tops. Arrange the stuffed tomatoes in an oiled pan just large enough to hold them; sprinkle them with the oil and dry bread crumbs. Bake in a preheated 350° F. [180° C.] oven for 40 minutes, or until lightly browned. Serve the tomatoes hot, lukewarm or cooled to room temperature.

EMANUELE ROSSI (EDITOR)
LA VERA CUCINIERA GENOVESE

Stuffed Tomatoes with Sour-Cream Sauce

Gefüllte Tomaten

For a spicier filling, add ⅓ cup [75 ml.] of finely chopped lean bacon, 1 tablespoon [15 ml.] of chopped capers or a few drops of lemon juice and a pinch of paprika to the stuffing.

	To serve 4	
8	large tomatoes	8
	salt and pepper	
1 lb.	boneless beef or pork, ground	½ kg.
6 tbsp.	butter	90 ml.
2	medium-sized onions, chopped	2
½ cup	long-grain white rice, boiled for 20 minutes and drained	125 ml.
1	egg	1
1 tbsp.	flour	15 ml.
1 cup	sour cream	¼ liter
2 tbsp.	finely cut fresh dill or chopped fresh parsley	30 ml.

Slice off a small lid from the top of each tomato and carefully scoop out the center pulp. Sprinkle the insides of the tomatoes with salt and pepper.

Fry the ground meat in 2 tablespoons [30 ml.] of the butter until lightly browned. Add half of the onions, and continue frying until the onions are transparent. Mix the meat and onions with the cooked rice, egg, salt and pepper, and use this mixture to stuff the tomatoes. Replace the tomato lids. Butter a baking dish and arrange the tomatoes in it. Melt 2 tablespoons of the butter and pour it over the tomatoes. Bake them in a preheated 400° F. [200° C.] oven for about 15 minutes, or until the tomatoes are cooked and the stuffing is heated through.

Meanwhile, make the sour-cream sauce. Cook the rest of the onions in the remaining butter until transparent. Stir in

the tablespoon [15 ml.] of flour, then the sour cream, and cook, stirring constantly, for one to two minutes.

Put the tomatoes in a serving dish, pour the sour-cream sauce over them and sprinkle with dill or parsley.

KULINARISCHE GERICHTE

French Stuffed Zucchini

Courgettes Farcies

	To serve 6	
	coarse salt	
6	small zucchini, trimmed, a slice ¼ inch [6 mm.] thick cut lengthwise from each one and reserved	6
¼ cup	olive oil	50 ml.
2 tbsp.	chopped onion	30 ml.
3	large mushrooms, chopped	3
1 oz.	ham, diced	30 g.
3	sage leaves, chopped	3
	salt and pepper	

Bring 2 quarts [2 liters] of water and 2 tablespoons [30 ml.] of coarse salt to a boil. Plunge the zucchini and the slices you cut from them into the water and boil them for six minutes. Drain them in a colander under cold running water. As soon as the zucchini are cool enough to handle, use a teaspoon to scoop out the interior, leaving a shell about ¼ inch [6 mm.] thick. Set the shells and the slices aside and chop the scooped-out flesh coarsely.

Heat 2 tablespoons of the olive oil in the pan you used to cook the zucchini. Add the onion and cook over low heat for seven or eight minutes, stirring frequently with a wooden spoon. When the onion is soft but not browned, add the mushrooms, ham and sage. Stir for five minutes, then add the chopped zucchini and a pinch of salt. Increase the heat and stir until the liquid from the zucchini has evaporated. Take care that the mixture does not stick to the bottom of the pan and burn. Taste, season with more salt if necessary, and add pepper.

Arrange the zucchini shells compactly in a shallow baking dish just large enough to hold them side by side. Sprinkle the interiors lightly with coarse salt. Use a teaspoon to fill the zucchini shells with the ham-and-mushroom mixture, smoothing it down evenly. Use the slices of zucchini for lids. Brush the zucchini with the remaining olive oil. Bake them in a preheated 400° F. [200° C.] oven for 35 minutes. Check the zucchini periodically. If their cooking liquid appears to be drying up, add 1 or 2 tablespoons [15 or 30 ml.] of warm water to the dish. Serve hot.

ROGER VERGÉ
ROGER VERGÉ'S CUISINE OF THE SOUTH OF FRANCE

Zucchini with Veal and Prosciutto Stuffing

Zucchini Ripieni

To serve 6

2 lb.	zucchini, ends trimmed	1 kg.
4 tbsp.	butter	60 ml.
	Veal and prosciutto stuffing	
¼ lb.	lean veal, cut into pieces	125 g.
1	onion, finely chopped	1
2 tbsp.	finely chopped parsley	30 ml.
1	celery rib, finely chopped	1
1	carrot, finely chopped	1
1 oz.	prosciutto, finely chopped	30 g.
2 tbsp.	olive oil	30 ml.
	salt and pepper	
about 2½ cups	water	about 625 ml.
4	slices firm-textured white bread, crusts removed	4
1 cup	milk or stock (recipe, page 163)	¼ liter
1 tsp.	ground allspice	5 ml.
1	egg	1
½ cup	freshly grated Parmesan cheese	125 ml.

Use an apple corer to scoop out the insides of the zucchini, to leave room for the stuffing. If the cavities do not seem big enough, carefully widen them with a small knife.

To make the stuffing, put the veal in a pan over medium heat with the onion, parsley, celery, carrot, prosciutto, olive oil, salt and pepper. Stir the mixture frequently, and when the meat has absorbed all of the liquid and has begun to brown, pour in a ladleful of water. Continue to simmer. When the water has been absorbed, pour in another ladleful and continue simmering. Pour in a ladleful of water two more times, waiting after each addition for the mixture to absorb it; the meat should now be tender and there should be a little cooking liquid left. Strain the liquid and reserve it.

Simmer the bread in the milk or stock with the ground allspice until all of the liquid has been absorbed—about 15 minutes. Chop the strained meat mixture very fine in a bowl and combine it with the egg, Parmesan cheese and bread paste. Use this stuffing to fill the zucchini.

In a skillet, heat the butter until it is almost nut brown in color. Sauté the stuffed zucchini until they are lightly colored. Add the reserved cooking liquid, cover, and simmer until the zucchini are tender—about 10 to 15 minutes.

PELLEGRINO ARTUSI
LA SCIENZA IN CUCINA E L'ARTE DI MANGIAR BENE

Stuffed Zucchini

The scooped-out centers of the zucchini can be used in the stuffing mixture. If you find you have made too much stuffing, use it to line the dish in which the zucchini are cooked.

To serve 4

8	small zucchini, ends trimmed	8
1 lb.	ground beef	½ kg.
1	egg	1
2	garlic cloves, finely chopped	2
2 tsp.	salt	10 ml.
½ tsp.	dried oregano leaves	2 ml.
2	slices firm-textured white bread, crusts removed, soaked in water and squeezed almost dry	2
¼ cup	olive oil	50 ml.
	chopped fresh parsley	

Use an apple corer to scoop out the centers of the zucchini. In a bowl, combine the ground beef, egg, chopped garlic, salt, oregano and bread. Put the meat mixture into a pastry bag fitted with a plain tube and pipe the mixture into the zucchini from both ends.

Heat the olive oil in a skillet and sauté the stuffed zucchini over high heat until lightly browned on all sides—about 10 minutes. Arrange them in a baking dish and pour on the oil remaining in the skillet. Bake the zucchini in a preheated 350° F. [180° C.] oven for about 20 minutes, or until tender. To serve, sprinkle with chopped fresh parsley.

JULIE DANNENBAUM
MENUS FOR ALL OCCASIONS

Stir-fried Mixed Vegetables

The Chinese white turnip, or icicle turnip, called for in this recipe, is a large, smooth-textured and pungent vegetable available where Asian vegetables are sold. If it is not obtainable, substitute about 1 pound [½ kg.] of ordinary turnips.

To serve 8 to 10

¼ cup	peanut oil	50 ml.
1	Chinese white turnip, cut into julienne	1
2	carrots, cut into julienne	2
4	celery ribs, cut into julienne	4
1 tsp.	salt	5 ml.
1 tbsp.	vinegar	15 ml.
	sesame-seed oil	

Heat the peanut oil in a wok or large skillet. Add the vegetables and stir fry them for three minutes over medium heat.

Add the salt and vinegar, and stir fry the vegetables for three minutes more. Place the vegetables in a bowl and let them cool. Cover and refrigerate them for 30 minutes. Sprinkle them lightly with sesame-seed oil before serving.

GLORIA BLEY MILLER
THE THOUSAND RECIPE CHINESE COOKBOOK

Vegetable Gratin

Le Gratin Provençal

This dish will be even more succulent if extra Parmesan cheese is sprinkled between the vegetable layers. One may also intersperse a couple of layers of small sweet peppers that have been seeded and cut into thin strips.

To serve 6

2	medium-sized onions, finely chopped	2
¼ cup	olive oil	50 ml.
2	medium-sized zucchini, peeled, sliced, parboiled for 3 or 4 minutes and drained	2
4	tomatoes, peeled, seeded and cut into thick slices	4
1	large eggplant, peeled, sliced, salted and drained for 30 minutes, then parboiled for 3 or 4 minutes and drained again	1
	salt and pepper	
⅔ cup	freshly grated Parmesan cheese	150 ml.
½ cup	dry bread crumbs	125 ml.

Sauté the onions in 3 tablespoons [45 ml.] of the oil until they are transparent. Spread a layer of the onions in a large gratin dish. Spread a layer of the zucchini on top, then a layer of tomatoes and a layer of eggplant. Sprinkle with pinches of salt and pepper and a little of the cheese. Repeat these layers until all of the vegetables have been used up; reserve the remaining cheese. Drain off any excess vegetable juice and boil it over high heat until it is reduced to about ¼ cup [50 ml.]. Pour this back over the vegetables in the gratin dish. Sprinkle the top with the reserved cheese, the bread crumbs and the remaining oil. Bake the vegetables in a preheated 350° F. [180° C.] oven for about 30 minutes, or until browned.

JEAN-NOËL ESCUDIER AND PETA J. FULLER
THE WONDERFUL FOOD OF PROVENCE

White Sausages with Chicken

Boudins Blancs de Volaille

The technique of making sausages is shown on pages 36-37. These white sausages may be made up to three days in advance and then broiled just before serving.

To make about 20 small sausages

⅔ cup	finely chopped onions	150 ml.
½ lb.	pork-kidney fat, finely diced	¼ kg.
7	slices firm-textured white bread, crusts removed, soaked in milk and squeezed dry	7
½ lb.	finely chopped chicken breast meat	¼ kg.
1 cup	thick white sauce *(recipe, page 162)*	¼ liter
½ cup	finely chopped truffles	125 ml.
2 cups	finely chopped fresh mushrooms, sautéed in butter	½ liter
7	egg yolks	7
	salt	
2 tsp.	mixed spices	10 ml.
about 2 yards	salted lamb sausage casings, soaked and drained	about 2 meters
	butter for grilling	

Parboil the onions for a few seconds, drain them and put them in a saucepan together with the pork-kidney fat. Cook over low heat for 10 to 12 minutes.

In a mortar, pound the bread with the chicken meat. Push the purée through a drum sieve into a bowl a little at a time. Add the onions, pork fat and white sauce gradually to the mixture. Then add the truffles and sautéed mushrooms, and beat in the yolks. Season this forcemeat with salt and mixed spices.

Using a funnel or pastry bag, stuff the forcemeat into the sausage casings, knotting the sausages at 3-inch [8-cm.] intervals. Put the sausages in a pan of warm water and heat slowly to just below the boiling point. Cover the pan and remove it from the heat; let the sausages cool in the liquid.

When cold, drain the sausages, wrap them and refrigerate them for at least six hours. To serve, prick the sausages with a larding needle, roll them in melted butter and broil them, turning them at frequent intervals, for seven minutes, or until well browned.

URBAIN DUBOIS AND ÉMILE BERNARD
LA CUISINE CLASSIQUE

White Sausages

Boudins Blancs

Boudins Blancs, eaten in France at Christmas time, are made in advance, then rolled in butter and broiled before serving. The technique of making sausages is shown on pages 36-37.

If you cook the sausages in milk rather than in water, they will be more delicate.

	To make 10 sausages	
3	sprigs fresh parsley	3
2	scallions, trimmed	2
1	sprig thyme	1
1	sprig basil	1
2	shallots	2
3	whole cloves	3
1	bay leaf	1
10 to 12	coriander seeds	10 to 12
12	onions, quartered	12
2½ cups	gelatinous meat stock *(recipe, page 163)*	625 ml.
	salt and pepper	
4	slices firm-textured white bread, crusts removed	4
⅔ cup	milk	150 ml.
¾ cup	almonds, blanched and peeled	175 ml.
2 cups	heavy cream, warmed	½ liter
8	egg yolks	8
½ lb.	fresh pork-kidney fat, cut into small dice	¼ kg.
1	roasted chicken breast, skinned, boned and finely chopped	1
	mixed spices	
2 yards	salted pork sausage casings, soaked in tepid water for 30 minutes and drained	2 meters

Tie the parsley, scallions, thyme and basil together, and wrap the shallots, cloves, bay leaf and coriander seeds in cheesecloth. Put them in a deep saucepan with the onion quarters and the stock, add salt and pepper, and simmer until the onions are tender and all of the liquid has been absorbed. Remove the onions from the pan and purée them.

Put the bread into a pan with the milk and cook, stirring constantly, until the bread has absorbed all of the milk and is reduced to a paste. Add the paste to the puréed onions.

Pound the almonds in a mortar. Mix them with the cream, adding it gradually. Then place the mixture in a colander lined with a tightly woven cloth and squeeze the cloth to extract all of the liquid. Mix the almond cream with the bread-and-onion paste. Add the egg yolks, pork-kidney fat, chicken meat, salt and mixed spices. Combine the ingredients thoroughly and stuff them into sausage casings. Tie the casings at 3-inch [8-cm.] intervals.

To cook the sausages, prick them in several places to prevent them from bursting. Start the sausages in cold or tepid milk or water and bring them to a simmer. Cook them for 40 minutes, or until they feel firm.

MENON
LES SOUPERS DE LA COUR

Chicken and Mushroom Stew

Cassolettes de Volaille à la Reine

This little stew is used to fill baked pastry shells. It can also be spooned into small porcelain dishes, sprinkled with bread crumbs, dotted with butter and lightly browned in the oven.

	To serve 4	
4 tbsp.	butter	60 ml.
2 tbsp.	flour	30 ml.
2½ cups	chicken stock *(recipe, page 163)*	625 ml.
	salt and pepper	
½ lb.	fresh button mushrooms	¼ kg.
½ cup	water	125 ml.
3 tbsp.	strained fresh lemon juice	45 ml.
2	egg yolks, lightly beaten	2
6 tbsp.	heavy cream	90 ml.
½ lb.	boneless cooked chicken, cut into 1-inch [2½-cm.] pieces	¼ kg.
2	truffles, sautéed in 1 tbsp. [15 ml.] butter (optional)	2

Melt 2 tablespoons [30 ml.] of the butter in a heavy saucepan. Stir in the flour and cook over low heat for two minutes. Pour in the stock, whisking constantly to prevent lumps from forming. Increase the heat and continue whisking until the mixture boils. Reduce the heat and simmer the sauce for 45 minutes, skimming occasionally. Season to taste.

Meanwhile, put the mushrooms in a pan with the water, lemon juice, salt and pepper, and the rest of the butter. Cook them over high heat for five minutes, or until they are tender. Drain the mushrooms and slice them.

Remove the sauce from the heat and let it cool slightly. Mix the egg yolks and heavy cream, and beat them into the sauce. Strain the sauce, return it to gentle heat, and add the chicken pieces, mushroom slices, and the truffles, if using. Cook until the mixture is heated through.

LE CORDON BLEU

Chicken and Almond Fritters

Frictelle d'Amandole

The author of this recipe, Maestro Martino, lived in the mid-15th Century and was the first Renaissance cook to publish his recipes. To make the almond milk, pound ¾ cup [175 ml.] of blanched and peeled almonds in a mortar or purée them in a food processor, and add 1 cup [¼ liter] of milk and 1 teaspoon [5 ml.] of rose water. Then strain the mixture through a cheesecloth-lined sieve. Squeeze the cloth to extract all of the almond milk. The residue left in the cloth can be reserved and used to mix with dough for an almond-flavored pastry.

To serve 4 to 6

1½ cups	chopped, cooked chicken breast, pounded to a paste	375 ml.
⅔ cup	almond milk	150 ml.
2 or 3	egg whites	2 or 3
1 tsp.	sugar	5 ml.
	salt and pepper	
about ½ cup	flour	about 125 ml.
12 tbsp.	lard or butter	180 ml.

Mix the pounded chicken breast, the almond milk, egg whites and sugar together. Season with salt and pepper, and add enough flour to make a firm batter.

Heat the lard or butter and drop spoonfuls of the batter into it. Sauté the fritters until they are golden brown, about three minutes on each side.

EMILIO FACCIOLI (EDITOR)
ARTE DELLA CUCINA

Chicken Wings, Shanghai-Style

Whole star anise is obtainable where fine spices or Asian foods are sold.

The chicken wings are best cooked the day before and refrigerated overnight. Three or 4 tablespoons [45 or 60 ml.] of oyster sauce may be added if you want, but then reduce the soy sauce to 3 or 4 tablespoons.

To serve 4 to 6

12	chicken wings	12
⅓ cup	soy sauce	75 ml.
2 tbsp.	sugar	30 ml.
1 tbsp.	dry sherry	15 ml.
2	slices fresh ginger	2
½	whole star anise	½

Put the chicken wings and the rest of the ingredients into a large saucepan with ⅓ cup [75 ml.] of water. Bring to a boil, cover, and simmer over low heat for 20 minutes—stirring occasionally. Then uncover the pan and cook, continually basting the wings, for 15 minutes, until about ½ cup [125 ml.] of the liquid remains. For a darker, even color, spoon the liquid on the wings and stir frequently while they are cooling. Serve cold.

JOYCE CHEN
JOYCE CHEN COOK BOOK

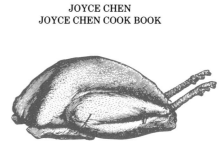

Molded Chicken Liver Mousse

The recipe can be halved easily and, of course, it is not necessary to mold the mousse.

To serve 20

¾ lb.	unsalted butter, softened	350 g.
1	medium-sized onion, finely chopped	1
1	garlic clove, finely chopped	1
1 lb.	chicken livers, trimmed	½ kg.
	salt and pepper	
¼ tsp.	ground mace	1 ml.
⅔ cup	heavy cream, whipped	150 ml.
3	small Savoy cabbage leaves	3
	paprika	

Melt 3 tablespoons [45 ml.] of the butter in a large skillet. Sauté the onion and garlic over low heat until transparent and soft, but not browned. Increase the heat, add the livers, and stir constantly until they brown on the outside but still retain a delicate pink interior. Remove from the heat, discard 2 tablespoons [30 ml.] of the cooking liquid, and season the livers with salt, pepper and the mace. Purée the livers in a blender or food processor with the remaining softened butter. Transfer the purée to a bowl, fold in the whipped cream and press plastic wrap directly onto the surface of the mousse. Refrigerate it until firm.

Arrange the cabbage leaves on a tray and shape the mousse into a large rose on top: Using a metal spatula—frequently dipped in hot water—make a central, coned core, then form individual leaves until the flower is complete.

Sprinkle the mousse with paprika and refrigerate it until needed. Store any leftover mousse in a crock and pour melted butter over the top to coat and preserve it. The mousse will keep for three or four days.

JUDITH OLNEY
SUMMER FOOD

Individual Liver Mousses

Mousse de Foies Blonds

The original version of this recipe calls for the pale-colored livers of chickens raised in the Bresse region of France. Ordinary chicken livers, soaked in milk, are a suitable substitute.

	To serve 6	
4	eggs	4
4	chicken livers, trimmed	4
1 cup	*crème fraîche* or heavy cream	¼ liter
1	whole clove, crushed	1
1 tsp.	salt	5 ml.
	freshly ground black pepper	

Break the eggs into a large electric blender; add the chicken livers, cream, clove, and salt and pepper. Blend until the mixture becomes an almost-liquid purée.

Pour the purée into six well-buttered 6-ounce [175-ml.] ramekins—they should be nearly full—and put the ramekins into a shallow baking dish. Fill the dish with enough boiling water to reach halfway up the sides of the ramekins, and transfer the dish to a preheated 325° F. [160° C.] oven. Cook the mousses for 40 minutes, or until they have set. To unmold, pass the blade of a knife around the insides of the ramekins and turn the mousses out onto warmed serving dishes. Serve very hot, coated with tomato sauce.

MICHEL OLIVER
MES RECETTES

Liver Mousse

Mousse au Foie

Instead of brioche, rusk crumbs or dry bread crumbs can be used, but the mousse, while still very good, will be less tasty.

	To serve 4 to 6	
1 cup	milk	¼ liter
¾ cup	stale brioche crumbs	175 ml.
1	goose or duck liver or 2 chicken livers, finely chopped	1
1 tbsp.	finely chopped fresh parsley	15 ml.
	salt and pepper	
3	eggs, the yolks separated from the whites, and the whites stiffly beaten	3
1¼ cups	tomato sauce *(recipe, page 162)*	300 ml.

Bring the milk to a boil and pour it over the brioche crumbs. Cool the softened crumbs.

Using a mortar and pestle, pound the liver to a purée with the parsley and a pinch each of salt and pepper. Press

the purée through a fine sieve to remove any remaining liver filaments that would prevent the mousse from rising. Mix the egg yolks with the liver purée and add the cooled crumbs. Fold in the beaten egg whites.

Pour the mixture into a buttered 1-quart [1-liter] charlotte mold. The mixture should not fill more than three quarters of the mold: It will rise during cooking.

Bake the mousse in a preheated 325° F. [160° C.] oven, or set it in a large pot filled with enough hot water to reach two thirds of the way up the sides of the mold and cook the mousse in a preheated 350° F. [180° C.] oven. The mousse is done when a skewer inserted in the mousse comes out clean—after about 45 minutes.

Run the blade of a knife around the inside of the mold to loosen the mousse. Unmold it while still hot onto a warmed serving dish. Serve it hot, accompanied by the tomato sauce.

M. ÉDOUARD NIGNON (EDITOR)
LE LIVRE DE CUISINE DE L'OUEST-ÉCLAIR

Chicken Liver Mousse

For a firmer mousse, the cream may be replaced by an additional 8 tablespoons [120 ml.] of butter.

	To serve 4	
1	shallot or small onion, finely chopped	1
8 tbsp.	butter, softened	120 ml.
½ lb.	chicken livers, trimmed	¼ kg.
	salt and freshly ground pepper	
	ground allspice	
½ tsp.	mixed dried thyme, savory, marjoram and oregano	2 ml.
2 tbsp.	Cognac	30 ml.
⅔ cup	heavy cream	150 ml.

Gently stew the shallot or onion in about one third of the butter until soft but not colored. Increase the heat, add the livers, and sauté them rapidly, seasoning with salt, a generous amount of pepper, a small pinch of allspice and the herbs. When the livers turn gray on the outside (and are still rare), add the Cognac. Carefully ignite the Cognac with a long match or tip the pan to set it aflame, then remove the pan from the heat.

Press some of the livers and their juices through a fine sieve, add the remaining butter, and continue to sieve the livers thoroughly, scraping the bottom of the sieve from time to time. You will obtain a warm, slightly liquid purée. Whip the cream until foamy and semifirm but pourable, and stir it into the purée. The cream must not be stiffly whipped or the resultant mousse will be dry and cottony, rather than firm, moist and velvety. Chill before serving.

PETITS PROPOS CULINAIRES

Three Mousses

Trois Mousses

For the following recipe you will need a total of about 1 quart [1 liter] of gelatinous veal stock and about 2 cups [½ liter] of heavy cream.

To serve 8 to 10

Chicken mousse

3 lb.	chicken, roasted and partially cooled	1½ kg.
1 cup	gelatinous veal stock (recipe, page 163), melted and cooled	¼ liter
	salt and pepper	
	freshly grated nutmeg	
1 cup	heavy cream, lightly whipped	¼ liter

Sorrel mousse

10 oz.	sorrel, picked over, washed, parboiled for a few seconds and drained	300 g.
2 tbsp.	butter	30 ml.
⅔ cup	gelatinous veal stock, melted and cooled	150 ml.
	salt and pepper	
½ cup	heavy cream, lightly whipped	125 ml.

Tomato mousse

1	medium-sized onion, finely chopped	1
1 tbsp.	butter	15 ml.
5 to 6 tbsp.	dry white wine	75 to 90 ml.
5	medium-sized firm ripe tomatoes, peeled, seeded and chopped, or canned tomatoes, drained	5
½ tsp.	sugar	2 ml.
	salt and pepper	
	cayenne pepper	
⅔ cup	gelatinous veal stock, melted and cooled	150 ml.
½ cup	heavy cream, lightly whipped	125 ml.

Jelly

1 cup	gelatinous veal stock	¼ liter

To prepare the chicken mousse, remove the skin from the chicken legs and breast, and scrape the bones free of the flesh. You should have a generous 2 cups [½ liter] of flesh: The remainder of the carcass and the cooking juices may be used to enrich a pilaf. Pound the chicken flesh in a mortar, adding—a small quantity at a time—about half of the stock. Season with salt, pepper and only a suggestion of nutmeg, and put the mixture through a food mill. Work in the remaining stock, beating the purée vigorously. Finally, incorporate the cream. Spread the mixture into the bottom of a glass or crystal bowl that will reveal the rose, pale green and white bands of the tiered mousses. Refrigerate until set—about one hour.

To prepare the sorrel mousse, gently stew the sorrel in the butter, stirring regularly with a wooden spoon for 20 minutes, or until fairly dry. Add about two thirds of the stock and reduce by something over half, stirring continuously, until the mixture is a smooth, semiliquid purée. Grind in pepper, then press the mixture through a fine sieve into a bowl, and stir in the remaining stock. Taste for salt, remembering that the addition of the cream will attenuate the saltiness. Embed the bowl in a larger bowl containing cracked ice, and stir until the mixture begins to thicken. Stir in the cream. Spread the sorrel mousse over the surface of the firm chicken mousse and refrigerate the bowl again until the sorrel mousse is firm.

To prepare the tomato mousse, cook the onion gently in the butter for 15 to 20 minutes, or until the onion is soft and lightly yellowed. Add the wine and reduce over high heat until the pan is nearly dry. Add the tomatoes, sugar, a little salt and pepper, and a pinch of cayenne pepper. Simmer, uncovered, for about 30 minutes, stirring occasionally. Then add about half of the stock, and reduce the mixture by half at a rapid boil, stirring. Using a wooden pestle, press the mixture through a fine sieve into a bowl, then stir in the remaining stock. Place the bowl over cracked ice and stir the contents until they begin to turn syrupy; then, just before the jelling point, fold in the cream. Pour the tomato mousse over the surface of the sorrel mousse, and refrigerate to set all of the mousses completely—about one to two hours.

Meanwhile, melt the stock for the jelly. Let it cool nearly to room temperature. Pour the liquid jelly over the tomato mousse, and leave to set in the refrigerator for several hours or overnight before serving.

RICHARD OLNEY
SIMPLE FRENCH FOOD

Deviled Bones

Roast goose or turkey bones and necks can be treated in a similar manner.

To serve 2 to 4

½ lb.	meaty bones left from a standing rib beef roast	¼ kg.
½ tsp.	cayenne pepper	2 ml.
2 tsp.	Dijon mustard	10 ml.

Brush the bones with a mixture of the cayenne pepper and mustard, and broil them for five minutes on each side; serve immediately. No forks and knives are required to eat them.

X. M. BOULESTIN AND A. H. ADAIR
SAVOURIES AND HORS D'OEUVRE

Thin-sliced Raw Beef with Spicy Sauce
Carpaccio

To serve 6

1 lb.	lean beef top round, trimmed of all fat	½ kg.
	Spicy sauce	
½ cup	vinaigrette (recipe, page 160)	125 ml.
2	salt anchovies, filleted, soaked in water for 30 minutes, drained and patted dry	2
1 tbsp.	capers, rinsed and drained	15 ml.
1 tbsp.	finely chopped onion	15 ml.
1 tsp.	Dijon mustard	5 ml.
1 tbsp.	chopped sour gherkins	15 ml.

Chill the meat in the freezer for about one hour until it is partially frozen; this facilitates the slicing. Slice the meat across the grain into paper-thin slices and arrange the slices side by side on a platter. Blend all of the sauce ingredients in a food processor for only one second (the sauce should be grainy). Serve the meat and sauce separately.

JOE FAMULARO AND LOUISE IMPERIALE
THE FESTIVE FAMULARO KITCHEN

Shaking Beef
Bò Lúc Lắc

The fish sauce called for is sold under the name "nuoc mam" in stores specializing in Southeast Asian and Chinese foods.

To serve 6

½ lb.	beef sirloin, porterhouse or tenderloin steak	¼ kg.
5	garlic cloves, chopped	5
1 tsp.	fish sauce	5 ml.
½ tsp.	sugar	2 ml.
½ tsp.	salt	2 ml.
1 tbsp.	vegetable oil	15 ml.
1	medium-sized onion, halved lengthwise, then cut crosswise into paper-thin slices	1
1 tbsp.	vinegar	15 ml.
	freshly ground black pepper	
1 tbsp.	olive oil	15 ml.
2 cups	watercress leaves	½ liter

Cut the beef into 1-inch [2½-cm.] cubes, and combine them with four of the chopped garlic cloves. Sprinkle on the fish

sauce, sugar, ¼ teaspoon [1 ml.] of the salt, and 2 teaspoons [10 ml.] of the vegetable oil. Mix thoroughly and allow to marinate for 30 minutes. In a separate bowl, marinate the onion in the vinegar for five to 10 minutes, then sprinkle on the pepper, the remaining salt and the olive oil. Add the watercress and arrange the mixture on a platter. Heat the remaining vegetable oil in a small skillet or wok over high heat. Add the remaining garlic clove, stir, then add the beef mixture. Fry the beef quickly until the cubes are seared on the outside and slightly pink in the center—about five minutes. Pour the beef over the watercress and serve at once.

BACH NGÔ AND GLORIA ZIMMERMAN
THE CLASSIC CUISINE OF VIETNAM

Raw Lamb and Wheat Balls
Houm Kiufta

The bulgur called for in this recipe is a form of dried, cracked wheat. It can be obtained from stores specializing in Middle Eastern foods.

Those who are fond of garlic will welcome this interesting version of a traditional Armenian dish.

To serve 4

¾ to 1 cup	fine bulgur	175 to 250 ml.
½ lb.	lean boneless leg of lamb, ground 3 times	¼ kg.
1 or 2	small garlic cloves, pounded to a paste	1 or 2
	salt and freshly ground black pepper	
	cayenne pepper	
½ cup	finely chopped fresh parsley	125 ml.
¼ cup	finely chopped scallions, including part of the green tops	50 ml.
2	medium-sized tomatoes, cut into eighths	2
1	lemon, cut into wedges	1

Rinse the bulgur thoroughly in a strainer under cold running water. Squeeze out the moisture and place the wheat in a mixing bowl. Add the lamb and the garlic, and season to taste with salt, pepper and cayenne pepper.

Moistening your hands now and then by dipping them into a bowl of ice water, knead the mixture vigorously for about 15 minutes, or until well blended, moist and smooth. Alternatively, pound the mixture in a stone mortar, adding 1 or 2 tablespoons [15 or 30 ml.] of cold water. Taste the mixture for seasoning.

Keeping your hands moist, form this mixture into 1-inch [2½-cm.] balls and arrange them on a serving platter. Sprinkle with the parsley and scallions, and garnish with the tomatoes and lemon wedges. Serve at once.

SONIA UVEZIAN
THE BEST FOODS OF RUSSIA

Lamb Rolls

Lammrullader

To prepare the kidneys called for in this recipe, wash them well, drain and parboil them for one minute. Remove their membranes and trim them of all fat and connective tissue.

To serve 4 to 8

1 lb.	lean leg of lamb, cut into 8 very thin slices	½ kg.
	salt and pepper	
4	lamb kidneys, trimmed and finely ground	4
½ cup	coarse bread crumbs	125 ml.
1 tbsp.	finely chopped dill pickle	15 ml.
½ tsp.	finely chopped fresh mint leaves	2 ml.
1 cup	milk or meat stock (recipe, page 163)	¼ liter

Pound the lamb slices until they are very tender and thin; season them with salt and pepper. Mix the ground kidneys with the other ingredients, using just enough milk or stock to moisten the mixture; season with salt and pepper. Spread a little of the kidney filling on each slice of lamb, and roll it up. Secure each roll with a string dipped in hot water.

Place the rolls in a roasting pan and roast them in a preheated 350° F. [180° C.] oven for about one hour. If they seem dry, baste the rolls with stock or milk. They should be brown and cooked through. Remove the strings before serving. Serve the lamb rolls hot with the deglazed pan juices or with currant jelly.

FLORENCE BROBECK AND MONIKA B. KJELLBERG
SMÖRGÅSBORD AND SCANDINAVIAN COOKERY

Raw Lamb with Wheat

Kibbeh Nayyeh

The bulgur called for in this recipe is a form of dried, cracked wheat. It can be obtained from stores specializing in Middle Eastern foods.

To serve 4 to 6

1 lb.	boned lamb shoulder, all fat, gristle and membranes removed	½ kg.
1	medium-sized onion, coarsely chopped	1
10	mint leaves, 6 coarsely chopped	10
5 oz.	fine bulgur, soaked in water for about 1 hour	150 g.
	salt and pepper	
about ½ cup	olive oil	about 125 ml.

Place the lamb, onion and chopped mint leaves in a large mortar and pound to a pastelike consistency. Squeeze the bulgur dry and add it to the lamb. Continue pounding until the mixture is quite smooth. Transfer the mixture to a large bowl, add salt and pepper to taste and a dribble of olive oil. Knead the mixture, add a little more oil, and continue kneading and adding oil until the mixture has the consistency of a smooth pâté. Add more salt and pepper if desired.

Mound the mixture on a serving platter. Shape it and flatten the top of the mound, then moisten your hand with a little olive oil and smooth the surface. Use a spoon handle to make wells in the top surface of the mound, and sprinkle a few drops of olive oil into each well. Garnish with the remaining mint leaves and serve.

PETITS PROPOS CULINAIRES

Viennese Sausage Salad

To serve 4 to 6

1½ tbsp.	cider vinegar	22½ ml.
½ tsp.	sugar	2 ml.
5 tbsp.	olive oil	75 ml.
4	knockwurst, boiled for 5 minutes, drained, peeled and thinly sliced	4
1	small red onion, thinly sliced	1
1 tbsp.	capers, rinsed and drained	15 ml.
2 tbsp.	finely chopped pimiento	30 ml.
1	small green pepper, halved, seeded, deribbed and diced	1
1	small dill pickle, thinly sliced	1
4	plum tomatoes, quartered	4
	salt and freshly ground black pepper	
1 to 2 tbsp.	chopped fresh parsley	15 to 30 ml.

In a serving bowl combine the vinegar, sugar and oil, and whisk until the sugar is dissolved. Then add the sliced knockwurst, the onion, capers, pimiento, green pepper, pickle and tomatoes. Season the salad with salt and pepper to taste and toss it lightly. Marinate the salad in the refrigerator for two to four hours.

Just before serving, correct the seasoning if necessary and sprinkle the salad with the parsley. Serve the salad chilled, but not cold.

PERLA MEYERS
THE PEASANT KITCHEN

Ham and Potato Balls

Skinbullar

To serve 4

2	medium-sized potatoes, boiled, peeled and mashed	2
½ cup	finely chopped cooked smoked ham	125 ml.
1 tsp.	finely chopped fresh parsley	5 ml.
⅛ tsp.	pepper	½ ml.
1 cup	fresh bread crumbs	¼ liter
1	egg, beaten	1
	fat for deep frying	
	Hot mustard sauce	
1½ cups	beef stock (recipe, page 163), boiled to reduce it to 1 cup [¼ liter]	375 ml.
1 tbsp.	dry mustard	15 ml.
1 tbsp.	vinegar	15 ml.
1 tsp.	sugar	5 ml.
1 tsp.	prepared mustard	5 ml.
½ tsp.	salt	2 ml.
½ tsp.	paprika	2 ml.

Mix the potatoes, ham, parsley and pepper. Shape the mixture into small balls. Roll them in the bread crumbs, then in the egg and then in the crumbs again. Heat the fat and deep fry the balls until delicately browned—two to three minutes. Drain the balls and serve them hot, with the mustard sauce. To make the sauce, mix the ingredients and, stirring constantly, bring to a boil. Serve the sauce immediately.

FLORENCE BROBECK AND MONIKA B. KJELLBERG
SMÖRGÅSBORD AND SCANDINAVIAN COOKERY

Creamed Belgian Endive with Ham

Endives au Jambon à la Crème

To serve 6

12	heads Belgian endive, trimmed	12
3 tbsp.	butter	45 ml.
1 tsp.	sugar	5 ml.
	salt and pepper	
12	slices ham	12
4 cups	white sauce (recipe, page 162), flavored with grated nutmeg	1 liter
½ cup	grated Gruyère or Parmesan cheese	125 ml.

With the point of a knife, cut out the bitter conical cores of the endive. Butter a casserole, put in the endive and sprinkle it with sugar, salt and pepper. Cover and bake the endive in a preheated 350° F. [180° C.] oven for one hour, or until it is very tender.

Let the endive cool slightly; then roll each head of endive in a slice of ham and arrange the packages diagonally in a buttered, shallow baking dish. Spoon the white sauce on top and sprinkle with the cheese. Bake the endive in a preheated 400° F. [200° C.] oven for 20 to 25 minutes, or until bubbling hot and browned.

FAYE LEVY
LA VARENNE TOUR BOOK

Fried Brain Cakes

Ausgebackener Hirnkuchen

The technique of preparing brains for cooking is demonstrated on pages 32-33.

To serve 6

¼ cup	flour	50 ml.
1¾ cups	milk	425 ml.
6	eggs, 5 with the yolks and whites separated, 1 lightly beaten	6
10 tbsp.	butter	150 ml.
1	pair calf's brains, soaked, cleaned and chopped	1
	salt and pepper	
1 tbsp.	finely chopped fresh parsley	15 ml.
	dry bread crumbs	

Stir the flour into the milk and heat it gently, stirring constantly. Bring the mixture to a boil; when it forms a smooth paste, remove it from the heat and let it cool slightly. Beat the egg yolks and stir them into the mixture with about 1 tablespoon [15 ml.] of the butter. Beat the whites until they form stiff peaks and fold them in. Line a 14-by-11-inch [35-by-28-cm.] jelly-roll pan with buttered parchment paper and pour the cake mixture into it. The mixture should be about ½ inch [1 cm.] deep. Bake in a preheated 375° F. [190° C.] oven for 15 to 20 minutes, or until firm to the touch.

Meanwhile, sauté the chopped brains in 2 tablespoons [30 ml.] of the butter until they are firm—about four or five minutes. Season the brains with salt and pepper, and sprinkle them with chopped parsley.

Remove the cake from the oven and turn it out onto a cloth. Spread it quickly with the calf's brains. While the cake is still warm, take hold of one end of the cloth and roll up the cake as you would a jelly roll. Place the roll in the refrigerator and chill it until firm—about two hours. Cut the roll into 3-inch [8-cm.] slices. Dip the slices in the lightly beaten egg and then in bread crumbs, and fry them in the remaining butter until golden on both sides—about five minutes.

ELEK MAGYAR
KOCHBUCH FÜR FEINSCHMECKER

Calf's Brain with Anchovies

Kalbshirn mit Sardellen

To serve 4

1	calf's brain, blanched in salted water for 5 minutes, membrane removed, parboiled, cooled and finely chopped	1
5	salt anchovies, filleted, soaked in water for 30 minutes, drained, patted dry and chopped	5
3 tbsp.	white wine	45 ml.
½ cup	heavy cream	125 ml.
1	egg yolk	1
1 to 2 tsp.	capers, rinsed and drained	5 to 10 ml.
2 tbsp.	almonds, blanched, peeled and slivered	30 ml.
¼ cup	dry bread crumbs	50 ml.
2 tbsp.	butter, cut into pieces	30 ml.

Mix the chopped brain thoroughly with the anchovy fillets, white wine, cream, egg yolk, capers and almonds. Butter four ramekins and fill them with the brain mixture. Sprinkle the tops with bread crumbs and dot them with the butter. Bake the ramekins in a preheated 400° F. [200° C.] oven for 12 to 15 minutes, or until the tops are browned.

LILO AUREDEN
WAS MÄNNERN SO GUT SCHMECKT

Pickled Lamb Tongues

To serve 6 to 8

8 to 10	lamb tongues, soaked for 3 hours in cold water and rinsed	8 to 10
2 or 3	sprigs parsley	2 or 3
2 tsp.	dried tarragon	10 ml.
1	bay leaf	1
1 tbsp.	salt	15 ml.
14	peppercorns	14
1	onion, sliced	1
2	garlic cloves	2
4	whole allspice	4
½ cup	white wine vinegar	125 ml.
½ cup	water	125 ml.
	salt	

Put the tongues into a large stockpot with the parsley, 1 teaspoon [5 ml.] of the tarragon, the bay leaf, salt, eight of the peppercorns, the onion, garlic and water to cover. Bring to a boil. Reduce the heat, cover and simmer for about one hour, or until the tongues are just tender. Drain the tongues and remove the skin and any gristle while the tongues feel warm to the touch. Cut the tongues in half lengthwise and place in a crock or jar.

Combine the remaining tarragon and peppercorns with the allspice, vinegar, ½ cup [125 ml.] of water and salt to taste in a nonreactive small saucepan. Boil for one minute. Pour the sauce over the lamb tongues and allow to cool. Store in the refrigerator overnight to let the flavors blend.

JANA ALLEN AND MARGARET GIN
INNARDS AND OTHER VARIETY MEATS

Skewered Sweetbreads

Des Hâtelets de Ris de Veau

This recipe was first published in 1787. The advance preparation of sweetbreads is demonstrated on pages 34-35. Wooden skewers should be presoaked in water for 30 minutes to prevent them from charring—or igniting—in the broiler.

To serve 4 to 6

1 tbsp.	flour	15 ml.
4 tbsp.	butter	60 ml.
3 tbsp.	finely chopped fresh parsley	45 ml.
3 to 4	scallions, finely chopped	3 to 4
1	pair veal sweetbreads, blanched, membranes removed, patted dry and cut into small pieces	1
½ lb.	veal liver or chicken liver, trimmed and cut into small pieces	¼ kg.
¼ lb.	sliced lean bacon, cut into strips and blanched for 2 minutes in boiling water	125 g.
	salt and pepper	
	bread crumbs	

Cook the flour in the butter over low heat until the flour is lightly colored. Stir in the parsley and scallions, then the sweetbread, liver and bacon pieces. Season with salt and pepper. Remove the pan from the heat when the liver has become slightly firm.

Thread the pieces of meat onto wooden skewers, coat with the remaining pan juices, and roll the skewered meats in bread crumbs. Lay the skewers on racks and refrigerate them for at least 30 minutes to firm the coating.

Broil the skewered meats, turning them two or three times during cooking, for eight to 10 minutes, or until they are light brown.

PIERRE JOSEPH BUC'HOZ
L'ART DE PRÉPARER LES ALIMENTS

Peruvian Skewered Heart

Anticucho

These skewered morsels have become Peru's national dish. They are sold on wooden skewers by street vendors, or cooked at home as a first course. Either way they are served rare, with a chili dip. To make the dip, seed and chop five or six dried hot red chilies, and pour 1 ¼ cups [300 ml.] of boiling water over them. Let them soak for two hours, then drain them thoroughly and purée them in a blender with ⅓ cup [75 ml.] of olive oil, one finely chopped garlic clove, a pinch of salt and 2 to 3 tablespoons [30 to 45 ml.] of hot stock or water.

If the skewers used are wood, they should be presoaked in water for 30 minutes to prevent them from charring in the heat of the coals or broiler.

Take care not to overcook the meat because it can easily become dry and hard.

	To serve 4	
1	calf's heart, halved, soaked in water for 1 hour, the tubes and tendons removed and the meat cut into 1-inch [2½-cm.] cubes	1
2 tbsp.	olive oil	30 ml.

Spicy marinade		
1 ¼ cups	wine vinegar	300 ml.
1 ¼ cups	water	300 ml.
1	onion, grated	1
1	garlic clove, crushed to a paste	1
½ to 1 tsp.	cayenne pepper	2 to 5 ml.
1	bay leaf	1
3	whole allspice, crushed	3
3	peppercorns, crushed	3
¼ tsp.	salt	1 ml.
¼ tsp.	sugar	1 ml.

Prepare a marinade with the vinegar, water, onion, garlic, cayenne pepper, bay leaf, crushed allspice and peppercorns, salt and a pinch of sugar. Put the cubed heart into the marinade—it should be submerged—toss it gently, cover and refrigerate it overnight.

On the following day, remove the meat from the marinade, arrange it on short skewers and brush it with the olive oil. Grill the meat over hot coals or under the broiler for about six minutes, turning the skewers once during cooking.

GRETE WILLINSKY
KULINARISCHE WELTREISE

Sweetbreads in a Rice Turban

The technique of preparing sweetbreads is demonstrated on pages 34-35. The cooked rice may be flavored with ½ cup [125 ml.] each of chopped fresh parsley and chives. To make the sauce less rich, omit the cream and thicken the sauce with a beurre manié made from 1 tablespoon [15 ml.] of softened butter kneaded with 1 ½ tablespoons [22½ ml.] of flour.

	To serve 8	
3 tbsp.	butter	45 ml.
1	large onion or 6 to 8 shallots, chopped	1
6 oz.	fresh mushrooms, stems removed and caps sliced (about 1 ¼ cups [300 ml.])	175 g.
2	pairs veal sweetbreads, soaked, blanched, membranes removed, and pressed flat under a weight	2
¼ cup	brandy	50 ml.
about 2 ½ cups	veal stock (recipe, page 163)	about 625 ml.
	salt and pepper	
	grated nutmeg	
1	bouquet garni of celery tops, parsley and a bay leaf (optional)	1
2 cups	heavy cream	½ liter
2 cups	white rice	½ liter

Melt the butter in a heavy skillet over medium heat. Add the chopped onion or shallots and the mushrooms, and cook until the onion softens—about 10 minutes. Lay the sweetbreads on top of the vegetables and pour the brandy over them. Ignite the brandy and let it burn until the flame dies. Reduce the heat and add 2 cups [½ liter] of the stock, salt and pepper to taste, and a pinch of nutmeg. Add the bouquet garni, if using. Cover and cook the sweetbreads for 30 minutes, basting them every 10 minutes and adding stock if needed. At the end of the cooking time, the pan juices should be syrupy.

With a slotted spoon, remove the sweetbreads from the skillet, slice them crosswise and put them on a warmed plate. Transfer the mushrooms and onion or shallots to the plate with the sliced sweetbreads. Add the cream to the skillet and cook until it is reduced to about 1 cup [¼ liter]. Remove the skillet from the heat and stir the mushrooms, onion and sliced sweetbreads into the reduced sauce.

Meanwhile, add the rice to 1 quart [1 liter] of lightly salted boiling water. Cover and cook the rice over low heat for 15 minutes, or until all of the water has been absorbed.

Lightly butter eight 1-cup [¼-liter] bowls. Press some hot rice into one bowl at a time, using a spoon to mold a shell of rice 1 inch [2½ cm.] thick. Fill the shells with some of the sweetbread mixture and cover with additional rice. Immediately unmold the filled bowls onto warmed, individual plates and pour any remaining sauce over the turbans.

COOKS' CLUB: FRENCH MENU V

Fish and Shellfish

Cold Anchovy Dish

Hamsi Buĝlamasi

Smelts or Baltic herring may be substituted for the anchovies.

	To serve 4	
2 lb.	fresh anchovies, gutted, washed and patted dry	1 kg.
½ cup	olive oil	125 ml.
1 ¼ cups	water	300 ml.
	salt	
¼ cup	finely cut fresh dill	50 ml.
¼ cup	finely chopped fresh parsley	50 ml.
3 tbsp.	strained fresh lemon juice	45 ml.

Lay the anchovies out side by side in a shallow heatproof dish. Add the olive oil, water, salt, dill and parsley. Cover the dish (using foil if it has no fitted cover) and cook in a preheated 400° F. [200° C.] oven for seven or eight minutes. Remove the anchovies from the oven, add the lemon juice shortly afterward, and serve cold.

ALAN DAVIDSON
MEDITERRANEAN SEAFOOD

Raw Anchovies with Lemon

Acciughe Crude al Limone

The technique of removing the backbone of a fish without cutting it in half is shown on page 54. If fresh anchovies are not available, substitute herring or smelts.

This simple recipe for an unusual fish hors d'oeuvre is from the Antica Osteria Pacetti restaurant in Genoa. It is essential to have anchovies almost straight from the sea.

	To serve 6	
18	fresh anchovies, cleaned, scaled, heads and backbones removed	18
1 cup	fresh lemon juice	¼ liter
1 cup	dry white wine	¼ liter
1	sprig parsley, finely chopped	1
	salt	
½ cup	olive oil	125 ml.

Place the anchovies in an oval dish, one beside the other, and cover them with the lemon juice and white wine. Let them steep for two to three hours to whiten them. Remove the anchovies from the marinade, drain them well, and place them side by side on a serving dish. Sprinkle them with the chopped parsley; salt them lightly and cover with the olive oil. Let them stand for three to four hours before serving.

LUIGI VOLPICELLI AND SECONDINO FREDA (EDITORS)
L'ANTIARTUSI: 1000 RECETTE

Stuffed Anchovies

Paupiettes d'Anchois a la Niçoise

To clean and bone anchovies as called for in this recipe, slit each one open along the belly with your thumb, then pull away the head with the gills and stomach sac attached. Pinch off the head, open the fish flat and peel away the backbone — pinching it off at the tail.

	To serve 4 to 6	
8 to 10	salt anchovies, soaked in water for 10 minutes, heads removed, cleaned and boned without separating the fillets, rinsed and patted dry	8 to 10
½ cup	dry white wine	125 ml.
⅓ cup	olive oil	75 ml.
1 tbsp.	vinegar	15 ml.
	Savory stuffing	
1 tbsp.	capers, rinsed, drained and finely chopped	15 ml.
1	sour gherkin, finely chopped	1
2	eggs, hard-boiled and finely chopped	2
2 tbsp.	fines herbes	30 ml.
1 to 2 tbsp.	mayonnaise (recipe, page 161), colored with puréed spinach	15 to 30 ml.

Marinate the anchovies for one hour in the wine. Then drain them and dry them.

Mix together the chopped capers, gherkin, eggs, fines herbes and mayonnaise. Stuff the anchovies with this mixture, shaping the fish around the stuffing. Arrange them on a small, shallow serving dish and sprinkle them with the oil and vinegar.

PROSPER SALLES AND PROSPER MONTAGNÉ
LA GRANDE CUISINE

Anchovy or Smoked Baltic Herring Hash

Ansjövisfräs och Böcklingfräs

So-called Swedish anchovies are in fact sprats preserved in spiced brine. They are much larger and milder in flavor than other preserved anchovies; other brine-packed sprats or small herring make appropriate substitutes. Baltic herring are smaller and leaner than Atlantic herring, which may be used instead.

	To serve 4	
1	large onion, finely chopped, or 1 or 2 leeks, white parts only, finely chopped	1
2 tbsp.	butter	30 ml.
8 to 10	Swedish anchovies or smoked Baltic herring, filleted, skinned and finely chopped	8 to 10
4	eggs, hard-boiled and coarsely chopped	4
	black pepper	

Sauté the onion or leeks in the butter until they are lightly browned. Add the anchovies and eggs. While stirring, fry the hash over high heat for about two minutes, or until it is heated through. Season with black pepper. Serve at once.

TORE WRETMAN
SWEDISH SMÖRGÅSBORD

Anchovies with Oil and Herbs

Anchois Toulonnais

	To serve 4	
¼ cup	olive oil	50 ml.
12	salt anchovies, filleted, soaked in water for 30 minutes, drained and patted dry	12
	freshly ground pepper	
1 tsp.	Dijon mustard	5 ml.
1 tbsp.	wine vinegar	15 ml.
2 tbsp.	chopped fresh parsley	30 ml.
1 tbsp.	finely chopped fresh chervil	15 ml.
1	garlic clove, finely chopped	1

Pour olive oil over the anchovies and let them marinate for two or three days. Remove them from the marinade, cut them in small pieces and dress them in the following manner: To the oil in which they have been soaked add the pepper, mustard, vinegar, parsley, chervil and garlic. Mix well, pour over the anchovies and serve.

X. M. BOULESTIN AND A. H. ADAIR
SAVOURIES AND HORS D'OEUVRE

Bluefish Seviche with Red Onion and Hot-Pepper Flakes

To extract more juice from limes, pour boiling water over them and let them stand for one minute, then rinse them under cold water.

	To serve 6	
one 2 to 3 lb.	bluefish, cleaned, filleted, skinned and cut into strips ¾ inch [2 cm.] wide	one 1 to 1 ½ kg.
1 tbsp.	tamari soy sauce	15 ml.
1 ½ tsp.	dried red hot-pepper flakes	7 ml.
1	large red onion, thinly sliced and separated into rings	1
about 1 cup	fresh lime juice (juice of 6 to 8 limes)	about ¼ liter
1 tbsp.	finely chopped fresh mint	15 ml.

Place the fish strips in a bowl, pour the soy sauce over them and toss the strips to coat them evenly. Place a layer of fish strips in the bottom of a glazed earthenware crock, or any deep ceramic or glass bowl with straight sides, such as a small soufflé dish. Sprinkle some of the hot-pepper flakes over the fish and then make a layer of onion rings. Repeat the layers until all of the fish and onions are used up, then pour in enough lime juice to cover the fish. Cover tightly with plastic wrap and refrigerate overnight. Add the mint just before serving.

SHERYL AND MEL LONDON
THE FISH-LOVERS' COOKBOOK

Marinated Smoked Cod

Morue Marinée

	To serve 6	
¾ to 1 cup	oil	175 to 250 ml.
1 lb.	smoked cod, cut into fillets ¼ inch [6 mm.] thick	½ kg.
2	onions, thinly sliced	2

Oil a glass baking dish and arrange a layer of one half of the cod fillets. Spread half of the sliced onions over the fish, then dribble half of the oil over the onions. Repeat with the other half of the ingredients to make a second layer. Cover tightly and let the cod marinate at room temperature for six to 12 hours; then refrigerate it for one week or more. Baste the cod occasionally with the oil in the dish. To serve, lift the cod fillets from the oil, arrange them in the center of a platter and surround them with the onion slices. Accompany the cod with thinly sliced dark bread.

CAROL CUTLER
HAUTE CUISINE FOR YOUR HEART'S DELIGHT

Baked Fish Ragout

Fischragout Überbacken

To steam cod, cook it in a covered steamer over boiling salted water for about 10 minutes. For a more elaborate version of this dish, replace the cod and capers with parboiled asparagus tips, flaked crab meat and lightly sautéed mushrooms.

To serve 6

1 lb.	cod fillets, skinned, steamed and flaked	½ kg.
1 tbsp.	capers, rinsed and drained	15 ml.
	salt and pepper	
1 tbsp.	fresh lemon juice	15 ml.
2 tbsp.	chopped fresh parsley	30 ml.
2	eggs	2
3 tbsp.	heavy cream	45 ml.
2 tbsp.	freshly grated Parmesan cheese	30 ml.
1 tbsp.	dry bread crumbs	15 ml.
1 tbsp.	butter, cut into small pieces	15 ml.
3	lemons, quartered	3

Butter six individual ovenproof dishes or scallop shells. Combine the fish with the capers and divide the mixture among the dishes. Season with salt, pepper and a few drops of lemon juice; sprinkle with the parsley. Beat the eggs with the cream and pour into the dishes. Sprinkle with the grated cheese and bread crumbs, and dot with the butter. Bake in a preheated 425° F. [220° C.] oven for 10 minutes, or until lightly browned. Serve with lemon wedges.

HEDWIG MARIA STUBER
ICH HELF DIR KOCHEN

Salt Cod Purée

Brandade de Morue Parmentière

This purée can be served with a garnish of fried bread triangles, or it can be used to fill pastry or bread cases.

To serve 6

1½ lb.	salt cod, soaked in 3 changes of water for at least 24 hours, skinned and boned	¾ kg.
1 cup	olive oil	¼ liter
1	small garlic clove, crushed to a paste	1
4	medium-sized potatoes, boiled, peeled and mashed to a purée (about 2½ cups [½ liter])	4
⅓ cup	scalded milk	75 ml.
	salt and pepper	

Put the cod into a pan and cover it with cold water. Bring the water to a boil, then reduce the heat and poach the cod for 10 to 12 minutes. Drain the cod, remove any remaining skin and bones, and use two forks to flake it. In a heavy saucepan over medium heat, heat all but 2 tablespoons [30 ml.] of the oil. Remove the pan from the heat and add the cod. Mash the fish and oil together with a fork and beat the mixture against the sides of the pan until it forms a fibrous mass.

Return the pan to the heat and, drop by drop as if making a mayonnaise, add the remaining oil, beating the paste constantly. Add the garlic and then alternate spoonfuls of puréed potato and milk, beating after each addition. Add the rest of the potatoes and beat until the mixture forms a soft, smooth paste. Add extra milk if needed. Season to taste.

ALBIN MARTY
FOURMIGUETTO

Herring Savory

To serve 2

2	salted herring, soaked overnight in water, skinned and filleted	2
¼ cup	dry bread crumbs	50 ml.
2 tbsp.	butter, cut into pieces	30 ml.
¼ cup	heavy cream	50 ml.
2 tsp.	chopped fresh chervil	10 ml.

Coat the fillets thoroughly with the bread crumbs, arrange the fillets in a buttered gratin dish and dot them with the butter. Bake the fillets in a preheated 375° F. [190° C.] oven for five to 10 minutes. Then pour the cream over the herring and bake them for a further 10 minutes, or until the herring are soft. Sprinkle them with the chopped chervil.

INGA NORBERG (EDITOR)
GOOD FOOD FROM SWEDEN

Smoked Herring and Eggs

To serve 6

6	smoked herring, filleted and skinned	6
	salt and pepper	
1 tbsp.	finely cut fresh dill	15 ml.
1 tbsp.	finely cut fresh chives	15 ml.
3	eggs	3
1 cup	milk or half-and-half cream	¼ liter

Butter an ovenproof casserole and cover the bottom with the fish fillets. Salt and pepper them sparingly and sprinkle them with the dill and chives. Beat the eggs and milk or cream together, season and pour the mixture over the fish. Bake in a preheated 400° F. [200° C.] oven for 15 to 20 minutes. The egg mixture should be set and lightly browned.

OSKAR JAKOBSSON (EDITOR)
GOOD FOOD IN SWEDEN

Herring Salad with Dill Cream

Haringsla met Dilleroom

To serve 10 to 16

5	fresh herring, filleted, coated with salt, refrigerated for 2 hours and wiped dry	5
1½ cups	sour cream	375 ml.
1	medium-sized onion, finely chopped	1
1 tbsp.	vodka	15 ml.
2 tsp.	finely cut fresh dill	10 ml.
1	garlic clove, pounded to a paste	1
¼ tsp.	pepper	1 ml.

Cut each herring fillet into six equal pieces. Combine the remaining ingredients in a mixing bowl and stir in the pieces of herring.

HUGH JANS
SLA, SLAATJES, SNACKS

Herring in Paper Cases

Hering in Papier-Hülle

To serve 4

4	fresh herring, cleaned, filleted and skinned, each fillet halved crosswise	4
3 tbsp.	butter	45 ml.
1 cup	finely chopped fresh mushrooms	¼ liter
2 tsp.	fines herbes	10 ml.
1	shallot, finely chopped	1
	salt and pepper	
⅔ cup	white sauce (recipe, page 162)	150 ml.
	oil or butter	

Sauté the herring fillets in 1 tablespoon [15 ml.] of the butter. Sauté the mushrooms, fines herbes and shallot in the remaining butter until the mushroom liquid has evaporated and the mixture begins to thicken. Add salt and pepper, then stir in the white sauce. Stir constantly until the mixture has thickened. Remove from the heat and let the mixture cool.

Cut parchment paper into eight heart shapes, each about 5 inches [13 cm.] wide and long. Brush oil or butter over the paper hearts. Spread half of the herring pieces with the filling. Cover with the rest of the pieces to make sandwiches, and put a herring sandwich on the left-hand side of each paper heart. Fold the right-hand half of the heart over the herring and fold the edges of the paper firmly closed, turning the edges inward several times so that the contents cannot leak out during cooking.

Cover a griddle with a sheet of oiled parchment paper to fit. Lay the packages on the heated griddle and cook them

over low heat, turning frequently, for 15 to 20 minutes. Alternatively, cook them in the same way in a heavy, oiled or buttered skillet, or bake them on an oiled baking sheet in a preheated 400° F. [200° C.] oven for 15 to 20 minutes.

SOPHIE WILHELMINE SCHEIBLER
ALLGEMEINES DEUTSCHES KOCHBUCH FÜR ALLE STÄNDE

Latvian Herring

Hors d'Oeuvre Livonien

To serve 6 to 8

5	large smelts, filleted	5
14 tbsp.	butter, 12 tbsp. [180 ml.] softened	210 ml.
5	eggs, the yolks separated from the whites, and the whites stiffly beaten	5
	salt and pepper	
	grated nutmeg	
2 tsp.	flour	10 ml.
2	large salt herring, filleted, soaked in milk for 30 minutes and diced	2

Fry the smelt fillets in 1 tablespoon [15 ml.] of the butter until slightly browned on both sides. Drain and set the smelts aside to cool.

In a bowl, work the softened butter into a paste and beat in the egg yolks, one at a time. Season with salt, pepper and a pinch of nutmeg, and beat in the flour.

Fold in the stiffly beaten egg whites. Add the diced herring and fried smelts to the egg mixture in the bowl.

Melt the remaining butter in an ovenproof omelet pan and pour the fish-and-egg mixture into the pan. Bake the omelet in a preheated 375° F. [190° C.] oven for 15 to 20 minutes, or until completely set.

Cut the omelet into wedges or strips, place them on small plates and serve.

A. PETIT
LA GASTRONOMIE EN RUSSIE

Dill-flavored Mackerel

Gravad Makrel

To serve 4

4	fresh mackerel, filleted	4
1 tbsp.	sugar	15 ml.
2 tbsp.	salt	30 ml.
	freshly ground white pepper	
3 tbsp.	finely cut fresh dill	45 ml.
	dill sprigs	

Mix together the sugar, salt and pepper, and sprinkle over both sides of each mackerel fillet. Next sprinkle the fillets with the finely cut dill. Lay a bed of dill sprigs in a dish and place the fillets on it in pairs, layering them head to tail so that they fill the dish evenly. Cover them with another layer of dill sprigs. Let them rest in the refrigerator under light pressure (for example, a wooden board with a 1-pound [½-kg.] weight on it) for at least 12 hours.

To serve, scrape the dill and seasonings off the fillets and cut them into thin slices, using a very sharp knife and starting at the tail. Lay the cut slices on a platter and sprinkle them with dill.

ALAN DAVIDSON
NORTH ATLANTIC SEAFOOD

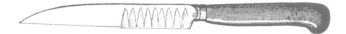

Scandinavian Pickled Salmon

Mackerel or trout may be used for this delicious dish.

To serve 6

1½ to 2 lb.	salmon, preferably cut from the tail section and divided into 2 fillets	¾ to 1 kg.
2 tbsp.	sea salt	30 ml.
1½ tbsp.	sugar	22½ ml.
1 tsp.	coarsely ground black pepper	5 ml.
1 tbsp.	brandy (optional)	15 ml.
1 cup	finely cut fresh dill leaves	¼ liter
Mustard sauce		
2 tbsp.	Dijon mustard	30 ml.
2 tsp.	sugar	10 ml.
1 tbsp.	wine vinegar	15 ml.
¼ cup	olive oil	50 ml.
	finely cut fresh dill leaves	
1	small garlic clove, crushed to a paste (optional)	1

Place one salmon fillet, skin side up, in a dish. Mix together the salt, sugar, pepper and brandy, if using. Rub about a quarter of this mixture into the skin of the fillet in the dish; then turn the fillet over and rub in half of the remaining mixture. Sprinkle with half of the dill leaves and put the second fillet on top, skin side up. Rub the rest of the mixture into the skin of the second fillet and sprinkle with the remaining dill.

Put a piece of foil on top, then two cans as weights. Let the fish marinate in the refrigerator for at least 12 hours and at most four days.

To serve, drain the fillets and slice them diagonally or horizontally, starting at the thick end. Serve with thinly sliced whole-wheat or rye bread and butter, lemon quarters

and mustard sauce. To make the sauce, combine all of the ingredients and mix them together until thick and smooth.

JANE GRIGSON
GOOD THINGS

Marinated Salmon

Gravlax

To serve 8

two 1 lb.	fresh salmon fillets, preferably center cut, with the skin left on	two ½ kg.
⅓ cup	salt	75 ml.
¼ cup	sugar	50 ml.
1 cup	finely cut fresh dill	¼ liter
20	white peppercorns, coarsely crushed	20
Mustard and dill sauce		
3 tbsp.	oil	45 ml.
1 tbsp.	red wine vinegar	15 ml.
1 tbsp.	sugar	15 ml.
½ tsp.	salt	2 ml.
	white pepper	
2 to 3 tbsp.	prepared mustard	30 to 45 ml.
2 to 3 tbsp.	finely cut fresh dill	30 to 45 ml.

Wipe the salmon fillets dry with a paper towel; do not rinse them. Mix the salt with the sugar and rub some of the mixture into the fish. Sprinkle some more of the salt mixture and some of the dill into a deep enameled or stainless-steel baking dish. Place one salmon fillet, skin side down, in the dish, and sprinkle generously with dill, crushed peppercorns and the salt mixture. Cover the fillet in the dish with the second fillet, skin side up. Sprinkle with the remaining salt mixture. Cover with aluminum foil and a light weight, for example a chopping board, and refrigerate for at least one or two days. Turn the salmon over every day.

To make the sauce, shake or beat together the oil, vinegar, sugar, salt, a pinch of white pepper and the mustard. The dill may be added after mixing or may be served in a separate bowl.

To serve the salmon, scrape off the marinade, cut it into slices free from the skin. (The skin may be sautéed, rolled up and used as a garnish.) Serve the sauce separately.

ASTA ÖSTENIUS AND BRITA OLSSEN (EDITORS)
SWEDISH COOKING

Raw Salmon with Herbs

Saumon Cru aux Herbes

To serve 6

1 lb.	salmon center cut, skinned	½ kg.
4	shallots, chopped	4
3 tbsp.	strained fresh lemon juice	45 ml.
2 tsp.	green peppercorns, crushed	10 ml.
1 tbsp.	finely cut chives	15 ml.
2 tbsp.	chopped fresh chervil leaves or 1 tbsp. [15 ml.] dried chervil	30 ml.
2 tbsp.	mild olive oil	30 ml.
1 tbsp.	Cognac	15 ml.

Slicing parallel to the backbone of the salmon, cut the flesh into thin slices. They should look like slices of smoked salmon. Mix together the remaining ingredients, add the salmon, and let it marinate for 30 minutes in the refrigerator. Without draining the salmon, arrange it attractively on individual small plates and distribute the herbs and marinade over the pieces again, but a bit sparingly. Serve with triangles of thin toast, unsalted butter and lemon wedges.

MADELEINE PETER (EDITOR)
FAVORITE RECIPES OF THE GREAT WOMEN CHEFS OF FRANCE

Sliced Raw Salmon Marinated in Olive Oil and Lime Juice

Émincé de Saumon Cru au Citron Vert

This recipe is from Georges Blanc, chef of the restaurant Chez la Mère Blanc at Vonnas, a village in the Saône valley of southeastern France.

To serve 8 to 10

½ cup	olive oil	125 ml.
½ cup	strained fresh lime juice	125 ml.
1 tbsp.	finely chopped mixed fresh tarragon, chives and chervil	15 ml.
	salt and freshly ground pepper	
2 lb.	fresh salmon, filleted and very thinly sliced	1 kg.

Cream and mustard sauce

½ cup	heavy cream	125 ml.
½ cup	mayonnaise (recipe, page 161)	125 ml.
1 tsp.	Dijon mustard	5 ml.
	salt and freshly ground pepper	

Mix all of the marinade ingredients together. Pour half of the marinade into a deep platter. Place the salmon slices in the platter and pour over the remaining marinade. Let stand for about two minutes, or until the slices whiten slightly. Drain the salmon slices and arrange them on a large chilled serving platter.

To make the mustard sauce, mix the cream and mayonnaise with the mustard, and season to taste with salt and pepper. Serve the sauce separately in a sauceboat.

LA CUISINE NATURELLE À L'HUILE D'OLIVE

Mediterranean Pickled Sardines

Sardines Marinées à la Niçoise

To grill the fish in the oven, first preheat the broiler. Arrange the fish on the rack of a broiler pan, set it 3 inches [8 cm.] from the heat source and grill for two minutes on each side.

Small mullet, anchovies and herring, all oily fish, lend themselves very well to this recipe.

To serve 3

2 lb.	fresh sardines, gutted, heads removed, rinsed and dried	1 kg.
	salt	
	olive oil	

Vinegar marinade

2 cups	white wine vinegar	½ liter
1	onion, thinly sliced	1
1	carrot, thinly sliced	1
4	shallots, thinly sliced	4
1	sprig thyme	1
1	bay leaf	1
1	celery rib, sliced	1
3	parsley sprigs	3
3	cloves	3
1 tsp.	peppercorns	5 ml.

Put the sardines side by side in a shallow dish and cover with a thin layer of salt. Let stand for three hours. Meanwhile, simmer the marinade ingredients for 25 minutes.

Take the sardines from the salt; wipe them and grill them for about two minutes on each side over glowing charcoal. Arrange the sardines in an earthenware dish and pour the marinade over them. Cover the dish tightly. Refrigerate for 48 hours, remove the fish from the marinade, drain them well, place them side by side in another earthenware dish and pour in enough olive oil to barely submerge them. Cover tightly and refrigerate the fish again.

Three days later the sardines will be ready, but they will keep for several days longer if they remain covered by oil.

PAUL BOUILLARD
LA CUISINE AU COIN DU FEU

Stuffed Sardine Rolls

Sarde a Beccafico

The technique of removing the backbone from a fish without cutting it in half is shown on page 54. Canestrato and caciocavallo are sharp-flavored Italian cheeses, obtainable where fine cheeses are sold.

	To serve 6	
2 lb.	fresh sardines, cleaned, scaled, heads and backbones removed	1 kg.
½ cup	wine vinegar	125 ml.
3 tbsp.	olive oil	45 ml.
4 cups	fresh bread crumbs	1 liter
3½ oz.	canestrato or caciocavallo cheese, diced	100 g.
2 tbsp.	pine nuts	30 ml.
½ cup	raisins, soaked in warm water for 15 minutes and drained	125 ml.
1	garlic clove, chopped	1
¾ cup	chopped fresh parsley	175 ml.
	salt and pepper	
	flour	
3	eggs, lightly beaten	3
	oil for deep frying	

Open out the sardines and marinate them in the vinegar for 15 minutes. In a skillet, heat the olive oil over low heat. Drain three of the sardines, add them to the pan and mash them with a wooden spoon. Add 1 cup [¼ liter] of the bread crumbs and cook them, stirring constantly, until brown. Remove the skillet from the heat, add the cheese, pine nuts, raisins, chopped garlic and parsley, and season the mixture to taste with salt and pepper. Mix thoroughly until this stuffing is smooth.

Drain the remaining sardines, place them skin side down, spread the stuffing on them and roll them up from head end to tail. To keep the sardines rolled, secure them—if you like—with wooden picks. Dredge the sardine rolls in flour, dip them in the beaten eggs, then coat them with the remaining bread crumbs. Deep fry the rolls in oil until golden brown—about three minutes.

As a variation, the sardine rolls—without being floured and coated with eggs and crumbs—can be arranged in an oiled baking dish, separated from each other with bay leaves, sprinkled with lemon juice and olive oil, and baked in a preheated 375° F. [190° C.] oven for 30 minutes.

PINO CORRENTI
IL LIBRO D'ORO DELLA CUCINA E DEI VINI DI SICILIA

Castilian-Style Stuffed Sardines

Popietas de Sardinas a la Catalana

The technique of removing the backbone from a fish without cutting it in half is shown on page 54. Anchovies or herring can be substituted for the sardines.

	To serve 4	
1½ lb.	fresh sardines, cleaned, heads and backbones removed	¾ kg.
1 or 2	garlic cloves, finely chopped	1 or 2
2 tbsp.	chopped fresh parsley	30 ml.
1	egg, hard-boiled and chopped	1
6 tbsp.	olive oil	90 ml.
	salt and white pepper	
1 tsp.	vinegar	5 ml.
⅔ cup	dry white wine	150 ml.
4	eggs	4
½ cup	dry bread crumbs	125 ml.
16	croutons	16
2	tomatoes, halved crosswise, brushed with oil and broiled for 5 minutes	2

For the filling, sauté one third of the sardines, the chopped garlic, parsley and hard-boiled egg in 4 tablespoons [60 ml.] of the oil until the flesh of the fish is firm—about four minutes. Mash the mixture with a fork. Add salt and white pepper to taste, the vinegar and 3 or 4 tablespoons [45 or 60 ml.] of the wine. Beat in one egg and stir the mixture over very low heat until it thickens. Let the filling cool.

Spread the remaining sardines open, cavities upward. Beat one egg and brush it over the cavities. Spoon some of the filling onto each of the open sardines, then close them. Beat the two remaining eggs, dip the sardines into the eggs and then the bread crumbs. Lay the coated sardines side by side in a shallow baking dish. Sprinkle them with the rest of the oil and the white wine, and bake them in a preheated 350° F. [180° C.] oven for 15 minutes, or until the flesh is firm when pressed. Serve sprinkled with the croutons and accompanied by the broiled tomato halves.

GLORIA ROSSI CALLIZO
LAS MEJORES TAPAS, CENAS FRÍAS Y PLATOS COMBINADOS

Sardines with Cheese Stuffing

Sardines Farcies au Brocciu

The original version of this recipe called for brocciu, a Corsican fresh curd cheese made from sheep's milk. Brocciu is not obtainable in America, but ricotta cheese makes a suitable substitute. The technique of removing the backbone from a fish without cutting it in half is demonstrated on page 54.

	To serve 4	
1 lb.	ricotta cheese	½ kg.
1	egg, beaten	1
	salt and freshly ground pepper	
12	large fresh sardines, cleaned, heads and backbones removed	12
½ cup	dry bread crumbs	125 ml.
3 tbsp.	olive oil	45 ml.

To make the stuffing, mix the ricotta with the egg, salt and pepper. Put a spoonful of stuffing into each sardine and arrange the sardines in a baking dish. Sprinkle them with the bread crumbs and oil, and bake them in a preheated 375° F. [190° C.] oven for 20 minutes, or until they are golden brown.

MARIA NUNZIA FILIPPINI
LA CUISINE CORSE

Marinated Smelts

Marides Marinates

Marinated smelts will keep for several days in the refrigerator. If desired, sliced garlic, shallots or onion may be added to the marinade.

	To serve 8 to 10	
2 lb.	smelts, scaled, gutted and rinsed	1 kg.
3 tbsp.	strained fresh lemon juice	45 ml.
¾ cup	flour	175 ml.
	olive oil for deep frying	
½ cup	dry white wine	125 ml.
¼ cup	wine vinegar	50 ml.
2 tbsp.	chopped fresh parsley	30 ml.
1 tbsp.	chopped fresh thyme or 1 tsp. [5 ml.] dried oregano	15 ml.
½ tsp.	dry mustard, mixed with 1 tsp. [5 ml.] cold water	2 ml.
2 tbsp.	olive oil	30 ml.
	salt and freshly ground pepper	

Sprinkle each smelt with lemon juice and roll it in the flour. Fry the smelts in small batches in about ½ inch [1 cm.] of hot oil for about two minutes on each side. Drain the smelts on absorbent paper.

Meanwhile, in a small saucepan, combine the wine, vinegar, parsley and the thyme or oregano with the mustard and olive oil. Season with salt and pepper. Simmer this marinade over low heat for eight minutes. Add the fried smelts, bring the marinade to a boil over high heat, then remove the pan from the heat and let the smelts cool.

Remove the smelts and arrange them in a deep serving dish. Pour the marinade over the smelts, then chill before serving. Serve cold.

VILMA LIACOURAS CHANTILES
THE FOOD OF GREECE

Escovitched or Caveached Fish

This is the Jamaican version of the pescado en escabeche of the Caribbean. Any white-fish fillets may be used instead of the snapper.

	To serve 8	
3	green peppers, halved, seeded, deribbed and sliced	3
2	medium-sized onions, thinly sliced	2
3	carrots, thinly sliced	3
1	bay leaf	1
½ tbsp.	finely chopped fresh ginger	7 ml.
6	peppercorns	6
⅛ tsp.	mace	½ ml.
	salt	
2 cups	water	½ liter
½ cup	olive oil	125 ml.
½ cup	vinegar, preferably malt or cane	125 ml.
2 lb.	snapper fillets	1 kg.
	olives	
	pimientos	

In a saucepan, combine the peppers, onions, carrots, bay leaf, ginger, peppercorns, mace, salt and water. Cover and simmer for 30 minutes. Add 2 tablespoons [30 ml.] of the olive oil and the vinegar to the pan, and simmer for a minute or two longer. Strain this sauce. Heat the remaining olive oil in a large, heavy skillet, and sauté the fish fillets until they are lightly browned on both sides; be careful not to overcook them. Drain the fillets and arrange them in a warmed serving dish. Pour the hot sauce over the fish and serve hot. Or chill the fish in its sauce and serve it cold, garnished with olives and pimientos.

ELISABETH LAMBERT ORTIZ
THE COMPLETE BOOK OF CARIBBEAN COOKING

Escovitched Fish

To serve 12

3 lb.	snapper, cut into ½-inch [1-cm.] slices	1 ½ kg.
4 tsp.	salt	20 ml.
4 tsp.	black pepper	20 ml.
½ cup	oil	125 ml.
2 cups	cane or malt vinegar	½ liter
2	large onions, sliced	2
½ tsp.	crushed hot red-pepper flakes	2 ml.
1 tsp.	whole allspice	5 ml.
½ tsp.	black peppercorns	2 ml.

Wash the fish slices in water to which the juice of two or three limes or lemons has been added. Dry the slices thoroughly. Combine the salt and black pepper, coat the fish slices on both sides with this mixture and set them aside on paper towels. Heat the oil in a skillet and fry the slices on both sides until they are nice and crisp. Place the fish in a deep dish. In a nonreactive saucepan, bring the vinegar, onions, red pepper, allspice and peppercorns to a boil. Simmer until the onions are tender—about 15 minutes. Cool the mixture, then pour it over the fish slices, cover the dish, refrigerate and let the fish marinate overnight.

LEILA BRANDON
A MERRY-GO-ROUND OF RECIPES FROM INDEPENDENT JAMAICA

Deep-fried Fish Rolls
Machhli ke Kofte

Use any firm white fish such as sole or cod for this recipe.

To serve 8 to 10

2 lb.	white fish, filleted, skinned and cut into 3-inch [8-cm.] pieces, parboiled for 5 minutes, drained and cooled	1 kg.
6	medium-sized potatoes, boiled, peeled and mashed to a purée	6
2 tsp.	ground coriander seeds	10 ml.
	salt	
	cayenne pepper	
1 cup	vegetable oil	¼ liter
2	medium-sized onions, chopped	2
2	eggs, beaten	2
1 tsp.	fresh lemon juice	5 ml.
¼ cup	finely chopped fresh coriander leaves	50 ml.
¼ cup	dry bread crumbs	50 ml.

Mash the fish with the potatoes and add the ground coriander, salt and cayenne pepper. In a skillet, heat 1 tablespoon

[15 ml.] of the vegetable oil. Add the fish-and-potato mixture. Stirring constantly, cook the mixture over medium heat until it is dry, taking care not to let it burn. Remove the mixture from the skillet and set it aside to cool.

Heat 1 tablespoon of the oil and fry the onions until brown. Strain the onions and add them to the fish with the beaten eggs and lemon juice. Sprinkle with the coriander.

Form the mixture into cylindrical rolls about 3 inches [8 cm.] long and ¾ inch [2 cm.] thick. Coat the rolls lightly with bread crumbs and fry them in the rest of the oil, a small batch at a time, for three or four minutes, or until they are uniformly light brown. Drain the rolls on paper towels.

KRISHNA PRASAD DAR
KASHMIRI COOKING

North Vietnamese Skewered Fish
Cha Ca Nuong

Nuoc mam, Vietnamese fish sauce, is obtainable from Asian grocers, but if it is not available, Chinese oyster sauce or fish gravy can be used. Shrimp paste is imported from Malaysia and obtainable in Chinese food markets, as is rice wine.

Any sea fish with firm flesh, such as mackerel or grouper, may be used in this recipe.

To serve 6

1 ½ lb.	fish, filleted, skinned and cut into 1 ¼-inch [3-cm.] cubes	¾ kg.
⅓ lb.	sliced lean bacon, cut into 1 ¼-inch [3-cm.] pieces	150 g.
3 tbsp.	oil	45 ml.
4	scallions, chopped	4
⅓ cup	dry-roasted peanuts, pounded	75 ml.
Fish marinade		
3 tbsp.	oil	45 ml.
3 tbsp.	*nuoc mam*	45 ml.
2 tbsp.	rice wine	30 ml.
	ground turmeric	
1 tbsp.	finely chopped fresh ginger	15 ml.
2 tsp.	shrimp paste	10 ml.

Combine the marinade ingredients, add the fish cubes and let them marinate for two to three hours. Thread 12 skewers with alternating pieces of fish and bacon.

Heat the oil and add the scallions. Brush the skewered ingredients with the oil-and-scallion mixture. Broil the fish, turning the skewers frequently and basting them for seven minutes, or until the fish cubes are white and firm. Sprinkle the pounded peanuts over the skewered fish before serving.

ALAN DAVIDSON
SEAFOOD OF SOUTH-EAST ASIA

Fish Sausages

Andouilles de Poisson

Any firm-fleshed white fish such as fresh haddock or cod can be used for the sausages. The author of this 18th Century recipe suggests stuffing the sausage mixture into eel skins; sausage casings make a suitable—and more readily obtained—substitute. The techniques of making and poaching sausages are demonstrated on pages 36-37 and 60-61. Before serving, the fish sausages are brushed with melted butter and broiled.

	To make 6 or 7 sausages	
2 lb.	white fish, cleaned, filleted and skinned, bones and trimmings reserved	1 kg.
1 cup	aromatic court bouillon (recipe, page 164), made with red wine	¼ liter
8	egg yolks	8
	salt and freshly ground black pepper	
1 tsp.	mixed spices	5 ml.
2 yards	sausage casings, soaked in tepid water for 30 minutes, rinsed and drained	2 meters
2 tbsp.	butter	30 ml.
4 cups	aromatic court bouillon, made with white wine	1 liter

Pound the fish bones and trimmings in a mortar, add them to the red-wine court bouillon and cook for 15 minutes, or until the liquid has reduced by two thirds. Strain the liquid. Chop the fish fillets or slice them into narrow strips, and mix them with the egg yolks, salt, pepper and mixed spices. Stuff this mixture into the casings to make sausages about 6 inches [15 cm.] long.

Prick the sausages all over with a fork. Add the butter to the cold white-wine court bouillon, put the sausages into the court bouillon and gradually heat until the liquid is just below boiling. Poach the sausages in the court bouillon for about 20 minutes, or until firm. Cool them in the poaching liquid, then drain them. Serve broiled.

MENON
LES SOUPERS DE LA COUR

Frogs' Legs Gratin

Cuisses de Grenouilles à la Façon de Jacques les Omelettes

	To serve 4	
2	shallots, finely chopped	2
1	garlic clove, chopped	1
2 tbsp.	chopped fresh parsley	30 ml.
2½ cups	dry bread crumbs	625 ml.
12 to 16	pairs medium-sized frogs' legs	12 to 16
	salt and pepper	
1 lb.	butter, melted and cooled	½ kg.

Mix the shallots, garlic and parsley with the bread crumbs. Season the frogs' legs with salt and pepper, and dip them in the cooled melted butter. Coat the frogs' legs thoroughly with the bread-crumb mixture.

Take a large, fairly deep gratin dish and butter it generously. Lay the frogs' legs in it, fill the spaces between them with the bread-crumb mixture, and pour in the rest of the melted butter. Bake in a preheated 400° F. [200° C.] oven for 15 to 20 minutes, or until the top is lightly browned.

AMICALE DES CUISINIERS ET PÂTISSIERS AUVERGNATS DE PARIS
CUISINE D'AUVERGNE

Frogs' Legs Provençal

Grenouilles à la Provençale

	To serve 4 to 6	
	flour	
24	pairs medium-sized frogs' legs	24
½ cup	olive oil	125 ml.
	salt and pepper	
1	garlic clove, finely chopped	1
1 tbsp.	finely chopped fresh parsley	15 ml.

Flour the frogs' legs. In a large skillet, heat half of the olive oil until it is very hot. Sauté half of the frogs' legs, shaking the pan regularly and turning the frogs' legs until they are golden brown on both sides—about eight to 10 minutes. Just before removing them from the pan with a slotted spoon, sprinkle them with salt, pepper, and half of the chopped garlic and parsley. Set the frogs' legs aside on a warmed platter and sauté the remaining frogs' legs in the same skillet, using the rest of the oil and seasonings.

BENOÎT MASCARELLI
LA TABLE EN PROVENCE & SUR LA CÔTE D'AZUR

Deep-fried Frogs' Legs

Grenouilles à la Vendéenne

The author recommends serving tomato sauce (recipe, page 162) flavored with lemon juice with the frogs' legs.

To serve 4 or 5

2	eggs, well beaten	2
	salt and pepper	
	grated nutmeg	
¼ cup	heavy cream	50 ml.
24	pairs medium-sized frogs' legs	24
1 cup	fresh bread crumbs	¼ liter
	oil for deep frying	

Put the beaten eggs into a bowl, mix in the salt, pepper, grated nutmeg and heavy cream, and stir well. Dip the frogs' legs in this mixture and then in the bread crumbs. Fry them in very hot oil so that they are nice and crisp—about four or five minutes.

AMBROSE HEATH
MADAME PRUNIER'S FISH COOKERY BOOK

Frogs' Legs with Garlic

Ancas de Rana al Ajo Arriero

To serve 4 to 6

24	pairs medium-sized frogs' legs	24
¼ cup	finely chopped onion	50 ml.
2	bay leaves	2
½ cup	wine vinegar	125 ml.
	salt and pepper	
8	garlic cloves, finely chopped	8
1 tbsp.	finely chopped fresh hot red chili	15 ml.
¼ cup	olive oil	50 ml.
2 tsp.	paprika	10 ml.
2	eggs, hard-boiled and chopped	2

Put the frogs' legs in a heavy pot with the onion, bay leaves and vinegar. Add water to barely cover them, season with salt and pepper, bring the liquid to a boil, reduce the heat to low and simmer the frogs' legs for five minutes. In a skillet, fry the garlic and the red chili in the oil. When they begin to brown, add the paprika—taking care not to let it burn—and pour the mixture over the frogs' legs. Scatter the chopped hard-boiled eggs over the mixture. Cover the pot, simmer the frogs' legs for another three minutes, season to taste and serve very hot.

ANA MARIA CALERA
COCINA CASTELLANA

Italian-Style Fried Frogs' Legs

Rane Dorate alla Milanese

To serve 12

48	pairs medium-sized frogs' legs, soaked in equal quantities of cold water and milk for 1 hour, drained and patted dry	48
	flour	
4	eggs, lightly beaten	4
8 tbsp.	butter	120 ml.
	salt and white pepper	

White wine marinade

2 cups	dry white wine	½ liter
½	onion, very thinly sliced	½
	salt	
	freshly ground white pepper	

Combine the marinade ingredients in a large dish. Put the prepared frogs' legs in the marinade for one hour, stirring occasionally. Remove them and pat them dry with a cloth. Coat them with flour and dip them in the beaten eggs.

Melt the butter in two large skillets and, when it is hot, sauté the frogs' legs until golden all over—about five minutes. Reduce the heat to low, cover, and continue cooking for about 15 minutes. Season the frogs' legs with salt and white pepper, and serve them at once.

GIANNI BRERA AND LUIGI VERONELLI
LA PACCIADA

Marinated Abalone

To serve 6

1 ½ lb.	abalone steaks, pounded and cut into cubes	¾ kg.
4	medium-sized tomatoes, peeled, seeded and diced	4
⅓ cup	chopped onion	75 ml.
½ cup	fresh lemon juice	125 ml.
¼ cup	olive oil	50 ml.
1	small cucumber, peeled, halved, seeded and diced	1
1 tbsp.	finely chopped fresh hot green chili	15 ml.
½	green or red sweet pepper, seeded, deribbed and diced	½

Combine the ingredients in a mixing bowl. Cover and marinate the abalone in the refrigerator for one to two hours.

JEAN F. NICOLAS
THE COMPLETE COOKBOOK OF AMERICAN FISH AND SHELLFISH

Baked Clams Oregano

To serve 4

2	garlic cloves	2
4	sprigs parsley	4
1 tsp.	chopped fresh oregano leaves, or substitute dried oregano	5 ml.
½ cup	fresh bread crumbs	125 ml.
8 tbsp.	butter, softened	120 ml.
	salt and pepper	
24	cherrystone clams, scrubbed, opened and left on the half shell	24
	rock salt	

Chop the garlic, parsley and oregano together very fine. Add the bread crumbs, butter, and salt and pepper to taste. Blend until very smooth. Spread 1 tablespoon [15 ml.] of the mixture over each clam on its half shell.

Spread the rock salt in a thick layer over the bottom of a shallow baking dish. Set the clams on this bed of salt and bake uncovered in a preheated 475° F. [250° C.] oven for about 10 minutes, or until the edges of the clams begin to curl. Do not overbake.

VICTOR BENNETT AND ANTONIA ROSSI
PAPPA ROSSI'S SECRETS OF ITALIAN COOKING

Marinated Oysters

Whole-wheat bread is especially good with these oysters.

To serve 6

1 pint	shucked oysters, with their liquor	½ liter
1 cup	dry white wine	¼ liter
½ cup	oil	125 ml.
⅓ cup	fresh lemon juice	75 ml.
2	bay leaves	2
⅛ tsp.	Tabasco sauce	½ ml.
2 tsp.	peppercorns	10 ml.
	lettuce leaves	
	chopped fresh parsley	
6	lemon wedges	6

Put the oysters and their liquor in a small nonreactive pot. Pour in the wine, oil and lemon juice. Add the bay leaves, Tabasco and peppercorns. Stir to blend the marinade. Put the pot over medium heat and bring the marinade to the boiling point. As soon as the liquid begins to boil, remove the pot from the heat. Cover, and let the oysters marinate for at least one hour at room temperature. Then refrigerate them for about two hours to chill them.

To serve, line six small bowls with lettuce leaves. Lift five or six oysters from the marinade and arrange them on the lettuce in each bowl. Spoon a little marinade over the oysters, then sprinkle them with chopped parsley. Add a lemon wedge to each bowl.

CAROL CUTLER
THE SIX-MINUTE SOUFFLÉ AND OTHER CULINARY DELIGHTS

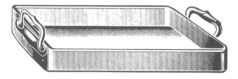

Oysters Rockefeller

For a finer-textured filling, the spinach used in this recipe may be parboiled. If you prefer a coarser texture, do not sieve the cooked filling. The technique of preparing Oysters Rockefeller is shown on pages 56-57.

To serve 6

6 tbsp.	butter	90 ml.
¼ lb.	spinach, stems removed and leaves finely chopped	125 g.
3 tbsp.	finely chopped fresh parsley	45 ml.
1	celery heart, trimmed and finely chopped	1
1	onion, finely chopped	1
5 tbsp.	dry bread crumbs	75 ml.
	Tabasco sauce	
½ tsp.	salt	2 ml.
½ tsp.	*pastis*, anisette or other anise-flavored liqueur	2 ml.
	coarse salt	
36	freshly shucked oysters, on the half shell	36

In a saucepan, melt the butter and stir in the spinach, parsley, celery, onion, bread crumbs, Tabasco, salt and *pastis* or anisette. Stirring constantly, cook the mixture over low heat for 15 minutes. Press the mixture through a sieve or food mill and set it aside.

Fill six piepans with a layer of coarse salt. Place six oysters in each pan. Put 1 teaspoon [5 ml.] of the vegetable mixture on each oyster. Broil the oysters 4 to 5 inches [10 to 13 cm.] under a preheated broiler for three to five minutes, or until the topping begins to brown. Serve the oysters at once, in the pans.

THE EDITORS OF AMERICAN HERITAGE
THE AMERICAN HERITAGE COOKBOOK

Mussels with Snail Butter

Les Moules au Beurre d'Escargot

The technique of steaming mussels is described on page 56.

	To serve 8	
96	live mussels, scrubbed, debearded and steamed open	96
	coarse salt	
	Snail butter	
1	salt anchovy, filleted, soaked in water for 30 minutes, drained and patted dry	1
2	garlic cloves, chopped	2
½ lb.	butter, softened	¼ kg.
2 tbsp.	coarsely chopped parsley	30 ml.
	salt and freshly ground pepper	
	cayenne pepper	
	anise-flavored liqueur	
3 tbsp.	fresh lemon juice	45 ml.

To make the snail butter, pound the anchovy fillet with the garlic. Add the butter, and gradually add the parsley, salt, pepper and a pinch of cayenne pepper. Beat in a few drops of anise liqueur and the lemon juice. When all are well blended, taste and correct the seasoning if necessary.

Remove the mussels from their shells. Fill the bottom of each half shell with a little snail butter. Put a mussel into each half shell and cover it with more snail butter.

Use coarse salt to cover the bottom of one gratin dish large enough to hold the mussels, or eight to 10 individual dishes. Lay the mussels carefully on the salt and bake them in a preheated 450° F. [230° C.] oven for 10 minutes.

ALEXANDRE DUMAINE
MA CUISINE

Pickled Mussels

	To serve 6 to 8	
72	large mussels, scrubbed and debearded	72
1	large onion, peeled and cut into slices ⅛ inch [3 mm.] thick	1
4	medium-sized garlic cloves, peeled and slightly crushed	4
½ cup	cider vinegar	125 ml.
2 tsp.	pickling spices	10 ml.
1 tsp.	salt	5 ml.

Combine the mussels with 1½ cups [375 ml.] of water in a heavy 4- to 6-quart [4- to 6-liter] pot and bring to a boil over high heat. Cover tightly, reduce the heat to low and let the mussels steam for about five minutes, turning them about in the pot once or twice with a slotted spoon. When steamed, all the shells should have opened; discard any mussels that remain shut.

With a slotted spoon, transfer the mussels to a platter, and remove and discard the shells. Strain the broth remaining in the casserole and the liquid that has accumulated around the mussels through a fine sieve lined with a double thickness of dampened cheesecloth. Measure 1½ cups of the broth into a small saucepan and set the pan aside. Place about ½ cup [125 ml.] of the mussels in a 1-quart [1-liter] widemouthed jar, spread about one fourth of the onion slices over them, and set a garlic clove on top. Repeat three more times, alternating layers of mussels with onions and garlic until you have arranged them all in the jar.

Add the vinegar, pickling spices and salt to the reserved mussel broth and bring to a boil over high heat. Cook briskly, uncovered, for two minutes, then pour the mixture slowly over the mussels and onions. Cool to room temperature, cover tightly and keep in the refrigerator for at least three days before serving.

Serve the mussels on chilled individual salad plates, mounded on fresh lettuce leaves if you like.

FOODS OF THE WORLD
AMERICAN COOKING: NEW ENGLAND

Shrimp Mornay

	To serve 4 to 6	
2 tbsp.	butter	30 ml.
2 tbsp.	flour	30 ml.
½ cup	fish stock *(recipe, page 163)* mixed with ½ cup [125 ml.] milk, or substitute 1 cup [¼ liter] milk	125 ml.
½ cup	grated Gruyère cheese	125 ml.
¼ cup	heavy cream	50 ml.
	salt and black pepper	
1 lb.	shrimp, poached for 1 to 3 minutes, shelled and deveined	½ kg.
2 tbsp.	freshly grated Parmesan cheese	30 ml.

Melt the butter over medium heat and blend in the flour. Gradually stir in the fish-stock mixture or the milk. Bring the mixture to a boil, stirring. When this sauce has thickened, add the Gruyère and stir until it melts. Add the cream and season to taste with salt and pepper.

Divide the shrimp among four to six buttered ramekins. Pour the sauce over the shrimp and sprinkle with the Parmesan. Place the ramekins under a preheated broiler, 4 inches [10 cm.] from the heat, and cook until the mixture is bubbly hot and lightly browned.

JEAN HEWITT
THE NEW YORK TIMES LARGE TYPE COOKBOOK

Shrimp Rémoulade

To serve 4 to 6

2 lb.	shrimp, shelled and deveined, shells reserved	1 kg.
1	bay leaf	1
1	celery rib with leaves	1
2	sprigs parsley plus 1 tbsp. [15 ml.] chopped fresh parsley	2
12	peppercorns	12
	salt and black pepper	
3 tbsp.	tarragon vinegar	45 ml.
3 tbsp.	Dijon mustard	45 ml.
5	flat anchovy fillets, finely chopped	5
¾ cup	oil	175 ml.
½ tsp.	chopped fresh tarragon leaves or ¼ teaspoon [1 ml.] dried tarragon	2 ml.
1	garlic clove, finely chopped	1
1	scallion, including the green top, chopped	1
3 tbsp.	prepared horseradish	45 ml.
	Tabasco sauce	

Place the shrimp, shrimp shells, bay leaf, celery, parsley sprigs, peppercorns and salt in a saucepan and add water to cover. Bring to a boil, then simmer for about five minutes. Drain and cool the shrimp. Place the shrimp in a mixing bowl. Chill. Combine the rest of the ingredients and pour the mixture over the shrimp. Cover and let the shrimp stand overnight in the refrigerator. Bring the shrimp to room temperature before serving them on a bed of lettuce.

JEAN HEWITT
THE NEW YORK TIMES LARGE TYPE COOKBOOK

Belgian Shrimp Gratin
Belgischer Garnelenauflauf

To serve 4

½ lb.	shrimp, peeled	¼ kg.
6	eggs, hard-boiled and sliced	6
1 tbsp.	flour	15 ml.
1 tsp.	dry mustard	5 ml.
1 tsp.	salt	5 ml.
1 cup	heavy cream	¼ liter
1 tbsp.	finely chopped fresh parsley	15 ml.
2 tbsp.	finely shredded Emmentaler cheese	30 ml.

Butter a shallow ovenproof dish, and fill it with alternate layers of the shrimp and sliced eggs. In a small pan, stir the flour, dry mustard and salt together, add the cream and bring to a boil, stirring constantly. Remove this sauce from the heat, add the parsley and cheese, and pour the mixture over the layered shrimp and eggs. Bake the dish in a preheated 425° F. [220° C.] oven for about 15 minutes, or until the top is golden and bubbling.

THEODOR BÖTTIGER AND ILSE FROIDL
DAS NEUE FISCHKOCHBUCH

Watercress Wine Scallops with Grapefruit

To serve 4

1½ lb.	scallops, rinsed and patted dry	¾ kg.
1½ cups	dry white wine	375 ml.
2	large grapefruits, peeled, divided into segments and membranes removed	2
8 tbsp.	butter, melted	120 ml.
	salt	
	paprika	
	finely chopped watercress plus watercress sprigs	

Put the scallops into a saucepan along with the wine; bring to a boil, then reduce the heat, cover, and simmer for eight minutes. Drain the scallops and cut them crosswise into slices about ¼ inch [6 mm.] thick. Arrange the scallops and grapefruit sections in four to six well-buttered scallop shells or individual baking dishes, or in a single shallow baking platter. Pour the melted butter evenly over the scallops and fruit. Sprinkle with salt and paprika. Bake in a preheated 350° F. [180° C.] oven for six minutes, or until heated through. Sprinkle generously with chopped watercress and garnish with watercress sprigs.

SHIRLEY SARVIS
CRAB & ABALONE: WEST COAST WAYS WITH FISH & SHELLFISH

Peruvian Scallops Seviche

To serve 6 to 8

2 lb.	shucked scallops, rinsed and sliced paper-thin	1 kg.
1¼ cups	fresh lemon juice	300 ml.
about 1 cup	fresh orange juice	about ¼ liter
2	large onions, thinly sliced	2
2	fresh hot red chilies, stemmed, seeded and cut into strips, or 2 dried hot red chilies, crumbled	2
	watercress	

Place the sliced scallops in a large colander and pour about 2 quarts [2 liters] of boiling water over them. Drain well.

Place the scallops in a bowl and cover them completely with the lemon and orange juices.

Soak the onions briefly in salted water. Rinse and drain them. Add the onions and hot chilies to the bowl and stir to distribute the flavors. Cover tightly and refrigerate for at least four hours.

To serve the scallops as a cocktail accompaniment, drain them, and place three or four slices on a sprig of watercress in each of several miniature shells. Serve with oyster forks.

MARIAN TRACY
THE SHELLFISH COOKBOOK

Egg Presentations

Stuffed Eggs with Herbs

	To serve 10	
10	eggs, hard-boiled and halved, the yolks separated from the whites	10
1 tbsp.	finely chopped fresh chervil leaves	15 ml.
2 tbsp.	finely cut fresh chives	30 ml.
1 tbsp.	finely chopped fresh tarragon leaves	15 ml.
	salt and pepper	
3 to 5 tbsp.	sour cream	45 to 75 ml.
6 tbsp.	butter, melted	90 ml.
	Chive cream sauce	
2 cups	sour cream	½ liter
	salt and pepper	
¼ cup	finely cut fresh chives	50 ml.

Sieve the egg yolks into a bowl. Add the chopped herbs, salt and pepper and mix well. Add 1 tablespoon [15 ml.] of sour cream to the contents of the bowl and begin to work the mixture with a wooden spatula or a fork. Continue to add the sour cream by the spoonful until the mixture is light and fluffy. Mound this mixture in the egg-white halves. Set the stuffed eggs as close together as possible in a buttered baking dish. Season the melted butter with salt and pepper and pour it over the eggs. Bake in a preheated 350° F. [180° C.] oven for seven to 10 minutes, or until the eggs are glazed and slightly browned, but still soft.

Meanwhile, prepare the sauce by first bringing the sour cream to a boil. Add salt and pepper and boil for two minutes, stirring constantly. Pour the sauce into a serving bowl and stir in the chives. Serve the eggs and sauce at once.

LOUISETTE BERTHOLLE
UNE GRANDE CUISINE POUR TOUS

Soft-boiled Eggs with Watercress Sauce

Oeufs Mollets Cressonière

A food processor may be used to purée the watercress.

	To serve 8	
8	eggs, at room temperature	8
1	bunch watercress, parboiled for 1 minute, drained and squeezed dry	1
1 cup	highly seasoned thick mayonnaise (recipe, page 161)	¼ liter

Lower the eggs into boiling water, reduce the heat so that the water simmers gently, and cook them for three to four minutes. Drain the eggs and cool them under cold running water; shell them very carefully. Press the watercress through a fine sieve. Beating vigorously, combine this purée with the mayonnaise. To serve, arrange the eggs in a circle on a round dish and coat them with the watercress sauce.

PAUL BOUILLARD
LA CUISINE AU COIN DU FEU

Hard-boiled Eggs in Green Sauce

Heuvos Duros en Salsa Verde

	To serve 4	
5	eggs, hard-boiled, plus 1 raw egg yolk	5
2 tsp.	vinegar	10 ml.
1	garlic clove, crushed to a paste	1
	salt and pepper	
about 1 cup	oil	about ¼ liter
1 tbsp.	capers, drained	15 ml.
1 cup	cooked spinach or 2 cups [½ liter] cooked lima beans, puréed	¼ liter
3	pickles, chopped	3
2	carrots, cooked and thinly sliced	2

Cut four of the five hard-boiled eggs crosswise into slices ½ inch [1 cm.] thick. Arrange them on a platter. In a bowl, mash the yolk of the remaining hard-boiled egg, and mix it with the raw egg yolk, the vinegar, garlic, salt and pepper. Slowly whisk in enough oil to form a thick mayonnaise. Add the capers and the puréed spinach or beans, and mix well. Stir in the pickles and season with salt and pepper to taste. Pour this sauce over the eggs, keeping the yolks uncovered. Before serving, arrange the carrots around the platter.

NURI FONSECA
RECETAS DE AMERICA LATINA

Poached Eggs Celestine

Oeufs Pochés à la Celestine

To fry bread, heat just enough oil or clarified butter in a skillet to half-cover the slices. Fry the slices gently for two or three minutes on each side; the color will darken when the bread is removed from the skillet. Drain on paper towels.

	To serve 6	
½ lb.	shrimp, peeled, poached for 3 to 5 minutes in salted water, drained and coarsely chopped	¼ kg.
1½ cups	velouté sauce (recipe, page 163), made with fish stock	375 ml.
6	bread slices, fried	6
6	eggs, poached	6

Stir the shrimp into the fish velouté. Lay the fried bread slices side by side in a lightly buttered gratin dish, cover each slice with shrimp sauce and a poached egg. Bake in a preheated 400° F. [200° C.] oven for two or three minutes, and serve the dish as hot as possible.

A. HERBERT KENNEY
FIFTY LUNCHES

Eggplant Flans

	To serve 6	
3	slices bacon, coarsely chopped	3
3	shallots, coarsely chopped	3
1	small garlic clove, coarsely chopped	1
½ cup	coarsely chopped fresh coriander leaves	125 ml.
2 tbsp.	olive oil	30 ml.
½ lb.	eggplant, trimmed, peeled and cut into 1-inch [2½-cm.] cubes	¼ kg.
¼ cup	dry white wine	50 ml.
1 cup	milk	¼ liter
3	eggs plus 1 egg yolk	3
½ cup	heavy cream	125 ml.
	coarse salt and freshly ground black pepper	
	freshly grated nutmeg	

Place the chopped bacon, shallots, garlic and coriander in an ovenproof casserole. Stir in the olive oil, eggplant and wine. Cover the casserole and bake the mixture in a preheated 375° F. [190° C.] oven for 45 minutes. Remove the casserole from the oven; reduce the oven temperature to 300° F. [150° C.]. Scrape the baked mixture into the bowl of a food proces-

sor with a spatula, and process the mixture until smooth. Rub it through a drum sieve or fine strainer to remove the seeds and form a silky purée. If you do not have a processor, simply press the mixture through a sieve.

Mix the milk, eggs, egg yolk, cream, salt, pepper and a pinch of nutmeg in a bowl. Stir in the eggplant purée; blend well. Pour into six buttered 6-ounce [175-ml.] ramekins.

Place the ramekins in a deep roasting pan. Add enough hot water to the pan to come halfway up the sides of the ramekins. Bake for 30 minutes, or until the flans feel firm to the touch. Let the flans rest in the water bath for at least 30 minutes before unmolding them.

When ready to serve the flans, unmold them onto individual plates or a platter. The flans will shrink slightly in the cooling and should slide easily from the ramekins. If not, return the flans to the oven for a few minutes to reheat before unmolding them.

TOM MARGITTAI AND PAUL KOVI
THE FOUR SEASONS

Lettuce Custard

Pain de Laitue

	To serve 4	
1½ lb.	Bibb, Boston, or leaf lettuce, trimmed	¾ kg.
1½ cups	chicken stock (recipe, page 163)	375 ml.
1 cup	thick white sauce (recipe, page 162)	¼ liter
3	large eggs, beaten	3
1 tbsp.	butter	15 ml.
	salt and white pepper	
2 cups	tomato sauce (recipe, page 162)	½ liter

Simmer the lettuce for 12 minutes in the chicken stock, drain, and squeeze the lettuce very dry. Coarsely chop the lettuce and simmer it in the white sauce for five minutes. Let it cool until tepid, then stir in the beaten eggs and butter. Season with salt and white pepper to taste. Pour the mixture into a buttered 1-quart [1-liter] charlotte mold, set it in a pan of hot water, and bake in a preheated 425° F. [220° C.] oven for 50 minutes. Unmold the custard and pour the tomato sauce over it. Serve at once.

JANET E. C. WURTZBURGER AND MAC K. GRISWOLD (EDITORS)
PRIVATE COLLECTIONS: A CULINARY TREASURE

Balkan Spinach Custard

Flan aux Épinards à l'Orientale

Kashkaval is a pungent, herb-flavored Balkan cheese made from sheep's milk. It is obtainable where fine cheeses are sold.

To serve 6

2	slices firm-textured white bread with crusts removed	2
1 cup	milk	¼ liter
2 lb.	spinach, trimmed and finely chopped	1 kg.
2	eggs, beaten	2
1 cup	farmer cheese	¼ liter
	salt and pepper	
2 tbsp.	lard	30 ml.
5 oz.	*kashkaval* or Parmesan cheese, grated (about 1¾ cups [425 ml.])	150 g.
½ cup	plain yogurt	125 ml.

Soak the bread in the milk and squeeze it almost dry. Put the spinach into a bowl with the bread, eggs and farmer cheese. Season with salt and pepper. Using a wooden spatula, beat the mixture until it forms a smooth, stiff paste. Grease a 10-inch [25-cm.] pie dish with the lard and fill it two thirds full with the mixture. Sprinkle the grated cheese on the top.

Bake the custard in a preheated 450° F. [230° C.] oven for 15 to 20 minutes, then reduce the heat to 400° F. [200° C.] and bake for a further 15 to 20 minutes. Remove the dish from the oven and let it cool a little before unmolding it. Serve it with the yogurt poured over it.

PIERRE ANDROUET
LA CUISINE AU FROMAGE

Little Mushroom Custards

Petits Pots aux Morilles

To serve 4

½ lb.	fresh mushrooms, trimmed	¼ kg.
2 oz.	dried morels (about ⅔ cup [150 ml.]), soaked in warm water for 30 minutes, drained, trimmed, halved lengthwise and rinsed thoroughly	60 g.
3	egg yolks	3
1 tsp.	fresh lemon juice	5 ml.
	sea salt	
	freshly ground pepper	
	grated nutmeg	
½ cup	*crème fraîche* or heavy cream	125 ml.

Put the fresh mushrooms, morels, egg yolks, lemon juice and a pinch each of salt, pepper and grated nutmeg into a blend-er. Blend the mixture until it is thick and creamy. Adjust the seasoning to taste, then add the cream and blend for three to five seconds more.

Butter four 6-ounce [175-ml.] molds and pour the mixture into them. Set the molds in a shallow pan and pour in enough hot water to cover the molds halfway. Bake the custards in a preheated 400° F. [200° C.] oven for about 15 minutes, or until they are set and a knife inserted into the center of a mold comes out clean.

DANIEL BOUCHÉ
INVITATION À LA CUISINE BUISSONNIÈRE

Maize Custards with Mushroom Purée

To serve 4

⅓ cup	finely ground yellow cornmeal	75 ml.
¼ tsp.	salt	1 ml.
	pepper	
2	eggs, beaten	2
¾ cup	heavy cream	175 ml.
Mushroom purée		
2 tbsp.	butter	30 ml.
¼ lb.	mushrooms, wiped, trimmed and finely ground in a blender or food processor	125 g.
	salt and pepper	
about ¼ cup	heavy cream	about 50 ml.
	lemon juice	

Mix the cornmeal, salt and pepper in a bowl. Make a well in the middle and slowly stir in the eggs and the cream. Let the mixture sit for 10 minutes, covered with a kitchen towel.

Butter a muffin pan with eight deep cups, or butter eight 6-ounce [175-ml.] soufflé dishes. Give the batter a good stir, then divide it equally among the buttered molds. Place a baking pan holding 1 inch [2½ cm.] of hot water in a preheated 325° F. [160° C.] oven and put the molds in the water. Bake for 30 minutes, checking once to make sure that the water is not boiling. Reduce the heat if necessary.

For the mushroom purée, melt the butter in a saucepan over fairly high heat, add the mushrooms and seasoning, and cook briefly until the mushrooms have given off all their water and appear very soft. Pour the cream into the purée, stirring until the mixture is smooth and syrupy. Remove the pan from the heat and add a small squeeze of lemon juice. Taste again for seasoning. Reheat the sauce just before serving, if necessary.

Gently pry the custards from their cups and place them, two to a serving and shiny side up, on each diner's plate. Spoon mushroom purée over the custards.

JUDITH OLNEY
COMFORTING FOOD

Chicken Liver Custard

Le Gâteau de Foies Blonds de Poulardes de la Bresse Baigné de la Sauce aux Queues d'Écrevisses

The original version of this recipe calls for the pale-colored livers from chickens raised in the Bresse region of France. Ordinary chicken livers, soaked in milk, are a suitable substitute. The custard is traditionally served with a crayfish-tail sauce. To make the sauce, cook live crayfish in a court bouillon (recipe, page 164), shell them and pound the shells with an equal weight of butter. Sieve the mixture and whisk it, off the heat, into a white sauce (recipe, page 162) or a velouté sauce (recipe, page 163) made with fish stock. Finally, add the whole crayfish tails to the sauce. The custard can also be served with a tomato sauce (recipe, page 162). The technique of making a savory custard is demonstrated on pages 66-67.

	To serve 4	
1	garlic clove	1
3 or 4	chicken livers, trimmed, soaked in milk for 2 or 3 hours and drained	3 or 4
2 oz.	beef marrow	60 g.
¼ cup	meat roasting juices, degreased, or 1 cup [¼ liter] meat stock (recipe, page 163), boiled until reduced to ¼ cup [50 ml.]	50 ml.
1 cup	milk	¼ liter
2	eggs	2
2	egg yolks	2
	salt and pepper	

Rub the bottom and sides of a large mortar with the garlic clove. In the mortar, pound the chicken livers with the beef marrow. Add the meat roasting juices or reduced stock and the milk; add the eggs and egg yolks. Whisk thoroughly, add salt and pepper, and press the mixture through a sieve.

Oil a 1-quart [1-liter] charlotte mold and line the bottom with a piece of oiled parchment paper. Pour the mixture into the mold. Stand the mold on a rack in a large pan and pour in enough hot, but not boiling, water to reach halfway up the sides of the mold. Cook the custard in a preheated 300° F. [150° C.] oven for one and one half hours, or until a knife inserted into the center comes out clean. Unmold the custard before serving it.

LUCIEN TENDRET
LA TABLE AU PAYS DE BRILLAT-SAVARIN

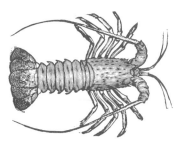

Baked Tomato Custards

Flanes de Tomates

	To serve 6	
6	small tomatoes, coarsely chopped	6
3 tbsp.	butter	45 ml.
	salt	
1 tsp.	sugar	5 ml.
3	eggs	3

Simmer the tomatoes until they are soft. Sieve them into a saucepan containing the butter. Add a pinch of salt and the sugar, and simmer gently for 10 minutes. Remove the purée from the heat and let it cool to room temperature.

Butter four individual 6-ounce [175-ml.] molds and set them side by side in a shallow baking pan. Beat the eggs well and season them with salt. Add the eggs to the cooled tomatoes and mix well. Fill the molds with the tomato-and-egg mixture and pour boiling water into the baking pan. Bake the custards in a preheated 375° F. [190° C.] oven for about 20 minutes, or until they are set.

VICTORIA SERRA
TÍA VICTORIA'S SPANISH KITCHEN

Cheese and Bacon Slices

Croque Lorraine

	To serve 8	
8	slices firm-textured white bread	8
3 tbsp.	butter	45 ml.
2	onions, coarsely chopped	2
4	thick slices bacon, diced	4
4	eggs, beaten	4
½ cup	heavy cream	125 ml.
1⅔ cups	finely shredded Gruyère cheese	400 ml.
	salt and pepper	

With a cookie cutter or the rim of a glass, cut the bread into eight rounds. In a skillet, fry the rounds in the butter until they are golden. Drain them and lay them in a buttered gratin dish. Fry the onions and bacon in the same skillet until golden brown. Then drain them and put them in a bowl with the eggs, cream, cheese, and salt and pepper. Mix well and spoon the mixture evenly over the rounds of bread. Bake in a preheated 425° F. [220° C.] oven for 10 minutes, or until the mixture is set and lightly browned.

NINETTE LYON
LES OEUFS

Pesto Soufflé

To serve 8

Pesto sauce

2 cups	chopped fresh basil leaves	½ liter
2 or 3	garlic cloves, chopped	2 or 3
¼ cup	pine nuts	50 ml.
⅓ cup	freshly grated Parmesan or pecorino Romano cheese	75 ml.
½ cup	olive oil	125 ml.
	salt	

Soufflé base

¾ cup	freshly grated Parmesan cheese	175 ml.
8 tbsp.	unsalted butter	120 ml.
⅓ cup	flour	75 ml.
1½ cups	milk	375 ml.
	salt and pepper	
	grated nutmeg	
8	egg yolks	8
4 to 6	scallions, finely chopped	4 to 6
8	medium-sized tomatoes, peeled, seeded and finely chopped	8
10	egg whites	10

To make the pesto sauce, mix all the pesto ingredients together, then beat them in an electric blender or food processor until they form a thick, smooth paste.

For the soufflé base, generously butter two 1½-quart [1½-liter] soufflé dishes and sprinkle the inside of each with about 1 tablespoon [15 ml.] of grated cheese. Set aside.

Melt 6 tablespoons [90 ml.] of the butter and, when the foam has subsided, blend in the flour. Cook over low heat for two minutes, stirring constantly. Remove the pan from the heat and blend in the milk with a whisk. Return the pan to the heat and cook, stirring, until the mixture has thickened and is smooth. Season to taste with salt, pepper and nutmeg. Add the egg yolks one at a time, beating after each addition to blend well.

Sauté the scallions in the remaining butter until they are soft; then add the tomatoes. Increase the heat and cook rapidly until the liquid has evaporated. Blend the scallions and tomatoes into the soufflé base, with the pesto and all but 2 tablespoons [30 ml.] of the remaining cheese. Correct the seasoning if necessary.

Beat the egg whites—preferably in a copper bowl—with a pinch of salt until stiff peaks form. Stir a quarter of them into the soufflé base, to lighten it, then gently fold the remaining whites into the sauce. Pour the mixture into the prepared soufflé dishes, smooth the tops with a spatula, and sprinkle with the remaining cheese.

Put the soufflés into a preheated 400° F. [200° C.] oven. Reduce the heat immediately to 375° F. [190° C.] and bake the soufflés for 30 to 35 minutes, until they are well puffed up and browned on top.

THE JUNIOR LEAGUE OF THE CITY OF NEW YORK
NEW YORK ENTERTAINS

Lettuce Soufflé

Soufflé de Laitues

To purée lettuce, blanch it for five minutes in boiling salted water, drain it well, and put it through a food mill or chop it in a processor.

This soufflé can also be made with spinach, green beans, peas, zucchini and many other vegetables. For every 2 cups [½ liter] of puréed vegetable that you use, add ¾ cup [175 ml.] of puréed potato.

	To serve 8	
5	medium-sized potatoes, baked in their skins	5
12	heads Bibb or Boston lettuce, puréed	12
	salt	
	grated nutmeg	
6	eggs, the yolks separated from the whites, and the whites stiffly beaten	6
14 tbsp.	butter, cut into pieces	210 ml.

Scoop out the flesh of the potatoes while they are still hot and push it through a sieve. Using a wooden spoon, beat the potato and lettuce purées together over medium heat for a few minutes to evaporate excess moisture. When the purée is well dried out, remove it from the heat and season it to taste with salt and grated nutmeg. Beat in the egg yolks and butter and fold in the egg whites. Pour the mixture into two buttered 1-quart [1-liter] soufflé dishes or charlotte molds. Place the dishes or molds in a water bath and bake in a preheated 350° F. [180° C.] oven for 25 minutes, or until the soufflé is well risen and lightly browned. Unmold and serve immediately.

LÉON ISNARD
LA GASTRONOMIE AFRICAINE

Asparagus Soufflé

To keep the asparagus tips intact, parboil them separately from the stalks; then sauté the stalks in a tablespoon [15 ml.] of butter for two or three minutes, and toss the tips briefly in the butter. Purée the stalks and incorporate them into the soufflé mixture. For baking, pour half of the soufflé mixture into the dish, add the asparagus tips and then pour in the rest of the soufflé mixture. To make individual soufflés, butter six 8-ounce [¼-kg.] baking dishes, pour in the soufflé mixture and bake it for 15 minutes at 400° F. [200° C.].

	To serve 6	
6 oz.	asparagus, stalks peeled, cut into short lengths, and parboiled for 2 or 3 minutes	175 g.
½ cup	thick white sauce (recipe, page 162), flavored with 1 whole garlic clove, later discarded	125 ml.
	grated nutmeg	
	salt and pepper	
3	egg yolks, beaten with 1 tbsp. [15 ml.] milk	3
4	egg whites, stiffly beaten	4

Using a food processor, purée the asparagus, then push it through a drum sieve to remove the fibers. Add the purée to the cooled white sauce with a pinch of nutmeg and salt and pepper to taste. Then beat in the egg yolks. As soon as the yolks are properly incorporated, fold in the egg whites, taking care that they are properly distributed. Use as light a hand as possible, stirring upward rather than downward.

Pour the whole thing into a well-buttered 1-quart [1-liter] soufflé dish and bake in a preheated 350° F. [180° C.] oven for 20 to 30 minutes. Do not be afraid to open the oven to look at it, but close the door gently. When the soufflé has risen well and is a deep golden brown, serve it without delay.

GEOFFREY BOUMPHREY
CUNNING COOKERY

Little Chicken Soufflés

Petits Soufflés de Volaille

	To make 8 to 10 small soufflés	
2 cups	chopped cooked chicken breast meat	½ liter
1¼ cups	thick white sauce (recipe, page 162)	300 ml.
5	eggs, the yolks separated from the whites, and the whites stiffly beaten	5
	grated nutmeg	
	salt and pepper	

Pound the chopped chicken in a mortar, then pass it through a very fine sieve. Mix the chicken purée with the thick white

sauce and let it cool. Gradually add the egg yolks to the cooled mixture, beating thoroughly after each addition. Season with a pinch of nutmeg, salt and pepper. Gently fold the egg whites into the mixture.

Butter eight to ten 6-ounce [175-ml.] ramekins, stand them side by side on a jelly-roll pan, and spoon the soufflé mixture into them. Bake the soufflés in a preheated 400° F. [200° C.] oven for 12 to 15 minutes, or until they are well risen and golden.

JULES GOUFFÉ
LE LIVRE DE CUISINE

Zucchini Soufflé

Soufflé aux Courgettes

The zucchini can be replaced by pumpkin or such winter squash as Hubbard or acorn.

	To serve 8 to 10	
2 lb.	zucchini	1 kg.
1 cup	thick white sauce (recipe, page 162)	¼ liter
⅔ cup	finely shredded Gruyère cheese	150 ml.
⅓ cup	freshly grated Parmesan cheese	75 ml.
9	eggs, the yolks separated from the whites, the yolks beaten, and the whites stiffly beaten	9
	salt and pepper	
	ground mace or grated nutmeg	
1	small onion, grated	1
	dry bread crumbs	

Put the whole zucchini into boiling salted water and cook them, uncovered, for five to 10 minutes, or until tender; do not let them disintegrate. Let them cool, then peel them and press them through the fine disk of a food mill. Put the resulting purée in a large, heavy-based skillet, and set it over low heat to dry out the purée. Stir frequently to make sure that the purée does not burn.

Cool the white sauce until it is tepid, then add the cheeses, egg yolks, salt and pepper, a pinch of mace or nutmeg, the puréed zucchini and finally the onion. Mix well. Fold the egg whites into the zucchini mixture.

Butter a 1½-quart [1½-liter] soufflé dish and sprinkle it with bread crumbs. Pour the zucchini mixture into the dish and bake the soufflé in a preheated 375° F. [190° C.] oven for 30 minutes, or until the soufflé is risen and golden.

NINETTE LYON
LES OEUFS

Ham Soufflé Alexandra

Soufflé de Jambon Alexandra

Note that paprika is an excellent seasoning with ham and that ¼ cup [50 ml.] of grated Parmesan cheese added to the ham mixture will make a very pleasant blend of flavors.

To serve 4

2 tbsp.	cold white sauce (recipe, page 162)	30 ml.
¼ lb.	lean ham, pounded in a mortar or very finely ground in a food processor	125 g.
¼ cup	hot thick white sauce (recipe, page 162), made with cream	50 ml.
2	egg yolks	2
3	egg whites, stiffly beaten	3
¾ lb.	very small asparagus tips, parboiled for 2 to 3 minutes in salted water	350 g.
1 tbsp.	butter	15 ml.

Preheat the oven to 400° F. [200° C.]. Mix the cold white sauce with the ham and put the mixture through a sieve into a saucepan. Warm the mixture over low heat. Remove the mixture from the heat and add the hot white sauce. Stir in the egg yolks one at a time and fold in the egg whites. Toss the asparagus tips rapidly in the butter, over high heat.

Pour half of the soufflé mixture into a buttered 1-quart [1-liter] soufflé dish, add the asparagus tips in one layer and then add the rest of the soufflé mixture. Reduce the oven temperature to 375° F. [190° C.] and bake the soufflé for 25 minutes, or until it is risen and golden. Serve at once.

AMBROSE HEATH
GOOD SAVOURIES

❖

Calf's Brain Soufflés

Paszteciki w Muszlach

The technique of preparing brains is shown on pages 32-33.

To serve 8

1	onion, grated	1
6 tbsp.	butter, 5 tbsp. [75 ml.] melted	90 ml.
2	pairs calf's brains, soaked, cleaned, parboiled, cooled and chopped	2
	salt and pepper	
¼ cup	dry bread crumbs	50 ml.
4	egg yolks	4
1	egg white, stiffly beaten	1
¼ cup	strained fresh lemon juice	50 ml.
2	lemons, sliced	2

Fry the grated onion in 1 tablespoon [15 ml.] of the butter. Off the heat, mix it with the chopped brains and add salt,

pepper, 2 tablespoons [30 ml.] of the bread crumbs and the egg yolks. Mix well and fold in the egg white. Taste the mixture and add more salt if necessary.

Butter eight 6-ounce [175-ml.] ramekins and fill them with the mixture. Sprinkle them with the rest of the bread crumbs and pour on 2 tablespoons of the melted butter. Bake the soufflés in a preheated 375° F. [190° C.] oven for 10 to 15 minutes, or until lightly browned. To serve, sprinkle lemon juice over the soufflés and serve them with the lemon slices and the remaining melted butter.

I. PLUCINSKA
KSIAZKA KUCHARSKA UDOSKONALONA

❖

Cheese Soufflés in Artichokes

To serve 6

6	artichokes, stems cut off and tough outer leaves discarded	6
2 tbsp.	butter	30 ml.
2 tbsp.	flour	30 ml.
1 cup	milk	¼ liter
1 cup	freshly grated Gruyère cheese	¼ liter
	salt and black pepper	
3	egg yolks, lightly beaten	3
4	egg whites, stiffly beaten	4

Bring a large pot of salted water to a boil and plunge the artichokes into it upside down. Depending on their size, cook them for 20 to 40 minutes, until tender. Drain and cool them. When they are cool enough to handle, pull out the center bunch of leaves from each artichoke, leaving a hollow space well enclosed with leaves. Scrape out the choke with a small, sharp spoon. Trim the stem ends, if necessary, so that the artichokes stand upright.

To make the soufflé mixture, melt the butter in a pan, stir in the flour and cook for two or three minutes. In a separate pan, heat the milk and pour it into the foaming butter-and-flour mixture. Blend and simmer gently for four or five minutes, stirring often, until you have a thick sauce. Stir in the grated cheese and season well with salt and pepper. Remove the pan from the heat and allow the contents to cool slightly before beating in the egg yolks. Then fold in the egg whites.

Quickly spoon the cheese mixture into the artichokes. Stand the artichokes on an oiled baking sheet and bake them in a preheated 400° F. [200° C.] oven for 15 minutes. The cheese mixture should be less set than the usual soufflé, resembling a thick, foamy sauce.

At the table, each diner pulls off the leaves of the artichoke one by one and dips them in the soufflé before eating them. The artichoke heart is then cut into pieces with a knife and fork and eaten.

ARABELLA BOXER
ARABELLA BOXER'S GARDEN COOKBOOK

Molded Harlequin Soufflé

Sformato di Legumi Arlecchino

Any number of vegetable purées can be used to make this soufflé as long as the proportions are kept the same: ⅔ cup [150 ml.] of purée to ⅓ cup [75 ml.] of white sauce and one egg—the yolk and white beaten separately. To make a white layer, use 1 cup [¼ liter] of white sauce—flavored, if you like, with some freshly grated Parmesan cheese—plus one egg. The technique of making a dish of this type is demonstrated on pages 40-41.

	To serve 6	
4	medium-sized carrots, sliced, boiled for 15 minutes, drained, and sautéed in 1 tbsp. [15 ml.] butter for 5 minutes	4
4	celery ribs, sliced, boiled for 15 minutes, drained, and sautéed in 1 tbsp. [15 ml.] butter for 5 minutes	4
¾ lb.	spinach, boiled for 1 to 2 minutes, drained, squeezed dry, and sautéed in 1 tbsp. [15 ml.] butter for 5 minutes	350 g.
1¼ cups	freshly shelled peas, boiled for 5 minutes, drained, and sautéed in 1 tbsp. [15 ml.] butter for 5 minutes	300 ml.
⅔ lb.	Belgian endive, leaves separated, boiled for 15 minutes, drained, squeezed dry, and sautéed in 1 tbsp. [15 ml.] butter for 5 minutes	300 g.
1⅔ cups	thick white sauce *(recipe, page 162)*	400 ml.
5	eggs	5
3 tbsp.	freshly grated Parmesan cheese	45 ml.
	salt and freshly ground pepper	
	flour	

Purée each vegetable separately in a food mill or a blender. Measure out ⅔ cup [150 ml.] of each purée. To each one add ⅓ cup [75 ml.] of white sauce, one beaten egg yolk and a little Parmesan cheese; season with salt and pepper. Fold one stiffly whipped egg white into each purée.

Butter and flour a 3-quart [3-liter] mold and carefully fill it with layers of the vegetable mixtures. Arrange the layers so that there is a pleasant contrast of colors. Cover the mold and put it on a rack in a pan partly filled with boiling water. Cook the soufflé in a preheated 350° F. [180° C.] oven for one hour. Remove the mold from the oven. Let it rest for a few minutes, then unmold it onto a warmed serving plate.

LUIGI CARNACINA
GREAT ITALIAN COOKING

Dutch Cheese Soufflé

Kaassoufflé

Dutch gin is a distilled spirit with a somewhat bitter taste and a malty aroma.

	To serve 4	
5	thin slices firm-textured white bread, crusts removed	5
⅓ cup	Dutch gin *(jenever)*	75 ml.
4	eggs, the yolks separated from the whites, the yolks lightly beaten, the whites stiffly beaten	4
¼ lb.	finely shredded Gouda or Edam cheese (about 1 cup [¼ liter])	125 g.
2 tbsp.	finely cut chives	30 ml.
1 cup	milk	¼ liter
	ground ginger	
¼ lb.	ham, finely chopped (about 1 cup [¼ liter])	125 g.

Butter a 6-cup [1½-liter] soufflé dish. Moisten the slices of bread with the gin, then use them to line the dish. Beat the egg yolks thoroughly with the cheese, chives, milk and a pinch of ground ginger. Add the chopped ham and fold in the egg whites. Pour the mixture into the dish.

Bake the soufflé in a preheated 350° F. [180° C.] oven for about 20 to 25 minutes, or until well risen and golden. Serve straight from the oven.

LILO AUREDEN
DAS SCHMECKT SO GUT

Herring Roe Soufflés

Herring roe is obtainable from March to May. Other fresh roes—shad, walleyed pike, mullet, salmon, flounder, tuna or halibut, for example—may be substituted.

	To serve 6	
	salt and pepper	
¾ lb.	herring roe	350 g.
⅔ cup	tepid milk	150 ml.
2	egg yolks, lightly beaten	2
2 tbsp.	butter, softened	30 ml.
1½ tbsp.	flour	22½ ml.
¼ cup	grated Gruyère cheese	50 ml.
1	egg white, stiffly beaten	1
	paprika	

Salt and pepper the herring roe, and poach it for one minute in the tepid milk. Drain it and divide it among six buttered

6-ounce [175-ml.] ramekins. Mix the egg yolks, butter, flour and cheese. Fold in the egg white and cover the roe with this mixture. Bake the soufflés in a preheated 425° F. [220° C.] oven for five minutes, or until set. Put a pinch of paprika on each soufflé before serving it.

RUTH LOWINSKY
MORE LOVELY FOOD

Soufflé Roll with Crab Meat

To serve 8 to 12

4 tbsp.	butter	60 ml.
½ cup	flour	125 ml.
	salt and white pepper	
2 cups	milk	½ liter
5	eggs, the yolks separated from the whites, and the whites stiffly beaten	5

Crab-meat filling

2 tbsp.	butter	30 ml.
¼ cup	finely chopped shallots	50 ml.
2 tbsp.	cream cheese, softened	30 ml.
½ cup	sour cream	125 ml.
12 oz.	crab meat, picked over to remove shell and cartilage, and flaked (about 2 cups [½ liter])	350 g.
	salt (optional) and pepper	
2 tbsp.	chopped fresh tarragon or 1 tbsp. [15 ml.] dried tarragon	30 ml.

Butter a jelly-roll pan, 15 by 10 by 1 inch [38 by 25 by 2½ cm.], and line it with buttered wax paper or parchment paper. Sprinkle the paper with flour and shake off the excess.

In a small saucepan, melt the butter. Blend in the flour and just a pinch each of salt and white pepper. Add the milk slowly and bring the mixture to a boil over medium heat, stirring constantly with a wire whisk. Cook for one minute, then set the mixture aside to cool slightly.

Add the egg yolks, return the pan to the heat, and cook for one or two minutes but do not let the mixture boil. Remove the pan from the heat and set it aside to cool until the sauce is lukewarm.

Fold the whites gently into the cooled sauce and pour this soufflé mixture into the jelly-roll pan, using a rubber spatula to spread it evenly. Bake the soufflé in a preheated 400° F. [200° C.] oven for about 20 minutes, or until it is lightly browned. Turn the soufflé out onto a clean kitchen towel; the greaseproof paper will peel off easily.

While the soufflé is baking, prepare the filling by first melting the butter in the top of a double boiler set over hot—not boiling—water. Add the chopped shallots, cream cheese and sour cream; stir and blend these ingredients. Add the crab meat, pepper, salt if you wish—remember that the sour cream and crab meat are both salty—and 1½ tablespoons [22½ ml.] of fresh tarragon or ¾ tablespoon [10 ml.] of dried tarragon.

Spread about three quarters of the filling over the soufflé. Roll the soufflé, keeping the roll as tight as you can, and transfer it, seam side down, to a warmed platter. Spread a streak of the reserved filling across the top of the roll. Sprinkle a dash of fresh or dried tarragon over the streak. Serve the soufflé roll warm and slice it at the table.

JOE FAMULARO AND LOUISE IMPERÍALE
THE FESTIVE FAMULARO KITCHEN

Ham Roulade with Mustard Sour-Cream Sauce

To serve 4

2 tbsp.	vegetable oil	30 ml.
1 lb.	boneless ham, finely ground (about 2 cups [½ liter])	½ kg.
6	eggs, the yolks separated from the whites, and the whites stiffly beaten	6
8 tbsp.	butter, melted and cooled	120 ml.
½ cup	flour	125 ml.
½ tsp.	salt	2 ml.
½ tsp.	freshly ground pepper	2 ml.
2 tbsp.	chopped fresh parsley	30 ml.
2 tbsp.	chopped fresh tarragon or 2 tsp. [10 ml.] dried tarragon	30 ml.
¼ cup	dry Madeira	50 ml.

Mustard sour-cream sauce

1 cup	sour cream	¼ liter
1 tbsp.	Dijon mustard	15 ml.
1 tbsp.	chopped fresh tarragon or 1 tsp. [5 ml.] dried tarragon	15 ml.

Brush a jelly-roll pan with vegetable oil, then line it with wax paper, letting the paper extend 4 inches [10 cm.] at each end. Brush the paper with vegetable oil and set the pan aside. In a bowl, mix together the ham, egg yolks, melted butter, flour, salt, pepper, parsley, tarragon and Madeira. Fold the egg whites into the ham mixture. Spread the mixture in the prepared pan and bake it in a preheated 375° F. [190° C.] oven for 20 minutes. Unmold it onto two overlapping sheets of wax paper, peel off the lining paper, and with the wax paper to help, roll it up like a jelly roll. Place the roll on a serving platter. Mix the sour cream with the mustard and tarragon, and serve this sauce with the ham roulade..

JULIE DANNENBAUM
MENUS FOR ALL OCCASIONS

Crusted Cheese Pie

To make one 9- or 10-inch [23- or 25-cm.] pie

10	eggs	10
1 cup	milk	¼ liter
¾ cup	flour	175 ml.
¼ tsp.	salt	1 ml.
¼ tsp.	pepper	1 ml.
2 tbsp.	grated onion	30 ml.
½ lb.	cheese, grated (mixture of Cheddar, Parmesan and Gruyère)	¼ kg.
	watercress	

Stir the eggs with half of the milk until smooth. Place the flour and salt in a mixing bowl, make a well in the middle, and gradually whisk the remaining milk into the flour. Then whisk in the egg mixture. Beat the batter until it is smooth. Add the pepper. Cover the mixing bowl with a towel and let the batter stand all day (or for at least six hours) at room temperature.

Stir the grated onion and half of the cheese into the batter. Butter or oil a 9- or 10-inch [23- or 25-cm.] spring-form pan and place the pan on a baking sheet. Pour in the batter and bake in a preheated 350° F. [180° C.] oven for 20 minutes. Remove the pie from the oven and sprinkle the remaining cheese on top. Put the pie back in the oven for another 25 to 30 minutes, or until the top is brown and firmly crusted.

The pie will expand greatly. Allow it to settle for 10 minutes and then run a knife around the edge and open the pan at the side. Run a spatula under the pie and serve, slightly warm, surrounded by watercress.

JUDITH OLNEY
COMFORTING FOOD

Scotch Woodcock

To make anchovy butter, soak a filleted salt anchovy in cold water for 30 minutes. Pat it dry with paper towels and pound it in a mortar with pepper, a garlic clove and 1 tablespoon [15 ml.] of butter. Chill the anchovy butter until needed.

To serve 4

4 tbsp.	butter	60 ml.
6	eggs, beaten	6
4	slices hot toast	4
2 tbsp.	anchovy butter	30 ml.
4	salt anchovies, filleted, soaked in water for 30 minutes, drained and patted dry	4
½ cup	finely shredded Cheddar cheese	125 ml.

Melt the plain butter and in it scramble the eggs until they have a creamy consistency. Spread the hot toast with the anchovy butter and cover it with a layer of scrambled eggs. Put two anchovy fillets over the eggs on each slice of toast, sprinkle with cheese, and glaze quickly under a hot broiler so that the cheese just melts.

X. M. BOULESTIN AND A. H. ADAIR
SAVOURIES AND HOT HORS D'OEUVRES

Crepe, Pastry and Bread Assemblies

Crepes with Ham and Mushroom Stuffing

Ficelle Picarde

The technique of making stuffed crepes is demonstrated on pages 74-75.

To serve 4

4	shallots, finely chopped	4
3 tbsp.	butter, 1 tbsp. [15 ml.] melted	45 ml.
⅓ lb.	fresh mushrooms, chopped	150 g.
	salt and cayenne pepper	
	grated nutmeg	
1¼ cups	white sauce (recipe, page 162)	300 ml.
3 tbsp.	heavy cream	45 ml.
8	6-inch [15-cm.] crepes (recipe, page 167)	8
4	thin slices ham, cut into halves	4
⅔ cup	crème fraîche or heavy cream	150 ml.
½ cup	grated Gruyère cheese	125 ml.

Cook the shallots in 2 tablespoons [30 ml.] of the butter over medium heat for two to three minutes, or until softened. Add the mushrooms and seasonings, cover, and cook for 15 minutes over low heat. Stir in the white sauce and cream.

Place the crepes side by side. Pour a little of the mushroom sauce onto each crepe and top with a slice of ham. Add the remaining sauce. Tightly roll up the crepes and put them into a buttered gratin dish just large enough to hold them.

Combine the *crème fraîche*, grated cheese and melted butter. Pour the mixture over the rolls. Brown the stuffed crepes under a preheated broiler for one or two minutes. Serve very hot.

DOMINIQUE WEBER
LES BONNES RECETTES DES PROVINCES DE FRANCE

Swiss Chard Crepes

Crêpes de Bettes

Serve these crepes as you would pancakes, allowing three or four per person.

	To make 16 to 18 crepes	
½ lb.	Swiss chard, ribs removed, leaves very finely chopped	¼ kg.
1	small head lettuce, trimmed and very finely chopped	1
2 tbsp.	chopped fresh parsley	30 ml.
3	slices lean bacon, very finely chopped	3
1	onion, very finely chopped	1
2	slices firm-textured white bread, crusts removed, soaked in water or milk and squeezed dry	2
2 cups	crepe batter (recipe, page 167)	½ liter
4 tbsp.	butter	60 ml.

Mix together the Swiss chard, lettuce, parsley, bacon, onion and bread. Stir this mixture into the crepe batter. Melt 1 tablespoon [15 ml.] of the butter in a skillet. When it is hot, pour in ¼ cup [50 ml.] of the crepe mixture. Cook the crepe for two minutes on each side, or until brown. Cook the rest of the mixture in the same way, adding butter as needed.

LA CUISINE LYONNAISE

Crepes from the Auvergne

Crêpe Cantalienne

	To serve 4	
⅓ cup	freshly grated cheese	75 ml.
2 tbsp.	fines herbes	30 ml.
1 cup	white sauce (recipe, page 162)	¼ liter
8	6-inch [15-cm.] crepes (recipe, page 167)	8
4	thin slices ham	4
¼ cup	dry bread crumbs	50 ml.
4 tbsp.	butter, melted	60 ml.

Mix the grated cheese and fines herbes with the white sauce. Lay four of the crepes in a buttered shallow baking dish. Spread each pancake with 1 tablespoon [15 ml.] of the white-sauce mixture, and place a slice of ham over it. Cover with the remaining crepes and pour the rest of the white sauce over them. Mix the bread crumbs with the melted butter and sprinkle them on top. Bake the crepes in a preheated 425° F. [220° C.] oven for 10 minutes, or until lightly browned.

AMICALE DES CUISINIERS ET PÂTISSIERS AUVERGNATS DE PARIS
CUISINE D'AUVERGNE

Seafood Crepes

Crepes de Fruits de Mer

	To serve 8	
3 cups	fish stock (recipe, page 163)	¾ liter
½ lb.	sole fillets, skinned and cut into strips	¼ kg.
	salt and pepper	
¼ lb.	scallops, sliced into halves if large, rinsed and patted dry	125 g.
1½ cups	quartered fresh mushrooms	375 ml.
1½ tbsp.	fresh lemon juice	22½ ml.
about 3½ cups	velouté sauce (recipe, page 163), made with the seafood and mushroom cooking liquids	about 875 ml.
¼ lb.	cooked lobster or crab meat	125 g.
¼ lb.	shrimp, poached for 1 to 3 minutes, shelled, deveined and halved lengthwise	125 g.
16	5-inch [12½-cm.] crepes (recipe, page 167)	16
½ cup	heavy cream	125 ml.
2	egg yolks (optional)	2

Bring the fish stock to a boil, add the sole strips, salt and pepper, and poach the fish for one or two minutes, or until slightly stiffened. Lift out the fish with a slotted spoon, add the scallops and poach these for one or two minutes until just opaque. Drain them, reserving the cooking liquid. Put the mushrooms into a saucepan with the lemon juice, season them with salt and pepper, and add a ¼-inch [6-mm.] layer of water. Cover and cook over high heat for two to three minutes until the liquid boils to the top of the pan and the mushrooms are tender. Drain the mushrooms and use their cooking liquid, along with that of the seafood, to prepare velouté sauce.

Mix half of the velouté sauce together with the sole strips, scallops, lobster or crab meat, shrimp and mushrooms. Put a spoonful of filling on each crepe, roll up the crepes like cigars and arrange them diagonally in a shallow buttered baking dish.

Stir the cream into the egg yolks, if using, add a little of the remaining sauce and stir this mixture back into the saucepan. Heat gently, stirring, until the sauce thickens slightly. If using only cream, bring the sauce just to a boil. Taste again and spoon the sauce over the stuffed crepes. Bake the stuffed crepes in a preheated 350° F. [180° C.] oven for 20 minutes, or until they are very hot and browned.

ANNE WILLAN AND JANE GRIGSON (EDITORS)
THE OBSERVER FRENCH COOKERY SCHOOL

Crepe Soufflé
Crêpes Soufflées

The technique of making crepes is shown on pages 74-75.

To serve 4

3 tbsp.	butter	45 ml.
¼ cup	flour	50 ml.
1¼ cups	milk	300 ml.
2 tsp.	freshly grated Parmesan cheese	10 ml.
⅓ cup	finely shredded Gruyère cheese	75 ml.
	salt and pepper	
3	eggs, the yolks separated from the whites, and the whites stiffly beaten	3
8	7-inch [18-cm.] crepes (recipe, page 167)	8
1 cup	tomato sauce (recipe, page 162)	¼ liter

In a small saucepan, heat the butter and the flour. As soon as the mixture turns golden, gradually whisk in the milk. When the sauce is creamy, add the cheeses and a pinch each of salt and pepper. Let the sauce cool.

Add the egg yolks to the cooled cheese sauce, then fold in the whites. Butter a 1-quart [1-liter] soufflé dish. Put the crepes and the cheese mixture into the dish in alternate layers, beginning and ending with a crepe. Bake the soufflé in a preheated 375° F. [190° C.] oven for 35 minutes, or until the top is golden. Run a knife around the inside edge of the dish to loosen the crepes. The soufflé can be served directly from the dish with tomato sauce on the side, or it can be unmolded and covered with the tomato sauce.

NINETTE LYON
LES OEUFS

Ham Crepes
La Biguenée de Nantes

To serve 6

2 cups	flour	½ liter
2	eggs, lightly beaten	2
1 cup	tepid beer	¼ liter
1 cup	tepid milk or water	¼ liter
3 tbsp.	oil	45 ml.
	salt and pepper	
4 tbsp.	butter	60 ml.
6	slices boiled ham, cut into 4- to 5-inch [10- to 13-cm.] rounds	6

In a bowl, mix the flour and eggs. Beat in the beer and milk or water little by little to prevent lumps from forming. Final-ly, add the oil, salt and pepper. Cover the bowl and leave it in a cool spot for two hours.

In a 6-inch [15-cm.] crepe pan, melt 1 tablespoon [15 ml.] of the butter. Pour in ¼ cup [50 ml.] of the batter. Tilt the pan to spread the batter evenly over the surface. Remove the pan from the heat as soon as the batter sets, and lay a slice of ham on it. Pour in another ¼ cup of batter, tilting the pan to cover the ham evenly with the batter. Cook the crepe over high heat for two minutes, or until the underside is golden. Slip the crepe onto a plate, invert the pan over the plate and turn them upside down. Return the crepe to the heat to brown the other side. When cooked, put the crepe in a warm place, and make the remaining five crepes in the same way.

LA CUISINE BRETONNE

Rolled Stuffed Crepes
Les Canelloni

Canelloni can be stuffed with meat, brains, fish and mush-rooms; they are an excellent way of using up leftovers.

To make 12 stuffed crepes

1¼ cups	chopped roasted meat	300 ml.
¼ cup	chopped ham (optional)	50 ml.
2 lb.	spinach, stems and coarse ribs removed, parboiled in salted water for 1 minute, drained, squeezed dry and chopped	1 kg.
	salt and pepper	
	mixed spices	
2	egg yolks, beaten	2
12	6-inch [15-cm.] crepes (recipe, page 167)	12
1 cup	meat roasting juices, degreased, or tomato sauce (recipe, page 162)	¼ liter
⅔ cup	freshly grated Parmesan cheese	150 ml.

To make the stuffing, mix the chopped meat and ham, if using, with the spinach. Season with salt and pepper and mixed spices. Bind the mixture with the egg yolks.

Take a crepe and put two heaping spoonfuls of stuffing in the center. Fold two opposite sides of the crepe to meet in the center, over the stuffing. Then roll up the crepe like a jelly roll, at right angles to the folded sides. Proceed in the same manner with the rest of the crepes.

Arrange the rolled crepes seam side down in a buttered gratin dish just large enough to hold them. Pour the meat juices or tomato sauce over the crepes and sprinkle them with the Parmesan cheese. Bake in a preheated 450° F. [230° C.] oven for 10 to 15 minutes, or until the sauce begins to bubble. Then slide the dish under a hot broiler for one min-ute until the top is golden brown.

ÉDOUARD DE POMIANE
LE CODE DE LA BONNE CHÈRE

Crepes St. Gabriel

To serve 4

4	crepes *(recipe, page 167)*	4
4	very thin slices ham, equal in size to the crepes	4
½ cup	duxelles *(recipe, page 164)*	125 ml.
½ cup	heavy cream	125 ml.
¼ cup	ground almonds	50 ml.

Place a slice of ham on top of each crepe. Combine the *dux-elles* with ¼ cup [50 ml.] of the cream and the ground almonds, and mix well. Spread the *duxelles* filling over each ham crepe. Carefully fold the crepe in half as for an omelet. Place 1 tablespoon [15 ml.] of cream on top of each folded crepe and brown the crepes under the broiler. Serve at once.

ALEXANDER WATT
PARIS BISTRO COOKERY

Pepper and Tomato Tart

Tarte aux Poivrons et aux Tomates

Short-crust and rough puff dough (recipe, page 166) also can be used for this recipe.

To make one 12-inch [30-cm.] tart

6	medium-sized tomatoes, peeled, seeded and chopped	6
½ cup	peanut oil	125 ml.
3	garlic cloves, finely chopped	3
	salt and pepper	
1	small dried hot chili, crushed to a powder	1
6	green peppers, broiled, peeled, halved, seeded, deribbed and sliced into thin strips	6
1 tbsp.	wine vinegar	15 ml.
12	oil-packed flat anchovy fillets	12
1	egg yolk, beaten with a little water	1
White-wine dough		
2 cups	flour, sifted	½ liter
½ tsp.	salt	2 ml.
4 tbsp.	butter, softened	60 ml.
¼ cup	olive oil	50 ml.
¼ cup	white wine	50 ml.
2 tbsp.	hot water	30 ml.

To make the dough, put the flour into a bowl and make a well in the center. Into the well, put the salt, butter and oil. Mix with your finger tips so that the fat is thoroughly incorporated into the flour. Add the white wine. Work the dough for another minute and add the hot water. Knead briefly. Let the dough rest for at least 15 minutes.

Sauté the chopped tomatoes in the oil. Add the chopped garlic. Season with salt and pepper and the crushed chili. Add the strips of green pepper to the tomatoes in the skillet. Cook over medium heat for 10 minutes, then add the vinegar. The mixture should be fairly dry.

Roll out the dough to a thickness of about ⅛ inch [3 mm.] and use about two thirds of it to line a 12-inch [30-cm.] tart pan. Reserve the remaining dough.

Pour the pepper-and-tomato mixture onto the dough in the tart pan. Arrange the anchovies on top. Roll out the remaining dough and cut it into strips about ¼ inch [6 mm.] wide. Lay the strips in a lattice pattern over the filling. Glaze the latticework and the borders of the dough with the egg yolk. Bake the tart in a preheated 425° F. [220° C.] oven for 30 to 40 minutes, or until the pastry is golden brown.

SYLVIE THIÉBAULT
TARTES SUCRÉES ET TARTES SALÉES

Asparagus Quiche

To make a 10-inch [25-cm.] quiche

2½ lb.	asparagus, tough ends removed	1¼ kg.
2 tbsp.	butter	30 ml.
2 tbsp.	olive oil	30 ml.
4	eggs, lightly beaten	4
1 cup	heavy cream	250 ml.
1 tbsp.	finely chopped fresh parsley	15 ml.
	salt and pepper	
	grated nutmeg	
1	partially baked tart shell, made from ¾ lb. [350 g.] short-crust dough *(recipe, page 166)*	1

Cut tips 2½ inches [6 cm.] long from the asparagus stalks. Slice the stalks thin, and sauté the slices in the butter and oil until just tender. Combine the asparagus stems, eggs, cream, parsley, salt, pepper and a little nutmeg. Pour the mixture into the tart shell and bake at 350° F. [180° C.] for 25 to 30 minutes, or until the filling has set.

Meanwhile, cook the asparagus tips in boiling salted water. When just tender, drain the tips, refresh them under cold running water and pat them dry. Arrange the tips around the edge of the baked quiche, with all of the tips pointed toward the center.

JUDITH OLNEY
SUMMER FOOD

Easter Pie

Torta Pasqualina

To make one 8-inch [20-cm.] deep-dish pie

2 lb.	olive-oil dough (recipe, page 166)	1 kg.
4 lb.	Swiss chard, ribs removed, leaves shredded, parboiled very rapidly for 1 minute and drained	2 kg.
4 tbsp.	butter	60 ml.
⅔ cup	freshly grated Parmesan cheese	150 ml.
1 cup	heavy cream	¼ liter
	dried marjoram leaves	
2 cups	farmer cheese	½ liter
2 tbsp.	flour	30 ml.
3 tbsp.	olive oil or melted butter	45 ml.
4	eggs	4

Divide the olive-oil dough into seven equal pieces. Join two of them together to make a larger piece. Let the dough rest for about 20 minutes before rolling it out.

For the filling, sauté the chard in 2 tablespoons [30 ml.] of the butter until the excess moisture has evaporated. Stir in the Parmesan cheese. Put the mixture in a bowl and combine it with the cream, a pinch of marjoram, the farmer cheese and the flour.

Roll out the large piece of dough into a sheet big enough to line a round baking dish 8 inches [20 cm.] across and 4 inches [10 cm.] deep. Roll out the remaining five pieces of dough into sheets to fit the diameter of the dish. Oil or butter the dish and line it with the large sheet of dough. Brush the dough with oil or melted butter. Spread about one fifth of the filling in the lined dish, and lay a small sheet of dough on top. Brush the dough with oil or butter, spread more filling on it and add another sheet of dough. Buttering or oiling each sheet, repeat with more filling and the third small sheet of dough. Spread the third sheet with filling, make four holes in the filling and break an egg into each hollow. Dot each egg with a piece of the remaining butter. Cover with the fourth small sheet of dough and the rest of the filling, and top with the last sheet of dough. Tuck in the edges of the dough. Cut a hole in the top sheet and insert a straw or a rolled tube of cardboard to let out steam during baking. Bake the pie in a preheated 350° F. [180° C.] oven for 45 minutes, or until the top is golden brown.

LUIGI VOLPICELLI AND SECONDINO FREDA (EDITORS)
L'ANTIARTUSI: 1000 RICETTE

Carrot Turnovers

Petits Pâtés aux Carottes

The fillings used for these little pastries can be varied infinitely. For example: cooked rice and hard-boiled eggs; chopped cabbage; chopped cooked fish; chopped cooked beef, veal or game; a little stew of mushrooms, morels, lobster or crayfish tails, etc.

To make twenty 3-inch [8-cm.] turnovers

9	medium-sized carrots, halved lengthwise, woody cores discarded, diced and parboiled in salted water for 1 minute	9
3 tbsp.	butter	45 ml.
2	eggs, hard-boiled and chopped	2
1 tbsp.	chopped fresh parsley	15 ml.
1 tbsp.	finely cut fresh chives	15 ml.
1 tbsp.	thick white sauce (recipe, page 162)	15 ml.
	salt and pepper	
1 lb.	rough puff dough (recipe, page 166)	½ kg.
1	egg, beaten with 2 tsp. [10 ml.] water	1

Fry the carrots in the butter until tender. Stir in the hard-boiled eggs, parsley and chives. Then add the white sauce, season with salt and pepper, and let the mixture cool.

Roll out the rough puff dough, and cut it into about twenty 3-inch [8-cm.] rounds. Put a tablespoonful of the carrot mixture into the center of each round. Moisten the edges of the rounds with a little water and fold each round in half to make a turnover. Crimp the edges to seal the turnovers.

Sprinkle a buttered baking sheet with water and lay the turnovers on the sheet. Brush the turnovers with the beaten egg and use a very sharp knife to make several parallel incisions in the top of each turnover. Bake the turnovers in a preheated 400° F. [200° C.] oven for 25 minutes, or until golden brown. Pile the turnovers in a pyramid on a dish and serve piping hot.

A. PETIT
LA GASTRONOMIE EN RUSSIE

Cheese and Potato Tart

Tourte de Châteaumeillant

Any soft cheese made from goat's milk—montrachet, pyramide or bucheron—may be used for this tart. If goat's-milk cheese is not obtainable, it can be replaced by feta cheese.

To make one 10-inch [25-cm.] tart

1	unbaked tart shell, made from ¾ lb. [350 g.] rough puff dough (recipe, page 166)	1
½ lb.	soft goat's-milk cheese	¼ kg.
	salt and pepper	
4	medium-sized potatoes, peeled and very thinly sliced	4
7 tbsp.	butter, cut into pieces	105 ml.

Prick the dough-lined pan all over with a fork. Remove the rind from the cheese and push the cheese through a sieve set over a bowl. Beat the sieved cheese until it forms a smooth paste. Season it.

Put the sliced potatoes into a saucepan of cold water, bring them to a boil and cook them for five minutes. Then drain them under cold, running water. Dry the potatoes on paper towels and put half of them in the dough-lined pan. Season, and dot with half of the butter pieces.

Spread the cheese paste over the potatoes, and arrange the rest of the potatoes on top. Season, and dot with the remaining butter. Bake the tart in a preheated 375° F. [190° C.] oven for 30 minutes, or until the top is browned. Serve the tart piping hot.

PIERRE ANDROUET
LA CUISINE AU FROMAGE

Cabbage and Chopped-Beef Pie

Coulibiac au Chou et au Boeuf Haché

Any type of puff-pastry dough is suitable for this recipe. The technique of making Cabbage and Chopped-Beef Pie, using olive-oil puff dough, is demonstrated on pages 80-81.

To make one 12-by-8-inch [30-by-20-cm.] pie

1 lb.	puff-pastry dough (recipe, page 167)	½ kg.
1	onion, finely chopped and cooked in butter until soft	1
½ cup	unprocessed long-grain white rice, boiled in 1 cup [¼ liter] water for 15 minutes, or until tender, and cooled	125 ml.
4	green cabbage leaves, ribs removed, parboiled for 3 minutes, drained and coarsely chopped	4
	salt and pepper	
7 tbsp.	butter	105 ml.
3	eggs, hard-boiled and chopped	3
⅓ cup	chopped leftover boiled beef	75 ml.
1	egg white, diluted with a few drops of water	1
2	egg yolks, diluted with 1 tbsp. [15 ml.] water	2

Divide the dough into two pieces, one double the size of the other. On a lightly floured work surface, roll the smaller piece into a rectangle about 12 by 8 inches [30 by 20 cm.]. Lay the dough rectangle on a buttered baking sheet.

Mix the onion with the rice and spread the mixture evenly over the dough rectangle, leaving a ¾-inch [2-cm.] border. Season the chopped cabbage leaves and scatter them over the rice mixture. Cut 4 tablespoons [60 ml.] of the butter into pieces and dot them over the top. Scatter the chopped hard-boiled eggs over the cabbage and season again. Add the chopped meat. Brush the dough edges with the egg white.

Roll out the remaining dough into a rectangle large enough to completely cover the lower rectangle. Lay it over the filling, and seal the top and bottom layers of dough by pressing the two edges firmly together. Glaze the pie generously with the egg yolks.

Cut a ½-inch [1-cm.] hole in the center of the pie to let the steam escape during cooking. Bake the pie in a preheated 425° F. [220° C.] oven for 35 minutes, or until it is golden brown. Melt the remaining butter and, when the pie is cooked, pour in the butter through the hole in the top.

MIRIAM CENDRARS AND NINETTE LYON
GRATINS, TOURTES ET TARTES

Leek Tart

Porrea

This recipe was created in about 1405 by the monks of San Lorenzo in Florence.

To make one 8-inch [20-cm.] tart

1 cup	olive oil	¼ liter
¼ lb.	prosciutto, diced	125 g.
½ lb.	boneless fatty pork, ground	¼ kg.
½ lb.	veal or lamb, ground	¼ kg.
	salt and pepper	
	grated nutmeg	
¼ tsp.	powdered saffron, dissolved in 2 tbsp. [30 ml.] warm water	1 ml.
½ cup	red wine	125 ml.
6	large leeks, the white parts only, cut into quarters lengthwise	6
1 lb.	olive-oil dough (recipe, page 166)	½ kg.
⅓ cup	freshly grated Parmesan cheese, (optional)	75 ml.

In a pan, heat half the oil and brown the prosciutto and the ground meats. Add a little salt, pepper, nutmeg and the saffron. Cook for two minutes, then add the wine and cook for five more minutes, until the wine evaporates. In another pan, stew the leeks for a few minutes in the remaining oil. Take care not to let them disintegrate. Season with salt.

Roll out three quarters of the dough into a round and use it to line a buttered 8-inch [20-cm.] tart pan about 2 inches [5 cm.] deep. Pour in the meat mixture, adding a little more wine if it looks dry, and spread it out evenly. Arrange the leeks on top of the meat. Sprinkle with the Parmesan cheese, if using. Roll out the rest of the dough, slice it into strips and arrange these over the filling in a lattice pattern. Bake the tart in a preheated 375° F. [190° C.] oven for about 40 minutes, or until it is golden brown.

MASSIMO ALBERINI (EDITOR)
CENTO RICETTE STORICHE

Excellent Mushroom Tart

Torta de Fongi Bona e Perfettissima

This recipe is by Maestro Martino, a cook who lived in the 15th Century. He was the first Renaissance cook to have his recipes published.

To make one 12-inch [30-cm.] tart

⅓ cup	olive oil	75 ml.
1 lb.	mushrooms, cut into large pieces	½ kg.
¼ lb.	lean salt pork with the rind removed, blanched for 10 minutes, drained and diced	125 g.
⅔ cup	freshly grated Parmesan cheese	150 ml.
4	eggs, beaten	4
	salt and pepper	
	grated nutmeg	
	ground mace	
1	unbaked tart shell, made from ¾ lb. [350 g.] olive-oil dough (recipe, page 166)	1

Put the oil in a pan over low heat and fry the mushrooms and salt pork, adding a little water if necessary to prevent them from burning. When they are cooked, remove them from the pan with a slotted spoon and put them in a bowl. Add the cheese and eggs and mix well. Season the mixture with salt and pepper and a pinch each of nutmeg and mace.

Pour the mushroom mixture into the tart shell. Bake the tart in a preheated 400° F. [200° C.] oven for about 30 minutes, or until the filling is set and beginning to brown.

EMILIO FACCIOLI (EDITOR)
ARTE DELLA CUCINA

Leeks Baked in French Puff Pastry

Flamiche aux Poireaux

To make one 10-inch [25-cm.] pie

5	medium-sized leeks, white part and small part of green only, finely chopped	5
7 tbsp.	unsalted butter	105 ml.
3 to 4 tbsp.	water	45 to 60 ml.
⅓ cup	heavy cream	75 ml.
	salt and freshly ground pepper	
1 lb.	rough puff or puff-pastry dough (recipes, pages 166-167)	½ kg.
1	egg yolk, mixed with a little water	1

Gently stew the leeks in the butter, starting with half of the total amount of butter and adding the rest a little at a time.

When the leeks are translucent, moisten them with the water, cover the pan, and cook gently until the leeks are completely soft and all of the liquid has been absorbed—about 10 minutes. The leeks should not be allowed to brown. Add the cream and season well.

Divide the dough in half. Roll out one half into a thin round about 10 inches [25 cm.] in diameter and transfer it to a dampened baking sheet. Place the leek mixture in the middle, leaving a margin of 1 inch [2½ cm.] all around. Brush the margin with water. Roll out the rest of the dough in the same way and place it on top of the leek mixture. Press the edges firmly together so that they are well sealed. To help the puff-dough layers separate during cooking, cut a 1-inch slit at 1-inch intervals all around the edges of the pie. To let steam escape, cut several small slits in the top. Glaze the top by brushing it with the diluted egg yolk and make a trelliswork pattern on it with the point of a knife.

Bake the pie in a preheated 425° F. [220° C.] oven for 10 minutes, then reduce the heat to 325° F. [160° C.] and continue baking for another 20 to 25 minutes. When ready, the pie should be golden with no dark spots. Serve very hot.

LOUISETTE BERTHOLLE (EDITOR)
SECRETS OF THE GREAT FRENCH RESTAURANTS

Onion Tart

Tarte aux Oignons

To make one 8-inch [20-cm.] tart

1	partially baked tart shell, made from ½ lb. [¼ kg.] rough puff dough (recipe, page 166) made with equal quantities of butter and lard	1
4	large onions, thinly sliced	4
10 tbsp.	butter	150 ml.
3	slices lean bacon, diced	3
3	eggs, beaten	3
¼ cup	heavy cream	50 ml.

Put the onions into cold, salted water and bring them to a boil over high heat. When they have boiled for three minutes, remove them from the pot and drain them well.

Melt 2 tablespoons [30 ml.] of the butter in a pan and sauté the bacon until lightly browned. In a large saucepan, melt the rest of the butter, add the onions, and cook them over low heat until they are light brown—about 20 minutes. Add the bacon and mix. Drain off the excess fat, and let the onions and bacon cool until tepid. Mix the eggs and cream, and add them to the onions and bacon.

Fill the pastry shell with the onion mixture and bake the tart in a preheated 400° F. [200° C.] oven for about 15 minutes, or until the filling and pastry are lightly browned.

X. MARCEL BOULESTIN
A SECOND HELPING OR MORE DISHES FOR ENGLISH HOMES

Corn Pie

For a corn-clam pie, add ½ cup [125 ml.] of chopped raw clams to the corn filling in this recipe.

To make one 9-inch [23-cm.] pie

4 cups	corn kernels, cut from about 8 large ears	1 liter
4	eggs, lightly beaten	4
2 tsp.	sugar	10 ml.
1 tsp.	salt	5 ml.
	freshly ground pepper	
2 tbsp.	flour	30 ml.
8 tbsp.	butter, melted	120 ml.
1 lb.	short-crust dough *(recipe, page 166)*	½ kg.

Combine the corn, eggs, sugar and salt, pepper to taste, flour and butter. Roll out half of the dough to fit a 9-inch [23-cm.] piepan. Pour the mixture into the pie shell and roll out the rest of the dough to make a top crust; cut a vent for the steam to escape. Bake the pie in a preheated 350° F. [180° C.] oven for one hour, or until the pie is golden brown.

BETTY GROFF AND JOSÉ WILSON
GOOD EARTH & COUNTRY COOKING

Pumpkin Satchels

Barba Jouan

To prevent it from becoming too moist, the pumpkin can be baked instead of boiled—in which case it should be seeded, cut into quarters and cooked in foil. Winter squash such as Hubbard, acorn or butternut can replace the pumpkin.

In the countryside around Nice, a little strong *brousse* cheese is added. The satchels can be deep fried in olive oil.

To make 36 to 48 satchels

5 lb.	pumpkin, peeled, scraped and cut into pieces	2½ kg.
1	garlic clove, chopped	1
1	small onion, chopped	1
1 tbsp.	olive oil	15 ml.
½ cup	long-grain white rice, boiled	125 ml.
2	eggs, beaten	2
1 cup	freshly grated Parmesan cheese	¼ liter
	salt and pepper	
2 lb.	olive-oil dough *(recipe, page 166)*	1 kg.

In enough boiling salted water to cover it, cook the pumpkin the night before for about 20 minutes, or until it begins to soften; drain it overnight. The pumpkin should have released all of the cooking liquid by morning.

Cook the garlic and onion in the olive oil until they are transparent. Chop the pumpkin or mash it in a bowl. Add the garlic and onion, the rice, eggs and grated Parmesan cheese. Season with salt and pepper and mix well.

On a floured surface, roll out the dough. Using a biscuit cutter or a glass, cut out rounds about 3 inches [8 cm.] in diameter. Put a heaping spoonful of stuffing in the center of each circle. Pull up the edges of the dough and pinch them together in the center to form satchels.

Place the satchels on oiled baking sheets, spacing them well apart to permit even baking. Brush the satchels with olive oil and bake them in a preheated 425° F. [220° C.] oven for 25 to 30 minutes, or until the pastry is light brown and the pinched edges are dark gold.

RAYMOND ARMISEN AND ANDRÉ MARTIN
LES RECETTES DE LA TABLE NIÇOISE

Rich Tomato Tart

The original version of this recipe calls for anchovy essence, which is a liquid flavoring unavailable in America. Diluted anchovy paste makes a suitable substitute.

To make one 8-inch [20-cm.] tart

1	unbaked tart shell, made from ½ lb. [¼ kg.] short-crust dough *(recipe, page 166)*	1
6	tomatoes, peeled, halved and seeded	6
	salt	
3 tbsp.	fresh bread crumbs, browned in the oven	45 ml.
1 tsp.	chopped mixed fresh herbs (chives, thyme, parsley, rosemary)	5 ml.
⅓ cup	heavy cream	75 ml.
1 cup	grated Gruyère cheese	¼ liter
1 tsp.	anchovy paste, dissolved in 2 tsp. [10 ml.] boiling water	5 ml.
	grated nutmeg	

Sprinkle the halved tomatoes with salt and leave them for 30 minutes. Tip away any liquid and dry the halves well with paper towels.

Cover the bottom of the unbaked tart shell with the bread crumbs and arrange the tomatoes on top. Dust with the herbs. Mix the cream and grated cheese together, season with the dissolved anchovy paste and a little grated nutmeg, and spoon the mixture over the tomatoes.

Bake the tart in a preheated 400° F. [200° C.] oven for 30 minutes, or until the top is golden brown. Serve hot.

DORSET FEDERATION OF WOMEN'S INSTITUTES
WHAT'S COOKING IN DORSET

Savory Herb Tart

Pour Faire une Tourte

This recipe comes from "a treatise on morals and domestic economy," written anonymously about 1393 by "un bourgeois Parisien." Farmer or ricotta cheese can be used for the soft cheese; Cheddar or Gruyère are suitable for the semihard cheese, and Parmesan or a similar hard grating cheese can be used for the old pressed cheese.

To make one 8-inch [20-cm.] tart

1	partially baked tart shell, made from ½ lb. [¼ kg.] short-crust dough (recipe, page 166)	1
¼ cup	finely chopped fresh parsley	50 ml.
2 tbsp.	finely chopped fresh chervil	30 ml.
1	small fennel heart, preferably from a young wild fennel bulb, finely chopped	1
½ lb.	Swiss chard, ribs removed, leaves parboiled for 3 minutes, squeezed dry and finely chopped	¼ kg.
¼ lb.	spinach, parboiled for 3 minutes, drained, squeezed dry and finely chopped	125 g.
¼ lb.	soft cheese (about ½ cup [125 ml.])	125 g.
¼ lb.	semihard cheese, cut into small cubes (about 1 cup [¼ liter])	125 g.
4	eggs, beaten	4
2 tsp.	mixed spices or 1½ tsp. [7 ml.] fresh ginger, peeled and finely chopped	10 ml.
	salt and pepper	
2 oz.	old pressed cheese, grated (about ⅔ cup [150 ml.])	60 g.

Mix the chopped herbs and vegetables together. In a bowl, mix the soft and semihard cheeses with the beaten eggs; then put the vegetables into the bowl and mix all together; add the mixed spices. Alternatively, before mixing the vegetables, cheeses and eggs, pound the ginger in a mortar; then add the cheeses, eggs and vegetables to the mortar and mix them. Season to taste, pour the mixture into the tart shell, and sprinkle it with the grated cheese.

Bake the tart in a preheated 375° F. [190° C.] oven for about 20 minutes, or until set. Serve it hot.

LE MÉNAGIER DE PARIS

Spinach or Chard Pie

Tourte aux Épinards ou aux Feuilles de Blettes

To make one 12-inch [30-cm.] pie

2 lb.	spinach or Swiss chard, stems and large ribs removed, green parts blanched for 1 minute, drained, squeezed dry and chopped	1 kg.
⅓ cup	chopped fresh parsley	75 ml.
4 or 5	garlic cloves, chopped	4 or 5
7 tbsp.	butter	105 ml.
6	eggs, beaten	6
1⅔ cups	finely shredded Gruyère cheese	400 ml.
2 cups	milk	½ liter
	salt and pepper	
1 lb.	short-crust dough (recipe, page 166)	½ kg.

Chop the spinach or chard with the parsley and garlic, and sauté the mixture in the butter for seven to eight minutes. Let it cool slightly, then beat in the eggs, grated cheese and milk. Season to taste. Use half of the dough to line a 12-inch [30-cm.] piepan. Fill the pan with the spinach or chard mixture. Roll out the rest of the dough and use it to cover the filling. Cut a small hole or several slits in the lid to let steam escape. Bake the pie in a preheated 375° F. [190° C.] oven for 45 minutes, or until the pastry is golden brown.

HENRI PHILIPPON
CUISINE DE PROVENCE

Spinach Pies from Crete

Spanakokalitsoyna

The original version of this recipe calls for mizithra or manouri cheese, Greek cottage cheeses unavailable in America. You may use ricotta or sieved cottage cheese instead.

To make about twenty 4-inch [10-cm.] tartlets

4 cups	flour	1 liter
4 tsp.	salt	20 ml.
½ cup	olive oil	125 ml.
1 cup	cold water	¼ liter
2 lb.	spinach, stems removed and leaves chopped	1 kg.
1 lb.	ricotta or cottage cheese	½ kg.
3	eggs, 2 beaten, 1 beaten separately with 2 tsp. [10 ml.] water	3
	pepper	
6 tbsp.	sesame seeds	90 ml.

Sift the flour and 1 teaspoon [5 ml.] of the salt into a large bowl. With your fingers, rub in half of the oil. Gradually mix in the water. Knead the dough on a floured pastry board for about 10 minutes, or until it is smooth and elastic. If necessary, add extra flour to make the dough stiff. Cover and let it rest for one hour.

Sprinkle the spinach with the rest of the salt and rub it with your hands. Leave it for one hour, then squeeze it well and combine it with the cheese, the two beaten eggs, a pinch of pepper and the rest of the oil.

On a floured pastry board, roll the dough to a thickness of less than ⅛ inch [3 mm.]. Cut it into 4-inch [10-cm.] squares. Place 2 tablespoons [30 ml.] of the spinach mixture in the center of each square. Moisten the edges with water and fold the four corners toward the center; press them firmly together. Brush the pies with the remaining egg, sprinkle them with the sesame seeds and bake them on an oiled baking sheet in a preheated 350° F. [180° C.] oven for about 35 minutes, or until they are golden brown.

CHRISSA PARADISSIS
THE BEST BOOK OF GREEK COOKERY

———————◆———————

Spiced Beef Pies
Hackfleischtaschen

To make about 25 pies

2 tbsp.	vegetable oil	30 ml.
1	large onion, finely chopped	1
2	garlic cloves, finely chopped	2
1 lb.	boneless beef, ground	½ kg.
	salt	
¼ tsp.	cayenne pepper	1 ml.
1 tsp.	paprika	5 ml.
	ground allspice	
	freshly grated nutmeg	
	dried rosemary and thyme leaves	
2	eggs, 1 lightly beaten, 1 yolk separated from the white and both lightly beaten	2
1½ lb.	rough puff dough (recipe, page 166)	¾ kg.

Heat the oil and sauté the onion and garlic until they are transparent. Add the ground beef and cook for five minutes. Add salt to taste and season with the cayenne pepper, paprika and a pinch each of allspice, nutmeg, and rosemary and thyme leaves. Let the mixture cool slightly, then stir in the beaten egg.

Roll out the dough thin and cut it into about twenty-five 5-inch [12-cm.] squares. Brush the squares with the beaten egg white. Put 2 tablespoons [30 ml.] of the filling in the center of each square and fold the corners to the center, pressing the edges to seal them. Brush the pies with the beaten egg yolk. Place them on a baking sheet sprinkled with water and bake them in a preheated 425° F. [220° C.] oven for about 25 minutes, or until golden brown.

HEDWIG MARIA STUBER
ICH HELF DIR KOCHEN

———————◆———————

Livers in Red Wine Sauce
Les Foies de Volaille au Vin Rouge

The author recommends filling the tartlets while they are still hot from the oven, and adding 1 tablespoon [15 ml.] of meat glaze to the sauce. Meat glaze is rich meat stock that has been reduced to a syrupy consistency. To produce the spoonful of glaze, you would need to boil down about 2 cups [½ liter] of meat stock.

To serve 6

12	fully baked tartlet shells, made from 1 lb. [½ kg.] short-crust dough (recipe, page 166)	12
¾ lb.	chicken livers, trimmed and halved	350 g.
	salt and pepper	
2 tbsp.	butter	30 ml.
1	slice lean salt pork, ¼ inch [6 mm.] thick, cut crosswise into 12 strips	1
2 oz.	beef marrow, sliced and poached in water for about 10 minutes	60 g.
	Bordelaise sauce	
3	shallots, finely chopped	3
1½ cups	red wine	375 ml.
	freshly ground black pepper	
1	sprig thyme	1
⅔ cup	velouté sauce (recipe, page 163), made with veal stock	150 ml.

To make the sauce, put the shallots into a pan and add the wine, pepper and thyme. Cook until the liquid is reduced to one quarter its original volume. Add the veal velouté and simmer for 20 minutes. Strain the sauce through a muslin-lined sieve. Keep the sauce warm.

Season the livers and sauté them in half of the butter. Do not overcook them—they should be pink in the center. Remove the livers from the pan and sauté the salt pork until lightly browned and crisp. Drain the pork on paper towels. Stir the rest of the butter into the bordelaise sauce, then stir in the poached marrow. Fill the tartlet shells with livers and salt pork, and pour the sauce over them.

ÉDOUARD NIGNON
LES PLAISIRS DE LA TABLE

Meat Rolls

Maultaschen

The rolls are usually served in their cooking liquid, but they can also be drained, sprinkled with dry bread crumbs, matzo meal or fried chopped onion, and fried until golden brown.

To make 25 to 30 rolls

4 cups	flour	1 liter
4	eggs	4
	salt	

Pork and spinach filling

2	slices bacon, finely chopped	2
4	medium-sized onions, finely chopped	4
½ lb.	boneless pork, finely ground or chopped	¼ kg.
2 lb.	spinach, stems and coarse ribs removed, ½ cup [125 ml.] finely chopped raw and the rest parboiled for 1 minute, drained, squeezed dry and chopped	1 kg.
2	bratwurst, skinned and finely chopped	2
¾ cup	chopped fresh parsley	175 ml.
	salt and pepper	
	freshly grated nutmeg	
1½ quarts	meat stock *(recipe, page 163)*	1½ liters

To make the dough, sift the flour onto a board, make a well in the center, and put in the eggs and salt. Gradually work the flour into the eggs, squeezing the ingredients until they form a homogeneous dough. Knead the dough until it is firm and smooth—about 12 minutes. Divide it into six equal-sized pieces and roll out each piece into a very thin round.

To make the filling, fry the bacon and onions until lightly colored. Mix them with the pork, raw and cooked spinach, bratwurst and parsley, and season with salt, pepper and a pinch of nutmeg. Spread the mixture over the rounds of dough. Roll up each round as you would a jelly roll. With the side of your hand, make deep depressions in each roll at 2½-inch [6-cm.] intervals. Then slice the rolls at each depression; pressing with your hand prevents the cut ends of the rolls from opening during cooking.

Season the stock well and flavor it with a pinch of nutmeg. Bring the stock to a boil, add the rolls, and simmer them over low heat until they float to the surface—about 10 minutes. Serve the rolls in the stock.

HANS KARL ADAM
DAS KOCHBUCH AUS SCHWABEN

Chicken Vol-au-vent

Bouchées à la Reine du "Dauphin"

These vol-au-vent have always been associated with Alsace-Lorraine because they were the favorite of Maria Leszczyńska, wife of Louis XV and daughter of the Duke of Lorraine, the former King Stanislas of Poland. This recipe was created by the Dauphin restaurant in Strasbourg.

The method of preparing sweetbreads for cooking is shown on pages 34-35, and the making of vol-au-vent cases is demonstrated on pages 82-83.

To serve 6

3 lb.	chicken, with giblets	1½ kg.
1	leek, trimmed	1
1	carrot	1
1	medium-sized onion	1
2	bay leaves	2
2	whole cloves	2
1 tbsp.	salt	15 ml.
	pepper	
3	pairs sweetbreads, soaked, membranes removed	3
10 oz.	fresh button mushrooms	300 g.
1 tbsp.	strained fresh lemon juice	15 ml.
10 tbsp.	butter	150 ml.
1¼ cups	flour	300 ml.
1½ cups	heavy cream	375 ml.
6	fully baked 6-inch [15-cm.] vol-au-vent cases, made from 2 lb. [1 kg.] puff-pastry dough *(recipe, page 167)*	6

Put the chicken into a pot with its giblets and cover it with cold water. Bring the water to a boil over medium heat, and skim the surface to remove the scum. Meanwhile, tie the leek and carrot together; cut slits in the onion and stick the bay leaves through them, then stud the onion with the cloves. Add the leek and carrot and the onion to the pot. Season with salt and pepper. Reduce the heat to low, cover the pot and cook the chicken for 30 minutes. Add the sweetbreads and continue cooking for a further 30 minutes, or until the chicken is completely tender.

Cook the mushrooms in ½ cup [125 ml.] of salted water and the lemon juice for five minutes; drain the mushrooms, reserving the cooking liquid, and set them aside. In a saucepan, melt the butter, add the flour and cook this roux over low heat for 10 minutes, stirring constantly with a wooden spatula. Remove the roux from the heat and set it aside to cool in the pan.

Remove the chicken and sweetbreads from their cooking liquid and let them cool. Return the cooking liquid to the heat and boil it, uncovered, over high heat to reduce it to about 1 quart [1 liter]; strain it into the roux. Beat this sauce until smooth and simmer it for 30 minutes.

Warm the vol-au-vent cases in a preheated 300° F. [150° C.] oven for about 10 minutes. Skin and bone the chicken. Then cut the chicken meat, sweetbreads and mushrooms into ½-inch [1-cm.] dice.

Stir the cream into the sauce and simmer it slowly, uncovered, until it is reduced and thickened to the consistency of a pouring custard. If the sauce becomes too thick, thin it with some of the mushroom cooking liquid. Strain the sauce through a fine sieve into a pan and add the diced chicken, sweetbreads and mushrooms. Bring the mixture to a boil over medium heat, taste, and adjust the seasoning. Spoon the mixture into the heated vol-au-vent cases. Any leftover sauce can be served separately from a sauceboat.

FRANÇOIS VOEGELING
LA GASTRONOMIE ALSACIENNE

Tongue-and-Cider Turnovers

Empenadas de Galicia

The raisins are improved if they are plumped out first in a little sherry.

To serve 4

½ lb.	short-crust dough (recipe, page 166)	¼ kg.
¼ cup	milk or 1 egg, beaten with 2 tsp. [10 ml.] water	50 ml.

Tongue-and-cider filling

½ lb.	cooked beef tongue, finely chopped	¼ kg.
¼ cup	hard cider	50 ml.
¼ cup	pine nuts or blanched, peeled and crushed almonds	50 ml.
½ cup	raisins	125 ml.
1 tsp.	sugar	5 ml.
	salt	
	grated nutmeg	
	ground cloves	

Roll the dough out thin and cut it into eight 4-inch [10-cm.] rounds. Make the filling by blending all of the ingredients together thoroughly. Put about 1 tablespoon [15 ml.] of the mixture in the center of each round of dough, dampen the edges, fold the round in half and press down the edges. Make

two shallow, diagonal cuts in each turnover and brush the top with the milk or beaten egg. Grease a baking sheet and put the turnovers on it. Bake them in a preheated 375° F. [190° C.] oven for 15 to 20 minutes, or until the pastry is crisp and golden.

ANNA MACMIADHACHÁIN
SPANISH REGIONAL COOKERY

Chard, Sausage and Ricotta Pie

Torta di Verdura

To make one 10-inch [25-cm.] deep-dish pie

½ lb.	Italian sausages, peeled and the meat crumbled	¼ kg.
1 to 2 tbsp.	olive oil (optional)	15 to 30 ml.
2	medium-sized onions, finely chopped	2
4 lb.	Swiss chard, ribs removed, parboiled for 10 minutes, squeezed dry and chopped	2 kg.
1 ¼ cups	freshly grated Parmesan cheese	300 ml.
½ lb.	ricotta cheese	¼ kg.
4	eggs, lightly beaten	4
	salt	
	freshly ground black pepper	
1 lb.	short-crust dough (recipe, page 166)	½ kg.
1	egg white, lightly beaten	1

Fry the sausage meat, in the olive oil if the meat is lean, until it is browned—about eight to 10 minutes. Remove the sausage meat with a slotted spoon and set it aside. Remove all but 2 tablespoons [30 ml.] of the fat from the pan. Sauté the onions until they begin to color—about five minutes. Remove the pan from the heat, add the chard and mix it with the onions. Then add the Parmesan cheese, ricotta, eggs and sausage meat, and mix well. Add salt and pepper to taste.

Divide the short-crust dough in half. Return one half to the refrigerator, and roll out the other half to fit a 10-inch [25-cm.] pie plate. Brush the bottom and sides of the dough with the beaten egg white; reserve a small amount of the white to brush the top crust. Add the filling to the pie. Then roll out the other half of the dough and cover the pie with it, working as quickly as you can but taking time to make a decorative edge. With a small, sharp knife, make short cuts in the center of the lid so that steam can escape during cooking. Any remaining dough can be used to make decorative shapes for the lid. Brush the remaining egg white on the lid.

Bake the pie in a preheated 400° to 425° F. [200° to 220° C.] oven for 30 to 40 minutes. The pie will be a rich, golden color when it is done.

JOE FAMULARO AND LOUISE IMPERIALE
THE FESTIVE FAMULARO KITCHEN

Petit Patties

To make 12 tartlets

½ lb.	boneless ground veal	¼ kg.
8	slices bacon, finely chopped	8
½ lb.	finely chopped beef suet	¼ kg.
½ tsp.	salt	2 ml.
	pepper	
1 tbsp.	fines herbes	15 ml.
1 cup	chopped fresh mushrooms	¼ liter
1½ lb.	short-crust dough (recipe, page 166)	¾ kg.
1	egg yolk, beaten	1

In a bowl mix the veal, bacon and suet. Season with the salt, pepper and fines herbes; add the mushrooms. Put the mixture into a saucepan and, stirring, cook over medium heat for eight to 10 minutes, or until the mixture begins to brown.

Roll two thirds of the dough to a thickness of about ¼ inch [6 mm.] and use it to line 12 tartlet pans. Fill the pans with the meat mixture. Roll the rest of the dough and cut it to cover the tartlets. Cut a slit in the top of each tartlet. Glaze with the egg yolk and bake the tartlets in a preheated 400° F. [200° C.] oven for 30 minutes, or until they are golden brown.

WILLIAM AUGUSTUS HENDERSON
THE HOUSEKEEPER'S INSTRUCTOR, OR, UNIVERSAL FAMILY COOK

Small Hot Pies

Petits Pâtés Chauds

To make four 5-inch [13-cm.] pies

1 lb.	short-crust dough (recipe, page 166)	½ kg.
2	salt anchovies, filleted, soaked in water for 30 minutes, drained, patted dry and chopped	2
2	shallots, finely chopped	2
1	garlic clove, finely chopped	1
1 tbsp.	chopped fresh parsley	15 ml.
1 tbsp.	finely cut chives	15 ml.
2 tbsp.	olive oil	30 ml.
½ cup	finely chopped cooked veal	125 ml.
¼ lb.	ham, finely chopped	125 g.
2 oz.	beef marrow, finely chopped	60 g.
2	egg yolks, 1 beaten	2
	salt and pepper	
1 tbsp.	brandy	15 ml.

Roll out the dough and cut it into eight 5-inch [13-cm.] rounds. To make the filling, mix the anchovy fillets, shallots, garlic, parsley and chives, and pound them in a mortar. Add the oil and let the mixture marinate for 15 to 20 minutes.

Drain the anchovy mixture of excess oil and combine the mixture with the chopped meats and the beef marrow; mix well and bind with an egg yolk. Season with salt and pepper; take care not to oversalt. Moisten with the brandy. Spoon the filling onto four of the dough rounds. Cover with the remaining rounds. Moisten the edges of the dough with a little water and seal them carefully.

Place the pies on a buttered baking sheet. Then glaze them with the beaten egg yolk and bake them in a preheated 425° F. [220° C.] oven for 20 to 25 minutes, or until they are golden brown on top.

MICHEL BARBEROUSSE
CUISINE PROVENÇALE

Poor Man's Pie

Tourte au Pauvre Homme

To make one 9-inch [23-cm.] pie

1 lb.	short-crust dough (recipe, page 166)	½ kg.
3 tbsp.	butter or lard	45 ml.
1	onion, chopped	1
2 or 3	tomatoes, peeled, seeded and chopped	2 or 3
about 3 tbsp.	flour	about 45 ml.
8	Mediterranean-style black olives, pitted	8
1¼ cups	sliced fresh mushrooms	300 ml.
	chopped dried thyme leaves	
2 tbsp.	chopped fresh parsley	30 ml.
	salt and freshly ground black pepper	
1 lb.	mixed ground pork and finely chopped lean bacon (about 2 cups [½ liter])	½ kg.

Divide the dough into two pieces, one twice the size of the other. Use the larger piece to line a 9-inch [23-cm.] piepan.

Melt the butter or lard, and in it cook the onion until softened—about 10 minutes. Add the tomatoes and sprinkle in the flour; stir constantly until the sauce thickens. Add the olives, mushrooms, a pinch of thyme, the parsley, and salt and pepper. Simmer the mixture for 15 minutes. Remove it from the heat and stir in the pork and bacon.

Pour the mixture into the lined piepan. Roll out the reserved dough and use it to make a lid for the pie. Trim and seal the edges. Cut a ½-inch [1-cm.] hole in the center to let the steam escape. Bake the pie in a preheated 375° F. [190° C.] oven for 40 minutes, or until it is golden brown.

HUGUETTE CASTIGNAC
LA CUISINE OCCITANE

Anchovy Tart

Tarte aux Anchois

This is a Provençal dish. There, they call it *pissaladière*. They make it with bread dough instead of short-crust dough.

To make one 8-inch [20-cm.] square tart

¾ lb.	short-crust dough (recipe, page 166)	350 g.
2 cups	chopped onions	½ liter
6 tbsp.	olive oil	90 ml.
10	salt anchovies, filleted, soaked in water for 30 minutes and drained	10
7	ripe olives, preferably Mediterranean-style black olives, halved and pitted	7
2	small tomatoes, thinly sliced (optional)	2
	freshly ground black pepper	

Roll out the dough to a thickness of ¼ inch [6 mm.] and cut it into an 8-inch [20-cm.] square. Lay it on a buttered or oiled baking sheet. Roll the edges of the square inward to make a narrow rim. Prick the dough all over with a fork.

In a skillet, cook the onions in 4 tablespoons [60 ml.] of the olive oil until they are golden. Spread the onions over the dough. Arrange the anchovies over the onions in a lattice pattern and place a halved olive in the center of each square formed by the anchovies. Add tomato slices, if you like. Pepper the tart and sprinkle it with the remaining olive oil.

Bake the tart in a preheated 400° F. [200° C.] oven for about 30 minutes, or until the pastry is crisp and golden.

ÉDOUARD DE POMIANE
LE CARNET D'ANNA

Valencian Fish Turnovers

Empanadillas Valencianas

To make eight 4-inch [10-cm.] turnovers

2	medium-sized tomatoes, peeled, seeded and chopped	2
½ lb.	smoked haddock, poached in milk for 10 minutes, boned, skinned and flaked	¼ kg.
	salt and pepper	
1 lb.	olive-oil dough (recipe, page 166), 1 tbsp. [15 ml.] water replaced by 1 tbsp. anisette or Pernod	½ kg.
	olive oil (optional)	

Put the tomatoes in a skillet. Stirring frequently, simmer for 10 to 15 minutes to make a thick purée. Stir in the fish; season with salt and pepper. Let this filling mixture cool.

On a cool, floured work surface, roll out the dough into a thin sheet and cut out eight 4-inch [10-cm.] rounds with a pastry cutter. Measure 2 tablespoons [30 ml.] of the filling onto one side of each round. Moisten the edges of the rounds and fold over the dough to form turnovers, sealing the edges with the tines of a fork. Roll out the remaining dough again. Continue making turnovers until all the dough and filling have been used. Deep fry the turnovers in hot olive oil for five minutes on each side or bake them in a preheated 400° F. [200° C.] oven for 15 to 20 minutes, or until golden brown.

JAN READ AND MAITE MANJÓN
FLAVOURS OF SPAIN

Stuffed Fillets of Sole in Pastry Cases

Mignonettes de Soles Sultanes

The mushrooms can be poached with a little butter and lemon juice in enough water to cover them halfway, and their cooking liquid added to the liquid in which the fillets are poached.

To serve 8

1 lb.	sole fillets, skinned and halved lengthwise	½ kg.
¼ lb.	whiting fillets, made into a mousseline (recipe, page 164) with 1 egg white and 6 tbsp. [90 ml.] heavy cream	125 g.
½ cup	dry white wine	125 ml.
⅔ cup	fish stock (recipe, page 163)	150 ml.
8	fully baked tartlet shells, made from ½ lb. [¼ kg.] short-crust dough (recipe, page 166)	8
⅓ cup	pistachios, blanched, peeled, pounded and sieved or ground in a food processor	75 ml.
7 tbsp.	butter, cut into pieces	105 ml.
⅓ lb.	shrimp, poached for 3 minutes and shelled	150 g.
½ lb.	fresh button mushrooms, sliced and sautéed in 1 tbsp. [15 ml.] butter	¼ kg.

Lightly score the skin side of the halved sole fillets with parallel incisions spaced about 1 inch [2½ cm.] apart. Spread the scored side of the fillets with the whiting mousseline, and roll up the fillets. Put the fillets in a buttered shallow pan just large enough to hold them. Pour the wine and fish stock over them. Cut parchment paper to cover the pan. Butter it and fit it over the pan. Put a lid on the pan and poach the fillets very gently until they are cooked—about 12 minutes. Drain them, reserving the liquid, and keep them warm.

Put the tartlet shells into a preheated 250° F. [120° C.] oven to warm. In a saucepan over high heat, boil the fish cooking liquid until it is reduced to a syrupy consistency. Stir in the pistachios. Remove the pan from the heat and whisk in the butter. Place the shrimp and mushrooms in the warmed tartlet shells. Put a stuffed fillet of sole in each shell and pour the sauce over the fillets.

LE CORDON BLEU

Turbot Vol-au-vent

Steinbuttpastetchen

The technique of making vol-au-vent cases is demonstrated on pages 82-83. Any firm-fleshed white fish, such as halibut, angler or bass, can be substituted for turbot.

	To serve 4	
½ lb.	turbot fillets, skinned and cut into small pieces	¼ kg.
1 tbsp.	butter	15 ml.
2 tsp.	fresh lemon juice	10 ml.
1 to 2 tbsp.	water	15 to 30 ml.
6	fully baked 6-inch [15-cm.] vol-au-vent cases, made from 2 lb. [1 kg.] puff-pastry dough (recipe, page 167)	6
1¼ cups	hollandaise sauce (recipe, page 162)	300 ml.
½ tsp.	paprika	2 ml.

Place the turbot in a saucepan with 1 tablespoon [15 ml.] of the butter, the lemon juice and 1 tablespoon of water. Cook over very low heat for about 15 minutes, or until the fish is cooked through; add another spoonful of water, if necessary.

Warm the vol-au-vent cases in a preheated 250° F. [130° C.] oven. Remove any bones from the fish and coarsely flake the flesh. Place the vol-au-vent cases on a warmed platter and fill them with the flaked fish. Flavor the hollandaise sauce with paprika, and pour it over the fish. Put the pastry caps on the cases. Serve any remaining sauce separately.

ARNE KRÜGER AND ANNETTE WOLTER
KOCHEN HEUTE

Pye (à la Oli, the Provençal Way)

The author of this recipe, Vincent La Chapelle, was head cook to Lord Chesterfield. Although he was French, his cookery book was first published in English, in London, in 1733. Two years later, La Chapelle published a French translation. He is considered the leading French chef of his generation.

	To make one 8-inch [20-cm.] pie	
1 lb.	olive-oil puff dough (recipe, page 166)	½ kg.
3	salt anchovies, filleted, soaked in water for 30 minutes, drained, patted dry, finely chopped and pounded	3
1 lb.	fresh anchovies, cleaned, filleted and halved	½ kg.
	salt and pepper	
1	egg, beaten with 1 tsp. [5 ml.] water	1

Make the olive-oil puff dough, working in the pounded anchovies as you mix the flour with the liquid ingredients.

Then roll out half of the dough to a thickness of about ¼ inch [6 mm.] and use it to line an 8-inch [20-cm.] pie dish. Lay the halved fresh anchovies over the bottom of the pie shell until the surface is covered. Season them with salt and pepper.

From the remaining dough, roll out a strip the breadth of a thumb and put it around the edge of the pie. Roll out the rest of the dough until it is ⅛ inch [3 mm.] thick and cut it into 2-inch [5-cm.] squares; cover the anchovies with these squares. Glaze the pie with the beaten egg and bake it in a preheated 400° F. [200° C.] oven until golden brown but not too dry—about 35 minutes.

VINCENT LA CHAPELLE
THE MODERN COOK

Stargazey Pie

There are all kinds of variations on the basic recipe. Sometimes the undercrust is omitted, and the fish laid on a bed of bread crumbs, chopped onion and herbs, the plate being well buttered first. Sometimes cider or a custard of egg and cream is poured over the fish to make a moister pie.

	To make one 9-inch [23-cm.] pie	
1 lb.	short-crust dough (recipe, page 166)	½ kg.
8	large fresh sardines or medium-sized herring, gutted, boned and cleaned, heads left on	8
	salt and pepper	
6 tbsp.	finely chopped onion, mixed with 1 tbsp. [15 ml.] finely chopped fresh parsley and 1 tbsp. finely cut chives, or 2 tbsp. [30 ml.] Dijon mustard	90 ml.
8	slices bacon (optional)	8
2	hard-boiled eggs, chopped (optional)	2
3 tbsp.	warm milk mixed with ⅛ tsp. [½ ml.] powdered saffron, or 1 egg, beaten	45 ml.

Roll out half the dough in a circle and use it to line a 9-inch [23-cm.] buttered pie plate. Season each fish lavishly inside with salt and pepper, then either with the finely chopped onion and herbs or with the Dijon mustard. Fold them into shape again and arrange them on the dough so that the heads lie evenly around the rim. If you like, put the bacon slices and the hard-boiled eggs between the fish. Roll out the rest of the dough and cut a round blanket to cover the fish, all but their heads, so that the dough lid is the diameter of the plate less the rim. Press the dough down firmly between each pair of fish. Brush with saffron milk or beaten egg. Bake the pie in a preheated 400° F. [200° C.] oven for 30 minutes, then reduce the heat to 350° F. [180° C.] and bake for a further 15 minutes.

JANE GRIGSON
FISH COOKERY

Shrimp Quiche with Almonds

To roast almonds, place blanched and peeled almonds on a baking sheet and—stirring occasionally—bake them in a preheated 400° F. [200° C.] oven for 10 minutes, or until they are lightly browned.

To make one 10-inch [25-cm.] tart

½ lb.	shrimp, shelled, deveined and coarsely chopped	¼ kg.
¼ cup	chopped roasted almonds	50 ml.
1 cup	heavy cream	¼ liter
2 tbsp.	clam juice	30 ml.
2	eggs, lightly beaten	2
1	egg yolk, lightly beaten	1
⅛ tsp.	grated nutmeg	½ ml.
	salt	
1	fully baked tart shell, made from ¾ lb. [350 g.] short-crust dough (recipe, page 166)	1

Combine the shrimp, almonds, cream, clam juice, eggs, egg yolk, nutmeg and salt. Pour into the tart shell. Bake in a preheated 400° F. [200° C.] oven until light brown—25 to 30 minutes. Let the tart stand at room temperature for at least five minutes before serving.

BERT GREENE
BERT GREENE'S KITCHEN BOUQUETS

Vol-au-vent with Bay Scallops

The making of vol-au-vent cases is shown on pages 82-83.

To serve 6

1 cup	fish stock (recipe, page 163)	¼ liter
½ cup	dry vermouth	125 ml.
½ cup	heavy cream	125 ml.
1½ tbsp.	butter	22½ ml.
1 lb.	bay scallops, rinsed and patted dry	½ kg.
3 tbsp.	fresh chervil leaves	45 ml.
	coarse salt	
	freshly ground black pepper	
6	fully baked 6-inch [15-cm.] vol-au-vent cases, made from 2 lb. [1 kg.] puff-pastry dough (recipe, page 167)	6

Place the fish stock and vermouth in a nonreactive 1-quart [1-liter] saucepan. Bring to a boil and reduce to a glaze—this will take about 20 minutes. Add the cream. Stir and cook until this sauce is fairly thick—about 10 minutes.

Over moderately high heat, melt the butter in a skillet. When the butter is foamy, add the scallops and cook just until opaque—about two minutes. With a slotted spoon, remove the scallops to a dish and keep them warm. Pour the liquid from the skillet into the saucepan with the cream sauce. Cook until the sauce is reduced to its original thickness. Add 2 tablespoons [30 ml.] of the chervil, the scallops, and salt and pepper to taste.

Slice the tops off the vol-au-vent cases and place the bottoms on individual serving plates. If the pastry is not cooked through, pull out and discard the uncooked middle. Divide the scallop mixture among the cases. Top with the remaining chervil and freshly ground black pepper. Brush the browned pastry tops with softened butter and place them over the filled bottoms.

TOM MARGITTAI AND PAUL KOVI
THE FOUR SEASONS

Poached Eggs Skabeleff

Oeufs Pochés Skabeleff

The technique of poaching eggs is shown on pages 64-65.

To serve 4

1½ cups	mayonnaise (recipe, page 161)	375 ml.
1 tsp.	anchovy paste	5 ml.
5 oz.	shrimp, poached in 3 cups [¾ liter] boiling salted water for 4 to 5 minutes, drained, peeled and coarsely chopped (about ⅔ cup [150 ml.])	150 g.
2 tsp.	puréed tomato	10 ml.
4	fully baked 4-inch [10-cm.] tartlet shells made from ½ lb. [¼ kg.] short-crust dough (recipe, page 166)	4
4	eggs, poached	4
1	thin slice smoked salmon (about 2 oz. [60 g.])	1

Mix 6 tablespoons [90 ml.] of the mayonnaise with the anchovy paste. Stir in the chopped shrimp and taste for seasoning. To the rest of the mayonnaise, add enough puréed tomato to color and flavor it. Divide the shrimp mixture among the four tartlet shells. Place one poached egg in each tartlet shell. Coat the eggs with the tomato mayonnaise. Cut the smoked salmon into thin strips and use them to decorate the tartlets.

ANNE WILLAN AND JANE GRIGSON (EDITORS)
THE OBSERVER FRENCH COOKERY SCHOOL

Cantal Cheese Tart

Flan de l'Aubrac

The tart shell can also be baked blind as demonstrated on page 76. Cantal cheese is a hard, pressed French cheese; if it is not available, either Cheddar or Gruyère cheese can be substituted.

To make one 10-inch [25-cm.] tart

1	unbaked tart shell, made from ¾ lb. [350 g.] short-crust dough (recipe, page 166)	1
2 tbsp.	butter	30 ml.
1 cup	heavy cream	¼ liter
	salt and pepper	
	grated nutmeg	
⅓ cup	flour	75 ml.
3	eggs, the yolks separated from the whites, and the whites stiffly beaten	3
5 oz.	Cantal cheese, finely shredded (about 1¼ cups [300 ml.])	150 g.

In a saucepan, gently heat the butter and cream. Season with salt and pepper and a pinch of nutmeg. Sprinkle the flour into the pan and, stirring constantly, cook over low heat until the mixture thickens. Remove the pan from the heat and beat in the egg yolks and cheese. Fold in the egg whites gently.

Pour the cheese mixture into the tart shell and bake the tart in a preheated 350° F. [180° C.] oven for 45 minutes, or until the top is golden brown.

SUZANNE SIMONET
LE GRAND LIVRE DE LA CUISINE OCCITANE

Lorraine Tart

Flan Lorrain

To make one 8-inch [20-cm.] tart

1	partially baked tart shell, made from ½ lb. [¼ kg.] rough puff dough (recipe, page 166)	1
5	slices lean bacon, finely chopped	5
1 tbsp.	butter	15 ml.
½ cup	finely diced Gruyère cheese	125 ml.
1	egg, lightly beaten	1
2	egg yolks, lightly beaten	2
1 cup	heavy cream	¼ liter
	salt and white pepper	

Over low heat, fry the bacon in the butter until lightly browned. Remove it from the heat and add the Gruyère

cheese. Beat the egg and egg yolks into the cream, and season with salt and pepper to taste.

Spread the bacon-and-cheese mixture evenly over the bottom of the tart shell. Pour in the cream-and-egg mixture. Bake the tart in a preheated 350° F. [180° C.] oven for about 20 minutes, or until the pastry is golden brown and the filling just set. Serve immediately.

PAUL BOUILLARD
LA CUISINE AU COIN DU FEU

Auvergne Cheese Soufflé

Soufflé au Bleu d'Auvergne

If bleu d'Auvergne cheese is not available, use another blue-veined cheese, such as Roquefort or Stilton. The technique of baking a pastry blind, or empty, is shown on page 76. If the soufflé is made in a cake pan with a removable bottom, the soufflé can be unmolded for serving. The soufflé can also be made without the pastry case.

To serve 5 or 6

½ lb.	short-crust dough (recipe, page 166)	¼ kg.
4	celery ribs, boiled for 5 minutes, cut into matchstick-sized strips	4
1 tbsp.	butter	15 ml.
2 cups	thick white sauce (recipe, page 162), cooled until tepid	½ liter
5	eggs, the yolks separated from the whites, and the whites stiffly beaten	5
	salt and pepper	
	nutmeg	
2½ cups	crumbled bleu d'Auvergne cheese	625 ml.

Roll out the pastry and use it to line a buttered 1-quart [1-liter] soufflé dish. Bake the pastry blind in a preheated 375° F. [190° C.] oven for 15 minutes, or until it is cooked but not colored.

Sauté the celery in the butter. To the thick white sauce, add the egg yolks, one at a time, stirring constantly, then season with salt, pepper and nutmeg. Stir in the celery and the crumbled cheese. Then fold the stiffly beaten egg whites into the mixture. Pour it into the pie shell and bake the soufflé in a preheated 325° F. [160° C.] oven for 35 to 40 minutes, or until golden brown and well risen.

AMICALE DES CUISINIERS ET PÂTISSIERS AUVERGNATS DE PARIS
CUISINE D'AUVERGNE

Neapolitan Escarole and Black-Olive Bread

Tortino Ripieno di Scarole e Olive

To make one 10-inch [25-cm.] round loaf

¼ oz.	package active dry yeast or ³/₅ oz. [18 g.] cake fresh yeast	7½ g.
½ tsp.	sugar, dissolved in ¼ cup [50 ml.] tepid water	2 ml.
2 cups	flour, sifted	½ liter
5 tbsp.	lard or butter, melted and cooled	75 ml.
1 tsp.	salt	5 ml.
¼ tsp.	freshly ground black pepper	1 ml.
1	egg white, lightly beaten with 1 tsp. [5 ml.] water	1

Escarole and olive filling

5 tbsp.	olive oil	75 ml.
3 or 4	very small heads escarole or 1 large head, cored and cut into thin shreds	3 or 4
1 cup	Mediterranean-style black olives, rinsed, pitted and chopped	¼ liter
½ cup	seedless white raisins, soaked in warm water for 15 minutes and drained	125 ml.
½ cup	pine nuts	125 ml.
1 tbsp.	capers, rinsed and drained	15 ml.
1	garlic clove, chopped	1
2 or 3 tbsp.	chopped fresh parsley	30 or 45 ml.
	salt and pepper	

Dissolve the yeast in the sugared tepid water. Set the mixture in a warm place until it is bubbly—about 15 minutes. Place the flour in a mixing bowl. Make a deep hollow in the center. Add the bubbling yeast mixture, 3 tablespoons [45 ml.] of the lard or butter, the salt and pepper. Work and knead for about 10 minutes to form a smooth, elastic dough, adding more flour or tepid water as necessary. Cover the dough lightly with a damp towel and let it rise in a warm place for one hour, or until doubled in bulk.

Meanwhile, in a large, heavy enameled saucepan or casserole, heat 4 tablespoons [60 ml.] of the olive oil. Add the shredded escarole and cook it, stirring, for 10 minutes or until most of the liquid in the pan has evaporated. Add the olives, raisins, pine nuts, capers, garlic and parsley. Continue cooking for about 10 minutes, stirring often. Season well with pepper and a little salt. Remove the mixture from the pan. Drain all excess liquid from the mixture and let it cool to room temperature.

Punch down the dough in the bowl, turn it out onto a lightly floured board and knead it for three minutes. Work in the remaining lard, and continue to knead until the dough is smooth, about five minutes. Divide the dough into two equal pieces. Roll out one piece into a round about 12 inches [30 cm.] across and lightly press it into an oiled 10-inch [25-cm.] cake pan. Spread the filling evenly over the dough and cover with the remaining piece of dough, rolled out to fit over the top. Press and push the dough to ensure that it covers the filling completely. Brush the top with the remaining 1 tablespoon [15 ml.] of oil, cover the bread with a towel and let it rise a second time in a warm place for about 20 minutes, until almost doubled in bulk. Then brush the top of the bread with the egg white beaten with water. This will make a shiny crust. Bake the bread in a preheated 375° F. [190° C.] oven for about 45 minutes, or until golden brown and well risen. Serve lukewarm or cold.

PAULA WOLFERT
MEDITERRANEAN COOKING

Cabbage and Mushroom Pie

Kulebiak z Kapusta i Grzybami

To make one 10-by-6-inch [25-by-15-cm.] pie

1	medium-sized cabbage	1
2 tbsp.	butter	30 ml.
1	medium-sized onion, sliced	1
1 oz.	dried Polish mushrooms (about ⅓ cup [75 ml.]), soaked for 1 hour in ⅔ cup [150 ml.] water	30 g.
4	eggs, 3 hard-boiled and chopped, 1 beaten	4
	salt and pepper	
1 lb.	rich egg-bread dough (recipe, page 165)	½ kg.

Parboil the whole cabbage in salted water for five minutes, drain and shred it. In a saucepan, melt the butter and add the cabbage and onion, then stew until the cabbage is tender—about 10 minutes. Remove the pan from the heat.

Simmer the mushrooms in their soaking water until tender, about 20 minutes, then chop them and add them to the cabbage. Add the hard-boiled eggs. Season to taste and mix thoroughly.

When the rich egg-bread dough has had its final rising, divide it in half and roll each piece into a 10-by-8-inch [25-by-20-cm.] rectangle. Lay one rectangle on a buttered and floured baking sheet. Spread the filling evenly over the rectangle, leaving a 2-inch [5-cm.] margin all around the dough. Cover with the second rectangle of dough and press the edges firmly together.

Brush the pie with beaten egg. Bake the pie in a preheated 425° F. [220° C.] oven for about 20 minutes, or until it is golden brown.

MARJA OCHOROWICZ-MONATOWA
POLISH COOKERY

Polish Rice and Mushroom Pie

Kulebiak z Ciasta
Krucho-Drożdżowego z Rýzem i Grzybami

To make one 12-by-4-inch [30-by-10-cm.] pie

1 oz.	dried Polish mushrooms (about ⅓ cup [75 ml.]), washed and soaked for 4 hours in ⅔ cup [150 ml.] water	30 g.
1 cup	white rice	¼ liter
	salt	
3 tbsp.	butter	45 ml.
⅓ cup	finely chopped onion	75 ml.
2	eggs, hard-boiled and chopped	2
	pepper	

Egg dough

¼ oz.	package active dry yeast or ⅗ oz. [18 g.] cake fresh yeast	7½ g.
1 tsp.	sugar	5 ml.
½ lb.	bread flour	¼ kg.
5 tbsp.	butter	75 ml.
2	whole eggs, plus 2 egg yolks, beaten separately	2
	salt	
¼ cup	heavy cream	50 ml.

First prepare the filling. Simmer the dried mushrooms in the soaking liquid for 20 minutes, or until they are tender. Drain the mushrooms, reserving the cooking liquid.

Place the rice in a saucepan and add 2 cups [½ liter] of liquid—use the reserved liquid from the mushrooms, plus enough boiling water to produce the right volume. Season the rice and liquid with salt, add half of the butter and bring the mixture to a boil. Simmer it for 20 minutes, or until all of the liquid has been absorbed.

Fry the onion to a light golden color in the remaining butter. Add the hard-boiled eggs to the cooked rice, together with the mushrooms, onion, salt and pepper.

To make the dough, first mix the cake yeast with the sugar and let stand for two or three minutes until the mixture liquefies. (If using active dry yeast, add 3 tablespoons [45 ml.] of tepid water.) Sift the flour onto a board. Using a knife, blend the butter with the flour. Add the egg yolks, one of the eggs, a pinch of salt, the yeast mixture and the cream. Continue chopping and folding the mixture with the knife until it forms a cohesive dough. Knead the dough until it is smooth—about five minutes—then roll it out into a rectangle about 12 by 8 inches [30 by 20 cm.] and ½ inch [1 cm.] thick. Lay it on a buttered and floured baking sheet.

Spread the filling down the center of the dough rectangle. Fold over the two longer sides of the rectangle to the center,

pinching them together firmly between thumb and finger, to make a raised, decorative seam.

Leave this pie in a warm place about one and one half hours until it rises to nearly twice its size. Brush the pie with the remaining beaten egg. Bake it in a preheated 350° F. [180° C.] oven for about one hour, until it is lightly browned. Place the pie on a warmed platter and let stand 15 minutes before slicing it into portions. Serve it hot with melted butter or with tomato or mushroom sauce.

HELEN HAWLICZKOWA
KUCHNIA POLSKA

Anchovy and Tomato Pie

Sardenaira

To make one 12-inch [30-cm.] pie

¼ oz.	package active dry yeast or ⅗ oz. [18 g.] cake fresh yeast	7½ g.
½ cup	tepid water	125 ml.
4 cups	flour	1 liter
½ cup	milk	125 ml.
3 tbsp.	olive oil	45 ml.

Anchovy and tomato filling

1 lb.	salt anchovies, filleted, soaked in water for 30 minutes, drained, patted dry and chopped	½ kg.
6	medium-sized tomatoes, peeled, seeded and finely chopped, or 1½ cups [375 ml.] tomato sauce (recipe, page 162)	6
1 tbsp.	capers	15 ml.
3 tbsp.	olive oil	45 ml.
12	Mediterranean-style black olives, halved and pitted	12
3	garlic cloves	3
1 tbsp.	crumbled dried oregano	15 ml.

Dissolve the yeast in 2 tablespoons [30 ml.] of the water. Put the flour on a board, make a well in the center, add the yeast, and mix to make a dough, gradually adding the remaining water, the milk and the olive oil. Knead the dough, cover it, and let it rise for one hour, or until doubled in bulk.

Meanwhile, prepare the filling. In a large bowl, mix the anchovies, tomatoes, capers and olive oil. When the dough has risen well, take a heavy, shallow piepan or pizza pan, or best of all, the Italian copper pan known as a *testo*, and oil it thoroughly. Spread the dough out in the dish with your hands, pressing it down with your fingers in a layer no more than ½ inch [1 cm.] thick. Spread a generous layer of filling over the dough. Dot the filling with the olive halves, pressing them down lightly. Finally, stick in the garlic cloves here and there, and finish with a sprinkling of oregano. Bake in a preheated 450° F. [230° C.] oven for 45 minutes to one hour, or until the edges of the dough are golden brown.

LUIGI VOLPICELLI AND SECONDINO FREDA (EDITORS)
L'ANTIARTUSI: 1000 RICETTE

———————◆———————

Neapolitan Turnover

Chausson à la Napolitaine

Pecorino Romano is a hard Italian sheep's-milk cheese obtainable at cheese specialty stores.

The *calzone*, a turnover made with olive-oil bread dough, is a specialty of the Campania region of Italy of which Naples is the chief town. Instead of one large turnover, several small ones may be made. In the latter case, the turnovers should be deep fried in very hot olive oil for only three minutes.

To make one 15-inch [38-cm.] turnover or 8 small turnovers

1 cup	ricotta cheese, sieved	¼ liter
1 cup	diced mozzarella cheese	¼ liter
1	egg	1
	salt and pepper	
⅔ cup	freshly grated pecorino Romano or Parmesan cheese	150 ml.
¼ lb.	Italian salami, thinly sliced, or prosciutto, cut into thin strips about 1 inch [2½ cm.] long	125 g.
1¼ lb.	basic bread dough *(recipe, page 165)*, made with 1 to 2 tablespoons [15 to 30 ml.] of olive oil	600 g.

Put the ricotta cheese into a bowl with the diced mozzarella, egg, salt and pepper to taste, the pecorino Romano or Parmesan cheese, and the salami or prosciutto. Mix lightly.

Oil a large baking sheet. Roll out the dough into a round about ¼ inch [6 mm.] thick and lay it on the baking sheet; slightly raise the edges of the dough to hold the filling. Spread the filling evenly over the dough. Then fold the dough in two to make a turnover. Moisten the edges of the dough and press them together securely. Bake in a preheated 425° F. [220° C.] oven for 30 minutes, or until the turnover is golden brown.

PIERRE ANDROUET
LA CUISINE AU FROMAGE

———————◆———————

Old-fashioned Quiche Lorraine

Fiouse è lè Flemme

This yeast-dough pie was originally baked on the embers of the oven before they had cooled sufficiently to make bread; *hence its name, which in English means "flame cake." This version comes from Metz, the capital of Lorraine. The author recommends making the filling with a very light oil, such as safflower or sunflower oil.*

To make one 10-inch [25-cm.] quiche

1 lb.	basic bread dough *(recipe, page 165)*	½ kg.
1	egg	1
3 to 4 tbsp.	oil	45 to 60 ml.
	salt	
5	slices lean bacon, diced (optional)	5
2	onions, finely chopped (optional)	2

Prepare the bread dough in the usual way and let it rise once.

To prepare the filling, beat the egg with the oil and a pinch of salt, and stir in the bacon and onions, if using. Roll out the bread dough into a fairly thick round about 10 inches [25 cm.] across, and press it into a buttered 10-inch tart or pizza pan. Pour in the filling. Bake the quiche in a preheated 425° F. [220° C.] oven for 15 minutes; then reduce the temperature to 375° F. [190° C.], cover the quiche with buttered aluminum foil and bake for 10 minutes longer. The dough should be browned and risen and the bacon and onions—if used—cooked through. Serve hot.

E. AURICOSTE DE LAZARQUE
CUISINE MESSINE

———————◆———————

Creamy Scrambled-Egg Brioches

The technique of making brioches is shown on page 88.

To serve 4

4	individual brioches, made with 1 lb. [½ kg.] rich egg-bread dough *(recipe, page 165)*	4
4	eggs, beaten	4
	salt and pepper	
4 tbsp.	butter, cubed	60 ml.

Warm the brioches in a preheated 325° F. [160° C.] oven. Meanwhile, season the beaten eggs with salt and pepper. Transfer the eggs to a saucepan. Place a rack inside a casserole, stand the pan of eggs on the rack and pour enough boiling water into the casserole to come two thirds of the way up the sides of the pan. Turn on the heat to keep the water at a simmer. Add the butter. With a wooden spoon, stir the eggs as the butter melts; scrape the bottom and sides of the pan where the eggs set first. When the eggs have thickened and become opaque and creamy, remove the pan from the water bath. Continue to stir the eggs for a minute or so. Remove the caps of the brioches and scrape out the interiors with a small spoon. Fill the hollowed-out brioches with the eggs, replace the caps and serve immediately.

MAPIE DE TOULOUSE-LAUTREC
LA CUISINE DE MAPIE

Stuffed Brioches

The technique of making brioches is shown on page 88.

	To serve 8	
8	individual brioches, made with 1 lb. [½ kg.] rich egg-bread dough *(recipe, page 165)*	8
2	eggs, beaten	2
1½ cups	fresh mushrooms, trimmed, blanched for 2 minutes, drained and cut into small pieces	375 ml.
1	thin slice ham, coarsely chopped	1
½ cup	sour cream	125 ml.
⅔ cup	grated Gruyère cheese	150 ml.
	salt	
	pepper	

Remove the tops of the brioches and scoop out most of the interior carefully, so as not to puncture the shell. Crush or grind half of the crumbs until fine and put them into a bowl. Add the beaten eggs, the mushrooms, ham, sour cream and cheese; mix well. Add salt and pepper to taste. Fill the brioches with this mixture and replace the tops. Heat the stuffed brioches in a preheated 325° F. [160° C.] oven for about 10 minutes. They should be very hot, but the filling should remain creamy.

MAPIE DE TOULOUSE-LAUTREC
LA CUISINE DE MAPIE

Sausage in Brioche

Saucisson Brioché

The original version of this recipe called for a truffled cervelas sausage, which is a large French poaching sausage. Any mild-flavored boiling sausage—2 to 3 inches [5 to 8 cm.] in diameter—can be substituted. The technique for making a sausage in brioche is demonstrated on pages 86-87.

	To make one 10-inch [25-cm.] brioche	
2 quarts	meat stock *(recipe, page 163)* or water	2 liters
1	boiling sausage (1 lb. [½ kg.]), pricked thoroughly with a fork	1
½ cup	flour	125 ml.
1 lb.	rich egg-bread dough *(recipe, page 165)*	½ kg.
1	egg yolk, beaten	1

Heat the stock or water, skim it, and bring it to a boil. Drop the sausage into the liquid, and reduce the heat immediately so that the cooking liquid is at a bare simmer. Cook the sausage for 30 to 40 minutes, depending on its thickness. Remove it from the cooking liquid, and peel it carefully by making a long incision down its length and pulling the skin away to either side. Dust the hot sausage liberally with flour and set it aside.

Roll out and trim the dough into two long strips approximately 4 inches [10 cm.] wide. Wrap the sausage by winding the dough strips around it in a spiral. Moisten the ends and seams of the dough with a little water, and seal them securely. Put the assembly on a buttered baking sheet, brush the dough with the egg yolk, diluted by a little water, and set the assembly aside in a warm place for about two hours, or until the dough has almost doubled.

Glaze the dough again and bake the brioche in a preheated 425° F. [220° C.] oven. The brioche should be golden brown and well risen. Transfer the brioche to a serving dish and serve it hot.

A. DELPLANQUE AND S. CLOTEAUX
LES BASES DE LA CHARCUTERIE

Standard Preparations

Vinaigrette

The proportion of vinegar to oil may be varied according to taste. Lemon juice may be substituted for the vinegar.

	To make about ½ cup [125 ml.] vinaigrette	
1 tsp.	salt	5 ml.
¼ tsp.	freshly ground pepper	1 ml.
2 tbsp.	wine vinegar	30 ml.
½ cup	oil	125 ml.

Put the salt and pepper into a small bowl. Add the vinegar and stir until the salt dissolves. Finally, stir in the oil.

Garlic vinaigrette. Pound half of a garlic clove to a purée with the salt and pepper before adding the vinegar.

Mustard vinaigrette. Mix about 1 teaspoon [5 ml.] of Dijon mustard with the salt and pepper. Add the vinegar and stir until the mustard dissolves before adding the oil.

Tomato vinaigrette. Add 2 tablespoons [30 ml.] of cooked, reduced puréed tomato to the prepared vinaigrette.

Green vinaigrette. Before adding the oil, stir in 2 tablespoons of cooked spinach, squeezed dry and puréed through a sieve, plus 1 tablespoon [15 ml.] of fines herbes.

Vinaigrette with egg. Before adding the oil, stir in the yolk of a soft-boiled egg. The egg white may be chopped and added to the prepared vinaigrette.

Other variations. Any vinaigrette may be combined with chopped fresh herbs (such as parsley, fines herbes, basil, mint, marjoram or hyssop), capers, chopped shallots or the juices from broiled sweet peppers.

Handmade Mayonnaise

To prevent curdling, the egg yolks and oil should be at room temperature and the oil should be added very gradually at first. The prepared mayonnaise will keep for several days if refrigerated in a covered container. Stir it well before use.

To make about 2 cups [½ liter] mayonnaise		
3	egg yolks	3
	salt and white pepper	
1 tbsp.	wine vinegar or strained fresh lemon juice	15 ml.
about 2 cups	oil	about ½ liter

Put the egg yolks in a bowl. Season with a little salt and pepper and whisk for about a minute, or until the yolks turn slightly paler in color. Add the vinegar or lemon juice and whisk until thoroughly mixed. Add the oil, drop by drop to begin with, whisking constantly. When the sauce starts to thicken, pour the remaining oil in a thin, steady stream, whisking rhythmically. The mayonnaise should be firm enough to hold its shape on the whisk.

Green mayonnaise. Parboil 1 cup [¼ liter] of trimmed spinach or watercress leaves for one to two minutes; drain the leaves, refresh them in cold water and squeeze them dry. Chop the leaves fine, then purée them in a food processor. Stir the purée into the prepared mayonnaise, along with 1 tablespoon [15 ml.] of mixed chopped tarragon, chives, chervil and parsley.

Mustard mayonnaise. Add 1 to 2 teaspoons [5 to 10 ml.] of Dijon mustard to the yolks with the vinegar or lemon juice.

Herb mayonnaise. Stir about 1 teaspoon [5 ml.] each of finely chopped fresh tarragon, chives, chervil and parsley into the prepared mayonnaise.

Red pepper mayonnaise. Prepare mayonnaise, using 2 teaspoons [10 ml.] of vinegar or lemon juice. Stir in one sweet red pepper that has been broiled, peeled, seeded, deribbed and either chopped fine by hand or puréed in a food processor.

Remoulade sauce. Combine ¼ cup [50 ml.] of chopped sour gherkins, ⅓ cup [75 ml.] of chopped fresh parsley, 2 tablespoons [30 ml.] of chopped capers, 1 tablespoon [15 ml.] of chopped fresh tarragon, 2 tablespoons of lemon juice, 1 tablespoon of Dijon mustard, salt and pepper. Stir the mixture into the prepared mayonnaise.

Blender or Processor Mayonnaise

To form an emulsion, the egg and oil should both be at room temperature. The basic mayonnaise may be turned into a rémoulade or green mayonnaise, or flavored with garlic, mustard, herbs or sweet red peppers as described for Handmade Mayonnaise *(left).*

To make about 1 ½ cups [375 ml.] mayonnaise		
1	egg	1
2 tsp.	vinegar or strained fresh lemon juice	10 ml.
	salt and white pepper	
1 to 1 ½ cups	oil	250 to 375 ml.

Combine the egg, vinegar or lemon juice, and salt and pepper in the jar of an electric blender or the bowl of a food processor. Cover and blend for a few seconds to mix the ingredients thoroughly. Without stopping the machine, pour in the oil in a slow stream through the hole in the lid of the blender or through the tube of the processor. Add 1 cup [¼ liter] of oil for a soft mayonnaise, up to 1½ cups [375 ml.] for a firm one.

Turn off the machine and use a rubber spatula to transfer the mayonnaise to a bowl. Taste and add more seasonings, vinegar or lemon juice if desired. Tightly covered, the mayonnaise can be kept refrigerated for three days.

Basil Sauce

Pesto

To make 1 ½ to 2 cups [375 to 500 ml.] sauce		
3	garlic cloves	3
2 cups	tightly packed fresh basil leaves	½ liter
1 cup	freshly grated Parmesan cheese	¼ liter
2 tbsp.	pine nuts	30 ml.
¾ to 1 cup	olive oil	175 to 250 ml.
	salt and pepper	

In a mortar, pound together the garlic cloves and basil leaves until the mixture is reduced to a pulp. Add the cheese and pine nuts, and continue pounding until the mixture forms a wet paste. Pound in the olive oil a little at a time to dilute the pesto to a thick sauce. Add salt and pepper to taste.

Alternatively, purée the garlic and pine nuts in a food processor. Add the basil and Parmesan cheese and process the mixture until it is smooth. Without stopping the machine, add ¾ cup [175 ml.] of the oil in a steady stream. If the sauce is too thick, mix in a little more oil. Season with salt and pepper to taste.

White Sauce

To make about 1 ½ cups [375 ml.] sauce

2 tbsp.	butter	30 ml.
2 tbsp.	flour	30 ml.
2 cups	milk	½ liter
	salt	
	pepper	
	freshly grated nutmeg (optional)	
	heavy cream (optional)	

Melt the butter in a heavy saucepan. Stir in the flour and cook, stirring, over low heat for two to five minutes. Pour in all of the milk, whisking constantly to blend the mixture smooth. Increase the heat and continue whisking while the sauce comes to a boil. Season with a little salt. Reduce the heat to very low and simmer for about 40 minutes, stirring occasionally to prevent the sauce from sticking to the pan. Add pepper and a pinch of nutmeg if desired; taste for seasoning. Whisk again until the sauce is perfectly smooth, and add cream if you prefer a richer and whiter sauce.

Thick white sauce for stuffings and soufflé bases. Make the sauce as above, but use double the amounts of butter and flour. Cook the sauce until it is almost too thick to pour—about 10 minutes—stirring constantly to prevent sticking.

Very thick white sauce for deep frying. Melt 8 tablespoons [120 ml.] of butter and stir in ⅔ cup [150 ml.] of flour. Cook the mixture, stirring constantly, for two minutes. Pour in 2 cups [½ liter] of milk and whisk for five minutes.

Tomato Sauce

When fresh, ripe summer tomatoes are not available, use canned Italian-style plum tomatoes.

To make about 1 cup [¼ liter] sauce

1	medium-sized onion, diced	1
1 tbsp.	olive oil	15 ml.
5	medium-sized ripe tomatoes, chopped	5
1	garlic clove (optional)	1
1 tsp.	chopped fresh parsley	5 ml.
1 tsp.	mixed basil, marjoram and thyme	5 ml.
1 to 2 tsp.	sugar (optional)	5 to 10 ml.
	salt and freshly ground pepper	

In a large enameled or stainless-steel saucepan, gently fry the diced onion in the oil until soft but not brown. Add the other ingredients and simmer for 20 to 30 minutes, or until the tomatoes have been reduced to a thick pulp. Sieve, using a wooden pestle or spoon. Reduce the sauce further, if necessary, to the required consistency, and check the seasoning.

White Butter Sauce

To make about 1 ½ cups [375 ml.] sauce

⅓ cup	dry white wine	75 ml.
⅓ cup	white wine vinegar	75 ml.
3	shallots, very finely chopped	3
	salt and pepper	
½ to ¾ lb.	unsalted butter, chilled and finely diced	¼ to ½ kg.

In a heavy, stainless-steel or enameled saucepan, boil the wine and vinegar with the shallots and a pinch of salt until only enough liquid remains to moisten the shallots. Remove the pan from the heat and let it cool for a few minutes. Season the mixture with pepper.

Place the pan on a heat-diffusing pad set over very low heat and whisk in the butter, a handful at a time, whisking after each addition until the mixture has a creamy consistency. Remove the sauce from the heat as soon as all of the butter has been incorporated.

Hollandaise Sauce

To make about 1 cup [¼ liter] sauce

3	large egg yolks	3
1 tbsp.	cold water	15 ml.
12 tbsp.	unsalted butter, chilled and cut into small pieces	180 ml.
	salt and white pepper	
	cayenne pepper	
1 tsp.	strained fresh lemon juice	5 ml.

Pour water to a depth of about 1 inch [2½ cm.] into the bottom of a double boiler—or a large pan or fireproof casserole, if you are making a water bath. Heat the water until it simmers, then reduce the heat to low. Place the top of the double boiler over the bottom, or set a rack or trivet into the pan or casserole and place a smaller pan on the rack or trivet. Put the egg yolks and the cold water in the upper pan and beat the yolks until they are smooth. Whisk a handful of the butter into the yolks and beat until the butter has been absorbed; continue adding butter in this way until all of it has been used. Beat until the sauce becomes thick and creamy. Season the sauce to taste with salt, white pepper and cayenne pepper. Then add the lemon juice.

Béarnaise sauce. In a small saucepan over high heat, combine ½ cup [125 ml.] of dry white wine, 2 tablespoons [30 ml.] of tarragon vinegar, 2 tablespoons each of finely chopped fresh tarragon, parsley and shallots, ¼ teaspoon [1 ml.] of salt and ⅛ teaspoon [½ ml.] of pepper. Bring the mixture to a boil, reduce the heat and simmer until the liquid is almost completely absorbed. Stir the herb mixture into the prepared hollandaise.

Velouté Sauce

To make about 1 cup [¼ liter] sauce

2 tbsp.	butter	30 ml.
2 tbsp.	flour	30 ml.
2 cups	meat or fish stock	½ liter

Melt the butter in a heavy saucepan over low heat. Stir in the flour to make a roux and cook, stirring, for two to three minutes. Pour the stock into the pan, whisking constantly. Increase the heat and whisk until the sauce comes to a boil.

Reduce the heat to low, and move the saucepan half off the heat so that the liquid on only one side of the pan simmers. A fatty skin will form on the still side. Remove the skin periodically with a spoon. Cook the sauce for 30 to 40 minutes to reduce it and to eliminate the taste of flour.

Egg-enriched velouté. In a small bowl, whisk together two egg yolks with 2 tablespoons [30 ml.] of strained fresh lemon juice. Stir in a few spoonfuls of the hot velouté sauce. Over low heat, stir the egg-velouté mixture into the remaining velouté sauce. Continue stirring until the sauce thickens to the consistency of pouring custard—two to three minutes.

Meat Stock

This general-purpose stock will keep for up to a week if refrigerated and brought to a boil every two days. Or it may be packed in containers and kept frozen for up to six months.

To make about 3 quarts [3 liters]

2 lb.	meaty beef shank	1 kg.
2 lb.	meaty veal shank	1 kg.
2 lb.	chicken backs, necks and wing tips	1 kg.
about 5 quarts	water	about 5 liters
1	bouquet garni, including leek and celery	1
1	garlic bulb, unpeeled	1
2	medium-sized onions, each stuck with 1 whole clove	2
4	carrots	4

Place a trivet or a rack in the bottom of a large stockpot to prevent the ingredients from sticking. Fit all of the meat, bones and chicken pieces into the pot and add cold water to cover by about 2 inches [5 cm.]. Bring slowly to a boil, skimming off the scum that rises. Keep skimming, occasionally adding a glass of cold water, until no more scum rises. Do not stir, lest you cloud the stock.

Add the bouquet garni, garlic, onions and carrots, and skim once more as the liquid returns to a boil. Reduce the heat to very low, cover the pot with the lid ajar, and simmer for five hours. If the meat is to be eaten, remove the veal after one and one half hours, the beef after three hours.

Ladle the stock into a colander lined with dampened muslin or cheesecloth and placed over a large bowl. Let the strained stock cool completely, then remove the last traces of fat from the surface. If the stock has been refrigerated to cool, lift off the solidified fat.

Lamb stock. Omit the beef bones and chicken pieces, and use 6 to 7 pounds [3 to 3½ kg.] of lamb bones, including the shank and neck, and a veal shank. Simmer for five hours.

Veal stock. Omit the beef, beef bones and chicken pieces, and substitute 4 pounds [2 kg.] of meaty veal trimmings (neck, shank or rib tips). For a richer, more gelatinous stock, add a calf's foot that has been cleaned, split and blanched for five minutes in boiling water. Simmer for five hours.

Beef stock. Substitute 4 pounds [2 kg.] of oxtail, beef shank or beef chuck for the veal shank and the chicken pieces, and simmer the stock for five hours. A veal knuckle or calf's foot can be added for a more gelatinous stock.

Chicken stock. Stewing chickens and roosters yield the richest stock. Use 5 pounds [2½ kg.] of carcasses, necks, feet, wings, gizzards and hearts, and simmer for two hours.

Fish Stock

To make about 2 quarts [2 liters] stock

2 lb.	fish trimmings (bones, heads, skin), rinsed and cut into pieces	1 kg.
about 2 quarts	water	about 2 liters
1	carrot, sliced	1
1	onion, sliced	1
2	celery ribs, sliced	2
2	garlic cloves, crushed	2
⅓ cup	parsley sprigs	75 ml.
1	large sprig thyme	1
3 or 4	wild fennel branches	3 or 4
1	bay leaf	1
	salt	
2 cups	dry white wine	½ liter
4	peppercorns (optional)	4

Put the fish trimmings into a large pan. Add the water to cover. Bring to a simmer over low heat. Skim off the scum that rises to the surface. When no more scum rises, add the vegetables, herbs and salt to taste. Partially cover the pan and simmer the contents for 15 minutes. Add the wine, return the liquid to a simmer and cook for 10 to 15 minutes. If you like, you may add the peppercorns 10 minutes before the end of cooking. Strain the stock through a colander lined with two layers of dampened muslin or cheesecloth.

Court Bouillon

This court bouillon is suitable for poaching meats, fish and shellfish. If the court bouillon is to be used as a marinade, or for poaching vegetables *à la grecque (pages 18-19)*, use 4 cups [1 liter] each of water and wine; add about ½ cup [125 ml.] of olive oil and 2 tablespoons [30 ml.] of fresh lemon juice to the water, and bring this mixture to a boil before adding vegetables and seasonings.

To make about 2 quarts [2 liters] court bouillon

1	large carrot, sliced	1
1	large onion, sliced	1
1	celery rib, diced	1
1	garlic clove, crushed	1
12	sprigs fresh parsley	12
2	sprigs thyme	2
2	sprigs dill (optional)	2
1	bay leaf	1
6 cups	water	1½ liters
	salt	
2 cups	dry white or red wine, or substitute ¾ cup [175 ml.] wine vinegar	½ liter
5 or 6	peppercorns	5 or 6

Put the vegetables, herbs, water and vinegar, if using, into a nonreactive pan and season them with a pinch of salt. Bring the mixture to a boil, then reduce the heat, cover, and simmer for about 15 minutes. Pour in the wine, if using, and simmer for 15 minutes more, adding the peppercorns for the last few minutes of cooking. Strain the court bouillon through a sieve into a bowl or a clean pan before using it.

Spinach-Ricotta Filling

To make 2½ cups [625 ml.] filling

6 oz.	ricotta cheese	175 g.
3 tbsp.	butter, softened	45 ml.
1	egg	1
	salt and pepper	
½ lb.	spinach, parboiled for 1 minute, drained, squeezed dry and finely chopped	¼ kg.
⅔ cup	freshly grated Parmesan cheese	150 ml.

Cream together the ricotta cheese and butter. Beat in the egg until no streaks of yellow appear. Add salt and pepper to taste; then stir in the spinach and gradually add the Parmesan cheese to form a stiff paste.

Duxelles

To make 2 cups [½ liter] duxelles

½ cup	finely chopped shallots or onions	125 ml.
7 tbsp.	butter	105 ml.
¾ lb.	mushrooms, finely chopped (3 cups [¾ liter])	350 g.
1 tsp.	salt	5 ml.
½ tsp.	freshly ground black pepper	2 ml.
¼ tsp.	freshly grated nutmeg	1 ml.
¼ cup	chopped fresh parsley	50 ml.
¼ cup	fresh lemon juice	50 ml.

Stirring frequently, cook the shallots or onions in the butter in a shallow pan over medium heat until they soften—about five minutes. Add the mushrooms, increase the heat to high and, still stirring, cook until the juices evaporate—about 10 minutes. Season with salt, pepper and nutmeg; then add the parsley and lemon juice. Cook over high heat until the lemon juice evaporates. Use the *duxelles* immediately.

Fish or Chicken Mousseline

To make about 2 cups [½ liter] mousseline

½ lb.	white or pink fish fillets, skinned, or boned chicken breast, skinned and the sinews removed	¼ kg.
	salt and pepper	
1	large egg white	1
1 cup	heavy cream	¼ liter

In a mortar, pound the fish or chicken to a smooth purée with a pestle. Season with salt and pepper and add the egg white a little at a time, pounding after each addition until it is completely incorporated. Alternatively, reduce the flesh to a purée in a food processor, add the seasoning and egg white and process the mixture again. A little at a time, rub the purée through a fine-meshed sieve, using a plastic dough scraper for a drum sieve or a wooden pestle for any other sieve. Pack the purée into a glass or metal bowl and press plastic wrap against the surface. Place the bowl in a larger bowl containing crushed ice, and refrigerate for at least one hour.

Pour off the water from the large bowl and add more crushed ice. Using a wooden spoon, work a little heavy cream into the purée. Return the bowls to the refrigerator for 15 minutes. Continue beating in small quantities of cream, refrigerating for 15 minutes after each addition and replacing the ice as necessary. Beat the mixture vigorously as soon as it becomes soft enough to do so. When about half of the cream has been incorporated, refrigerate the mixture for a few minutes. Lightly whip the remaining cream and incorporate it into the purée. Refrigerate until ready to use.

Sushi Rice

To make 6 cups [1 ½ liters] rice

3 cups	short-grain white rice, rinsed and drained	¾ liter
3⅓ cups	water	825 ml.
¼ cup	vinegar	50 ml.
¼ cup	sugar	50 ml.

Combine the drained rice and the water in a heavy pot. Cover tightly and bring to a boil over high heat—a process that will take about seven minutes. The pressure of the steam inside the pot will cause the lid to rattle when the water boils. (If the water foams over the rim, briefly slide the lid to one side to let the foam subside—then replace the lid.) Reduce the heat to low and, without removing the lid, cook the rice for eight minutes more, or until all of the water has been absorbed and the rice looks fluffy. Cover the top of the pot with a kitchen towel, replace the lid over the towel and let the rice rest off the heat for 10 to 15 minutes. Meanwhile, combine the vinegar and sugar.

Using a dampened wooden spatula or large wooden spoon, stir the rice until a grain yields to pressure when pinched. Empty the rice into a large stainless-steel or glass baking dish. Slide the spatula or spoon through the rice in a slicing motion to separate the grains, slowly adding the vinegar mixture as you work and gradually spreading the rice in the container. When the rice reaches room temperature—in about 20 minutes—transfer it to a bowl and cover it with a cloth until needed. *Sushi* rice should not be refrigerated and it should be used the day it is made.

Basic Bread Dough

To make about 2 ½ pounds [1 ¼ kg.] dough

¼ oz.	package active dry yeast or ⅗ oz. [18 g.] cake fresh yeast	7½ g.
about 1½ cups	tepid water	about 375 ml.
about 6 cups	flour	about 1½ liters
1 to 2 tsp.	salt	5 to 10 ml.

In a small bowl or a measuring cup, mix the yeast with 1½ cups [375 ml.] of the tepid water; if you are using active dry yeast, let it soften for about 10 minutes. Sift 5 cups [1¼ liters] of the flour and the salt into a large bowl. Pour the yeast mixture into the flour. Mix the flour and liquid together into a stiff, sticky dough, adding more flour or tepid water if necessary. Transfer the dough to a work surface and knead the dough until it is elastic and glossy—about 15 minutes.

Shape the dough into a ball and return it to a clean bowl. Cover the bowl with plastic wrap and let the dough rise in a warm, draft-free place until doubled in volume—from one to two and a half hours. The dough is ready when inserting a finger leaves a dent that does not immediately smooth out.

Punch the dough down with a blow of your fist, and put the dough on a work surface. Cut it into portions. Knead each portion into a ball, cover the balls with a cloth and let them rise for 10 to 15 minutes before shaping and baking.

Rich Egg-Bread Dough

The dough may be rolled out, cut into strips and wrapped around a sausage as shown on pages 86-87. Or it may be baked in individual or large brioche molds *(page 88)*. This recipe produces enough dough for sixteen 3-inch [8-cm.] individual brioches or two 8-inch [20-cm.] large brioches.

To make 2 pounds [1 kg.] dough

¼ oz.	package active dry yeast or ⅗ oz. [18 g.] cake fresh yeast	7½ g.
¼ cup	tepid water	50 ml.
about 4 cups	flour	about 1 liter
¼ cup	sugar	50 ml.
1 tsp.	salt	5 ml.
6	eggs	6
20 tbsp.	unsalted butter, softened	300 ml.
1	egg yolk, beaten with 2 tsp. [10 ml.] water	1

Mix the yeast with the tepid water, and let it stand for 10 minutes. Put the flour, sugar and salt into a bowl. Make a well in the center; add the yeast mixture and break in the eggs. Mix the eggs and yeast, gradually pulling flour from the sides of the well, until all of the flour has been moistened. The dough should be very soft and sticky.

Turn the dough out onto a cool, unfloured work surface. Using your hands and a pastry scraper, knead the dough thoroughly for about 10 minutes, or until it loses its stickiness and becomes smooth and elastic. Break off walnut-sized pieces of the butter and, using the pastry scraper or a spatula, fold them one at a time into the dough. Knead again until the dough is smooth. Put the dough into a bowl, cover it with plastic wrap, and leave it in a warm place for three or four hours, or until the dough has tripled in volume.

Punch the dough down several times to expel the air, then knead it lightly in the bowl for two or three minutes. Cover the bowl with plastic wrap and let the dough rise again. For best results, let the dough rise in the refrigerator for six to eight hours or overnight. If that is not possible, let the dough rise at room temperature until doubled in bulk—three or four hours—and then chill it for at least half an hour before shaping it.

Short-Crust and Rough Puff Dough

One simple formula produces dough for both plain short-crust pastry and for rough puff pastry. However, short-crust dough is made with 4 tablespoons [60 ml.] of butter or butter and lard, while rough puff dough requires 8 tablespoons [120 ml.]. Rough puff dough may be used in any recipe calling for puff-pastry dough. The amount of dough that this recipe yields will be sufficient to line an 8-inch [20-cm.] piepan or tart pan or eight 3-inch [8-cm.] tartlet pans.

To make ½ pound [¼ kg.] dough

1 cup	flour	¼ liter
¼ tsp.	salt	1 ml.
4 or 8 tbsp.	unsalted butter, or half butter and half lard, chilled and cut into small pieces	60 or 120 ml.
3 to 4 tbsp.	cold water	45 to 60 ml.

Mix the flour and salt in a bowl. Add the butter and cut it into the flour rapidly, using two table knives, until the butter is in tiny pieces. Do not work for more than a few minutes. Add half of the water and, with a fork, quickly blend it into the flour-and-butter mixture. Add just enough of the rest of the water to enable you to gather the dough together with your hands into a firm ball. Enclose the dough in plastic wrap or wax paper and place it in the refrigerator for at least one hour, or put it in the freezer for 20 minutes, until the surface is slightly frozen. The dough will keep in the refrigerator for two days or in the freezer for a month. If frozen, let the dough defrost in the refrigerator for one day.

To roll out short-crust dough: Unwrap the dough and put it on a cool, floured surface (a marble slab is ideal). Divide the ball if necessary; rewrap the excess portion and return it to the refrigerator. Press the dough out partially with your hand, then give it a few gentle smacks with the rolling pin to flatten and render it more supple. Roll out the dough from the center, turning it 90 degrees clockwise after each roll, until it forms a round about ⅛ inch [3 mm.] thick.

To roll out rough puff dough: Place the dough on a cool, floured surface and smack it flat with the rolling pin. Turn the dough over to make sure that both sides are well floured, and roll out the dough rapidly into a rectangle about 1 foot [30 cm.] long and 5 to 6 inches [13 to 15 cm.] wide. Fold the two short ends to meet each other in the center, then fold again to align the folded edges with each other. Following the direction of the fold lines, roll the dough into a rectangle again, fold it in the same way, enclose it in plastic wrap, and refrigerate it for one to two hours or freeze it for 15 to 20 minutes. Repeat this process two or three more times before using the dough. Always let the dough rest in the refrigerator or freezer between rollings.

To line a piepan or tart pan: Roll the dough onto the rolling pin, lift it up, and unroll it over the pan. Press the dough firmly against the bottom and sides of the pan. For a piepan, use a small knife to trim off the excess dough around the rim, leaving a margin ½ inch [1 cm.] wide. Fold this margin toward the center of the pan to create a double thick-ness, then crimp the edge. For a tart pan, roll the pin across the top to cut off the excess dough around the rim.

To line tartlet pans: Divide the dough into the required number of portions and roll out each one into a round about 2 inches [5 cm.] larger than the diameter of the pan. Place the rolled dough in the pans, pressing it against the bottoms and sides. Press the excess dough into the pan.

To prebake, or blind-bake, a pastry shell: Cut a piece of parchment paper, wax paper or foil slightly larger than the pan. Press the paper into the dough-lined pan, and fill the center with dried peas, beans or rice. Bake in a preheated 400° F. [200° C.] oven for about 10 minutes, or until the dough is set. Remove the filled paper or foil and, with a fork, lightly prick the bottom of the dough lining. For a partially baked pastry shell, return the pan to the oven for five minutes. For a fully baked shell, return the pan to the oven until the pastry is crisp and golden brown—10 to 15 minutes for a pie or tart shell or eight to 10 minutes for a tartlet. Cool the pastry in the pan for about five minutes. Then remove the fully baked shell and cool it on a wire rack before using it.

Olive-Oil Dough

With adjustments in the amount of water used, the same ingredients will yield either plain or rough-puff olive-oil dough. These doughs can be used interchangeably with plain or rough-puff short-crust dough in any recipe calling for one-crust pie shells or tart shells—unbaked, partially baked or fully baked.

To make 1 pound [½ kg.] dough

2 cups	flour	½ liter
	salt	
1	egg	1
½ cup	olive oil	125 ml.
4 tbsp.	tepid water	60 ml.

In a large bowl, mix the flour and salt. Break in the egg and add the olive oil and 3 tablespoons [45 ml.] of the tepid water. With a fork, stir the ingredients until they cohere in a mass; add the remaining tepid water, if necessary. Gather the dough into a ball. Knead it until it is smooth and comes away cleanly from the sides of the bowl. Cover it with plastic wrap and let it rest for at least one hour at room temperature before rolling it out thin as for short-crust dough.

Olive-oil puff dough. Reserve 1 tablespoon [15 ml.] of the oil and use the rest to make a dough, moistening it with 2 or 3 tablespoons [30 or 45 ml.] of water. Let the dough rest for one hour at room temperature.

Flour the work surface and roll out the dough into one long strip. Using a pastry brush, lightly paint two thirds of the strip with some of the reserved olive oil. Do not use too much oil, lest it be squeezed out when the dough is folded and make the work surface too greasy for rolling out the dough. Lift the unpainted end of the strip and fold it over the central third of the dough. Fold the remaining third of dough on top. Give the dough a quarter turn so that the open edges face you, roll it out again, and paint and fold it as before.

Let the dough rest for one hour before turning the dough and painting, rolling and folding it again. Let it rest for one hour and repeat the process before rolling it out to make a pastry crust.

Puff-Pastry Dough

To make 2 pounds [1 kg.] dough

3 cups	all-purpose flour	¾ liter
1 cup	cake flour	¼ liter
2 tsp.	salt	10 ml.
1 lb.	unsalted butter	½ kg.
10 to 12 tbsp.	water	150 to 180 ml.

Sift the flours and the salt into a bowl. Cut a quarter of the butter into small pieces and add them to the bowl. Using your finger tips, rub the butter into the flour. Add just enough cold water—a few tablespoonfuls at a time—to bind the ingredients, and work the dough into a ball. Wrap the dough in floured plastic wrap and chill it in the refrigerator for about 30 minutes.

Meanwhile, place the remaining butter between two sheets of parchment or wax paper and, with a rolling pin, flatten the butter into a slab about 6 inches [15 cm.] square and ½ inch [1 cm.] thick. Chill the butter in the refrigerator for about 30 minutes.

Place the dough on a lightly floured board and roll it into a 12-inch [30-cm.] square. Place the square of butter diagonally in the center of the dough and fold the corners of the dough over the butter so that they meet in the center. Roll the dough into a rectangle 12 by 18 inches [30 by 45 cm.].

Fold the dough into thirds and give it a quarter turn. Roll the dough again into a rectangle and fold it again into thirds. Wrap and chill the dough for at least one hour. Roll and turn the dough twice more, refrigerate for a few hours, and repeat, giving it six turns in all. After a final turn, refrigerate for four hours before using it. Tightly wrapped, the dough can safely be kept in the refrigerator for two or three days, or in the freezer for two or three months. If frozen, defrost it in the refrigerator overnight.

Tempura Batter

To make about 2 cups [½ liter] batter

2	eggs	2
1½ cups	ice water	375 ml.
2 cups	flour	½ liter

In a bowl set into a larger bowl of cracked ice, whisk the eggs lightly, then whisk in the ice water. Add the flour all at once, and stir just enough to incorporate it into the liquid. Use the batter immediately.

Crepes

To make ten to twelve 6-inch [15-cm.] crepes

½ cup	flour	125 ml.
1 tsp.	salt	5 ml.
3	eggs	3
1 cup	milk or water	¼ liter
2 tbsp.	brandy (optional)	30 ml.
¼ cup	fines herbes (optional)	50 ml.
3 tbsp.	unsalted butter, melted	45 ml.

Pour the flour and salt into a bowl, make a well in the center and break in the eggs. Pour the milk or water into the well. Working from the center, gradually whisk the eggs and milk or water into the flour. If you like, add the brandy or the fines herbes. Stir in the melted butter as soon as the batter is smooth and has the consistency of light cream. Do not whisk the mixture beyond this stage. Let the batter rest at room temperature for 30 minutes before cooking the crepes. If the batter thickens, dilute it with a little milk or water.

Heat a crepe pan or small skillet over medium heat. Grease it lightly with a little butter for the first crepe only. Pour in just enough of the batter to lightly coat the pan. The batter should sizzle as it touches the hot metal. As you pour, tilt and roll the pan to spread the batter as evenly and as thinly as possible. Pour excess batter that remains liquid back into the bowl.

Cook the crepe until the edges begin to curl and the underside is evenly colored—about 10 seconds. Then loosen the edges with a spatula and flip the crepe over, either with your fingers or with the spatula. Cook the underside of the crepe until it is lightly colored and dry—about 20 seconds.

Before making another crepe, stir the batter in case it has separated. Remove the pan from the heat for a few seconds to prevent it from overheating. As the crepes are made, stack them in a pile to keep them warm.

Recipe Index

169

General Index/ Glossary

Included in this index to the cooking demonstrations are definitions, in italics, of special culinary terms not explained elsewhere in this volume. The Recipe Index begins on page 168.

enclosed in olive-oil puff dough, 80-81; escarole, pine nut and raisin filling enclosed in yeast dough, 84-85

Pike: in mousseline, 60

Poaching: brains in court bouillon, 32-33; capon, 28; eggs, 64-65; sausages filled with mousseline, 60-61; white sausages, 36-37

Pork caul: *the lacy fat membrane that surrounds the stomach of the pig. Caul is obtainable fresh or salted at butcher shops. If bought salted, it must be soaked in tepid water for at least 15 minutes before use, then spread on a towel to dry.*

Poultry: marinating, 28; poaching, 28; removing breast, 28-29

Prosciutto: *the Italian name for salted and dried, but unsmoked ham;* 88

Puff pastry, 73; baking cases, 83; filling vol-au-vent cases, 83; kneading butter for, 82; rolling and folding dough, 82-83; shaping into cases, 82, 83; using cake flour for, 82

Puréeing: asparagus, 71; chicken, 40; chicken livers for custard, 66; chicken livers for mousse, 39; fish, 60; red peppers, 10; sorrel, 40; spinach, 10; tomatoes, 41

Quatre épices: *a French term for a mixture of ground spices, usually pepper, nutmeg and cloves and either cinnamon or ginger. Although available commercially, it can easily be assembled by combining ½ teaspoon [2 ml.] of ground cloves, 7 teaspoons [35 ml.] of ground white pepper, 2 teaspoons [10 ml.] of ground ginger and 1 teaspoon [5 ml.] of ground nutmeg. The proportions may be adjusted to taste.*

Rémoulade sauce: serving in seafood tartlets, 77

Rice: cooking for *sushi,* 48-49; filling grapevine leaves with, 20-21; flavoring with vinegar for *sushi,* 49; molding rings of, 34-35; molding for *sushi,* 48-51; in pie filling, 80-81

Rich egg-bread dough: amount of eggs in, 86; baking in molds, 86, 88; cutting into strips for wrapping sausages, 86-87; filling brioches with prosciutto, ham, mushrooms and shallots, 88; forming topknots in brioches, 88; kneading, 86-87; rising times, 86; shaping freestanding pie, 86

Rockfish: filleting, 44-45; in *sushi,* 48-50

Rough puff dough, 73; amount of butter in, 78; blind baking tart shells, 78; cooking a pepper and tomato filling for, 78-79; fillings for, 78; glazing with egg yolk and water, 78; rolling and folding, 78-79; shaping into a rectangular shell, 78

Roulades, 30-31; cuts of meat for, 30; fillings for, 30; freezing meat before slicing, 30; rolling veal, 30-31; sauces for, 30; of veal filled with leeks

and basil, 30-31

Saffron: coloring sauces with, 10

Salmon: filleting for *gravlax,* 52; marinating for *gravlax,* 52-53; puréeing for mousseline, 60-61; weighting for *gravlax,* 52

Salmon roe: in *sushi* assembly, 51

Salsify: boiling in acidulated water, 16

Salt anchovies: garnishing marinated herring, 55; pounding to a paste for snail butter, 56; topping a rough puff tart, 79

Sashimi, 46-47; arranging tuna slices in rosette, 47; cutting techniques for, 46; filleting fish for, 44-45; garnishes, 46, 47; serving, 46; shaping bundles from fish and cucumber wrapped in seaweed, 46, 47; slicing fish into rectangles for, 47; suitable fish for, 46

Sauces: béarnaise, 14, 15; green, 16; hollandaise, 6, 38, 39; mayonnaise, 11, 19; mustard-and-dill, 53; pesto, 14, 15; rémoulade, 77; serving with hors d'oeuvre, 5; tomato, 6, 7, 23, 25; using spices and vegetables to color and flavor, 10; velouté, 8-9, 21, 72, 88; vinaigrette, 17; white, 6, 32; white butter, 6, 7, 61, 75

Sausages: casings for, 36, 60; cleaning casings, 37; filling with chicken, 36, 37; filling with fish mousseline, 60-61; poaching, 36, 37, 60, 61, 86; wrapping in brioche, 86-87

Sea salt: *a salt distilled from sea water. Sea salt is sold in both coarse and fine crystals at health-food stores.*

Seafood hors d'oeuvre, 43, 44-61; clams baked in snail butter, 56-57; filleting fish for, 44-45; frogs' legs, 58-59; *gravlax,* 52-53; marinated sea bass (*escabèche*), 54-55; marinated, uncooked herring, 54-55; mousseline sausages, 60-61; oysters baked with spinach, bread crumbs and butter, 56-57; *sashimi,* 46-47; *sushi,* 42, 48-51

Semolina: *coarse, cream-colored granules milled from the heart of durum-wheat berries. Regular farina—not the quick-cooking type—can be substituted for semolina.*

Seviche: marinating raw herring, 54-55

Shellfish: baking clams with snail butter, 56-57; cleaning, 56; cooking and serving on the half shell, 56; obtaining fresh, 56; oysters baked with spinach, bread crumbs and butter, 56-57; steaming, 56

Short-crust dough, 73; binding with ice-water, 76; blind baking shell, 76; lining tartlet pans, 77; mixing, 76-77; relaxing gluten, 76; in seafood tartlets, 76-77; working butter in, 76

Shrimp: butterflying for *sushi,* 49; in fish mousseline, 60-61; parboiling, 76; peeling, 49; in seafood tartlets, 76-77; in *sushi,* 48, 50-51

Snail butter: baking clams in, 56-57; preparing, 56

Snow peas: coating with tempura and deep frying, 24-25; parboiling, 18; as vegetable filling, 12, 18-19

Sole: filleting, 44-45; making fish stock from trimmings, 8-9; puréeing for a mousseline, 60-61

Sorrel: coloring and flavoring sauces with, 10; in a layered custard of vegetables and herbs, 68-69; parboiling, 41; puréeing for a mousse, 40; shredding, 68

Soufflé: folding egg whites into base, 70; ingredients in, 63, 70; parboiling and puréeing asparagus for, 70-71; preparing white sauce base, 71; ratio of egg whites and yolks to purée, 70

Soy sauce: in marinade for flank steak, 30, 31; serving with *sashimi,* 46; with *sushi,* 48

Spinach: in coating for baked oysters, 56-57; in crepe filling, 74, 75; deep frying leaves for garnish, 24, 25; in a layered custard of vegetables and herbs, 68-69; parboiling, 10; puréeing to color and flavor sauces, 10; wrapping leaves around a stuffing, 20

Steaming: asparagus, 14-15; carrots, 14-15; mushrooms, 14-15; peppers, 14-15; shellfish, 56; vegetables, 14-15; vegetables on skewers, 14-15; zucchini, 15

Stock: clarifying with egg whites and shells, 9; combining with puréed meats and vegetables to make mousses, 40-41; combining with roux to make velouté, 8; fish, 8-9; gelatin in, 8; meat, 8; preparing aspics with, 9; removing fat from, 9; skimming, 8

Sushi, 42, 48-51; butterflying shrimp for, 49; encasing in seaweed, 50, 51; filleting fish for, 44-45; flavoring rice with vinegar, 49; garnishes, 48, 51; hand-shaping, 48-49; molds for, 48, 50-51; pressing in a mold, 50-51; rice for, 48-49; with salmon roe, 51; shaping with a bamboo mat, 50; suitable fish for, 48

Sweetbreads, 26; cooking, 34, 35; parboiling, 34; peeling, 35; selecting, 34; serving with rice rings, 34-35; soaking, 34; weighting, 35

Swiss chard: cleaning and trimming, 68; in a layered custard of vegetables and herbs, 68-69; parboiling, 69; wrapping leaves around stuffing, 20

Tamari sauce: *a soy sauce made without chemicals or preservatives. It is sold at health-food stores.*

Tart: blind baking the shell, 76; filled with shrimp and avocado, 76-77; lining tartlet pans, 77; rough puff, of tomatoes and peppers, 78-79

Tempura: deep frying snow peas, carrots and zucchini, 24-25; mixing batter for, 24

Tomatoes: baking stuffed, 22; basic

preparation, 32; coloring and flavoring sauces with, 10; enriching white sauce, 6; in filling for rough puff tart, 78-79; garnishing crepes with, 74; in gratin with brains, 32-33; puréeing tomatoes, 7; as vegetable cases, 18

Tomato sauce, 6, 7; with deep-fried eggplant, 25; enriching with cream, 6; puréeing tomatoes, 7; serving with chicken liver custard, 67; serving with stuffed fennel, 23

Tuna: cutting and arranging for *sashimi,* 46-47; in *sushi,* 50

Turmeric: coloring sauces with, 10

Turnips: parboiling before deep frying, 24

Veal: encasing leeks and basil, 31; making stock from bones, 8; pounding slices, 31; roulades, 30-31

Vegetable hors d'oeuvre, 13, 14-25; baked stuffed fennel, 22-23; baked stuffed mushroom caps, 22-23; boiled artichokes with vinaigrette, 16-17; deep-fried eggplant fans, 24-25; deep-fried vegetables in tempura batter, 24-25; filled artichoke bottoms, 18-19; filled red pepper cases, 18-19; steamed vegetables on skewers, 14-15; steamed zucchini julienne with pesto, 14-15; stuffed grapevine leaves, 20-21

Velouté: cleansing, 9; combining stock with roux, 9; with filled bread case, 72; fish-based, 8-9; serving with stuffed grape leaves, 21; stock for, 8-9; using spices and vegetables to color and flavor, 10; veal, 8, 88

Vinaigrette: serving with artichokes, 17

Vol-au-vent: baking cases, 83; filling for, 72, 73, 83; rolling and folding puff pastry for, 82-83; shaping cases, 83

Wasabi paste: garnishing *sushi,* 48, 49, 50, 51; preparing powder, 46; serving with *sashimi,* 46

White butter sauce, 6, 7; adding butter to vinegar and wine for, 7; serving with mousseline crepes, 75; serving with mousseline sausages, 61

White sauce, 6; adding *duxelles* to, 32; with brain gratin, 32-33; making a roux for, 6; preparing soufflé base, 71; using spices and vegetables to color and flavor, 10

Whiting: in mousseline, 60

Wine: in béarnaise sauce, 14; serving with hors d'oeuvre, 5; in white butter sauce, 6, 7

Yeast dough: in escarole pie, 84-85; glazing with egg white and water, 85; kneading, 84, 85; mixing, 84; temperature of ingredients, 84. See *also* Rich egg-bread dough

Zucchini: coating with tempura batter and deep frying, 24-25; making julienne, 14; serving with pesto, 14, 15; steaming, 15; as vegetable case, 18

Recipe Credits

The sources for the recipes in this volume are shown below. Page references in parentheses indicate where the recipes appear in the anthology.

Adam, Hans Karl, *Das Kochbuch aus Schwaben.* Copyright © 1976 by Verlag Wolfgang Hölker, Martinistrasse 2, D-4400 Münster(150).

Alberini, Massimo (Editor), *Cento Ricette Storiche.* Copyright Sansoni Editore, Florence, 1974. Translated by permission of G. C. Sansoni Editore Nuova S.p.A.(145).

Allen, Jana and Margaret Gin, *Innards and Other Variety Meats.* © Jana Allen and Margaret Gin, 1974. Published by 101 Productions, San Francisco. Published in England by Pitman Publishing as Offal. © Pitman Publishing 1976. By permission of 101 Productions(115).

American Heritage, the editors of, *The American Heritage Cookbook.* © 1964 American Heritage Publishing Co., Inc., New York. Published by American Heritage Publishing Co., Inc. By permission of American Heritage Publishing Co., Inc.(128).

Amicale des Cuisiniers et Pâtissiers Auvergnats de Paris, *Cuisine D'Auvergne.* © 1979 Denoël-Paris. Published by Éditions Denoël, Paris. Translated by permission of Éditions Denoël(126, 141, 156).

Androuet, Pierre, *La Cuisine au Fromage.* © 1978, Éditions Stock. Published by Éditions Stock, Paris. Translated by permission of Éditions Stock(133, 144, 159).

Armisen, Raymond and André Martin, *Les Recettes de la Table Niçoise.* © Librairie Istra 1972. Published by Librairie Istra, Strasbourg. Translated by permission of Librairie Istra(147).

The Art of Cookery, Made Plain and Easy. By a Lady. The Sixth Edition, 1758(99, 101).

Artusi, Pellegrino, *La Scienza in Cucina e L'Arte di Mangiar Bene.* Copyright © 1970 Giulio Einaudi Editore S.p.A., Torino. Published by Giulio Einaudi Editore S.p.A.(90, 94).

Aureden, Lilo, *Das Schmeckt so Gut.* © 1965 by Lichtenberg Verlag, München. Published by Lichtenberg Verlag, Munich, 1973. Translated by permission of Kindler Verlag, GmbH, Munich(103, 138). *Was Männern so Gut Schmeckt.* © 1954 Paul List Verlag, München. Published by Paul List Verlag, Munich. Translated by permission of Paul List Verlag(115).

Barberousse, Michel, *Cuisine Provençale.* Published by Librairie de la Presse, Biarritz. Translated by permission of Librairie de la Presse(152).

Bennett, Victor and Antonia Rossi, *Pappa Rossi's Secrets of Italian Cooking.* Copyright © 1981 by Victor Bennett and Antonia Rossi. Used by permission of Antonia Rossi(128).

Bertholle, Louisette (Editor), *Secrets of the Great French Restaurants.* Copyright © 1974 by Macmillan Publishing Co., Inc. Reprinted with permission of Macmillan Publishing Co., Inc.(146).

Bertholle, Louisette, *Une Grande Cuisine Pour Tous.* Coédition Albin Michel-Opera Mundi © Opera Mundi, Paris(131).

Böttiger, Theodor, *Das Grill-Buch.* Copyright © 1968 by Wilhelm Heyne Verlag, München. Published by Wilhelm Heyne Verlag, Munich. Translated by permission of Wilhelm Heyne Verlag(96).

Böttiger, Theodor and Ilse Froidl, *Das Neue Fischkochbuch.* Copyright © 1979 by Wilhelm Heyne Verlag, München. Published by Wilhelm Heyne Verlag, Munich. Translated by permission of Wilhelm Heyne Verlag(130).

Bouché, Daniel, *Invitation à la Cuisine Buissonnière.* Atelier Marcel Jullian, 1979. Published by Atelier Marcel Jullian, Paris. Translated by permission of Librairie Hachette, Paris(133).

Bouillard, Paul, *La Cuisine au Coin du Feu.* Copyright 1928 by Albin Michel. Published by Éditions Albin Michel,

Paris. Translated by permission of Éditions Albin Michel(122, 131, 156).

Boulestin, X. Marcel, *A Second Helping or More Dishes for English Homes.* Published by William Heinemann Ltd., London, 1928. By permission of A. D. Peters and Co., Ltd., London(146).

Boulestin, X. M. and A. H. Adair, *Savouries and Hors-d'Oeuvre.* © Marcel Boulestin and R. H. Adair 1956. Published by William Heinemann Ltd., London, 1932. By permission of William Heinemann Ltd.(111, 118, 140).

Boumphrey, Geoffrey, *Cunning Cookery.* Published by Thomas Nelson and Sons Limited, London, 1938. By permission of Thomas Nelson and Sons Limited(136).

Boxer, Arabella, *Arabella Boxer's Garden Cookbook.* Copyright © 1974 Arabella Boxer. Published by Weidenfeld and Nicolson Ltd., 1974. By permission of Weidenfeld and Nicolson Ltd.(137).

Brandon, Leila, *A Merry-Go-Round of Recipes From Independent Jamaica.* Second edition, 1963. Printed by Colour Graphic Printers, Jamaica(125).

Brera, Gianni and Luigi Veronelli, *La Pacciada.* © 1973 by Arnoldo Mondadori Editore S.p.a., Milano. Published by Arnoldo Mondadori Editore S.p.a., Milan. Translated by permission of Arnoldo Mondadori Editore S.p.a., Milan(127).

Brobeck, Florence and Monika B. Kjellberg, *Smörgåsbord and Scandinavian Cookery.* Published in 1948, Little, Brown and Company(113, 114).

Buc'hoz, Pierre Joseph, *L'Art de Préparer les Aliments.* 1787(115).

Calera, Ana Maria, *Cocina Castellana.* © Ana Maria Calera 1974. Published by Editorial Bruguera S.A., Barcelona, 1974. Translated by permission of Editorial Bruguera S.A.(127).

Carnacina, Luigi, *Great Italian Cooking.* (Edited by Michael Sonino.) Copyright in Italy by Garzanti Editore, Milan. Published by Abradale Press Publishers, New York. By permission of Aldo Garzanti Editore, S.p.A., Milan(138).

Castignac, Huguette, *La Cuisine Occitane.* © Solar, 1973. Published by Solar, Paris. Translated by permission of Solar(152).

Cendrars, Miriam and Ninette Lyon (Editors), *Gratins, Tourtes et Tartes (Les Carnets de Cuisine No. 9).* A. L.P.—Carnets de Cuisine. Published by Atelier Pratique, Paris. Translated by permission of Atelier du Livre et de la Presse, Paris and Ninette Lyon(145).

Chantiles, Vilma Liacouras, *The Food of Greece.* Copyright © 1975 by Vilma Liacouras Chantiles. Published by Atheneum Publishers, New York. By permission of Vilma Liacouras Chantiles(124).

Chen, Joyce, *Joyce Chen Cook Book.* Copyright © 1962 by Joyce Chen. Published by J. B. Lippincott Company, Philadelphia and New York. By permission of J. B. Lippincott Company(109).

Cooks' Club: French Menu V. Recipe by Joyce Piotrowski. Used by permission of Joyce Piotrowski(116).

Le Cordon Bleu, 1929, 1930 Vol I. Published by Le Cordon Bleu de Paris, 1932. Translated by permission of Le Cordon Bleu de Paris(108, 153).

Correnti, Pino, *Il Libro d'Oro della Cucina e dei Vini di Sicilia.* © Copyright 1976 Ugo Mursia Editore. Published by Ugo Mursia Editore, Milan. Translated by permission of Ugo Mursia Editore(123).

La Cuisine Bretonne. Used by permission of Les Presses de la Cite, Paris(142).

La Cuisine Lyonnaise. Published by Éditions Gutenberg, 1947(141).

La Cuisine Naturelle à l'Huile d'Olive. © 1978 Éditions De Vecchi S.A., Paris. Published by Éditions De Vecchi S.A. Translated by permission of Éditions De Vecchi S.A.(122).

Cutler, Carol, *Haute Cuisine for Your Heart's Delight.* Copyright © 1973 by Carol Cutler. Used by permission of Clarkson N. Potter, Inc.(118). *The Six-Minute Soufflé and Other Culinary Delights.* Copyright © 1976 by Carol Cutler. Used by permission of Clarkson N. Potter, Inc.(100, 102, 128).

Dannenbaum, Julie, *Menus for All Occasions.* Copyright © 1974 by Julie Dannenbaum. Bonanza Books,

New York(106, 139).

Dar, Krishna Prasad, *Kashmiri Cooking.* © Krishna Prasad Dar, 1977. Published by Vikas Publishing House Pvt. Ltd., New Delhi. By permission of Vikas Publishing House Pvt. Ltd., Sahibabad(125).

Davidson, Alan, *Mediterranean Seafood.* Copyright © Alan Davidson, 1972. Published by Penguin Books Ltd., London. By permission of Penguin Books Ltd.(117). *North Atlantic Seafood.* Copyright © Alan Davidson, 1979. Published by Penguin Books Ltd., London. By permission of Penguin Books Ltd.(120). *Seafood of South-East Asia.* Copyright © Alan Davidson, 1977. Published by Federal Publications, Singapore. By permission of Alan Davidson(125).

de Groot, Roy Andries, *The Auberge of the Flowering Hearth.* Copyright © 1973 by Roy Andries de Groot. The Bobbs-Merrill Company: New York and Indianapolis(92).

Delplanque, A. and S. Cloteaux, *Les Bases de la Charcuterie.* Editions-Jacques Lanore, Paris, 1975(160).

de Pomiane, Édouard, *Le Carnet d'Anna.* © Calmann-Lévy 1967. Translated by permission of Éditions Calmann-Lévy, Paris(153). *Le Code de la Bonne Chère.* Published by Albin Michel, Éditeur, Paris. Translated by permission of Éditions Albin Michel(142).

Dorset Federation of Women's Institutes, *What's Cooking in Dorset.* Published by the Dorset Federation of Women's Institutes, 1972. By permission of the Dorset Federation of Women's Institutes(147).

Dubois, Urbain and Émile Bernard, *La Cuisine Classique.* Volume I. Published by E. Dentu, Éditeur, Palais-Royal, Paris, 1881(107).

Dumaine, Alexandre, *Ma Cuisine.* © 1972 by Pensée Moderne, Paris. Published by Éditions de la Pensée Moderne, Paris. Translated by permission of Jacques Grancher, éditeur, Paris(129).

Escudier, Jean-Noël and Peta J. Fuller, *The Wonderful Food of Provence.* Copyright © 1968 by Robert Redstock and Peta J. Fuller. Reprinted by permission of Houghton Mifflin Company(107).

Faccioli, Emilio (Editor), *Arte della Cucina (Libri di Ricette, Testi Sopra lo Scalco il Trinciante ei Vini dal XIV al XIX Secolo).* © 1966 Edizioni Il Polifilo, Milano. Published by Edizioni Il Polifilo, Milan, 1966. Translated by permission of Edizioni Il Polifilo(109, 146).

Famularo, Joe and Louise Imperiale, *The Festive Famularo Kitchen.* Copyright © 1977 by Joe Famularo and Louise Imperiale. Published by Atheneum Publishers, New York, 1977. By permission of Atheneum Publishers(112, 139, 151).

Filippini, Maria Nunzia, *La Cuisine Corse.* Published by Société d'Éditions: Serena, Ajaccio, 1978. Translated by permission of Société d'Éditions: Serena(95, 104, 124).

Fonseca, Nuri, *Recetas de America Latina.* Copyright © 1978 Editorial Concepto, S.A., Mexico(131).

Foods of the World, *American Cooking: New England.* Copyright © 1970 Time Inc. Published by Time-Life Books, Alexandria, Virginia(129).

The Good Cooking School, *Penny-Wise, Party-Perfect Dinners.* Copyright © 1975 by The Good Cooking School. Reprinted by permission of Doubleday & Company, Inc.(99).

Gosetti, Fernanda, *In Cucina con Fernanda Gosetti.* © 1978 Fabbri Editori, Milano. Published by Fabbri Editori, Milan, 1978. Translated by permission of Fabbri Editori(94, 104).

Gouffé, Jules, *Le Livre de Cuisine.* Published by Librairie Hachette, Paris, 1867(136).

Graves, Eleanor, *Great Dinners From Life.* Copyright © 1969 Time Inc. Published by Time-Life Books, Alexandria, Virginia(93).

Greene, Bert, *Bert Greene's Kitchen Bouquets: A Cookbook of Favored Aromas and Flavors.* Copyright © 1979 by Bert Greene. Reprinted with permission of Contemporary Books, Inc., Chicago(155).

Grigson, Jane, *Fish Cookery.* Copyright © 1973 by Jane Grigson. Published by The International Wine and Food Society. Used by permission of Overlook Press, Lewis Hollow Road, Woodstock, New York(154). *Good Things.* Copyright © 1971 by Jane Grigson. Copyright © 1971 by

Alfred A. Knopf. Reprinted by permission of Alfred A. Knopf(121).

Groff, Betty and José Wilson, *Good Earth & Country Cooking.* Published by Stackpole Books, Harrisburg, Pennsylvania, 1974. By permission of Stackpole Books(147).

Guérard, Michel, *Michel Guérard's Cuisine Minceur.* English Translation Copyright © 1976 by William Morrow and Company. Originally published in French under the title *La Grande Cuisine Minceur.* Copyright © 1976 by Éditions Robert Laffont S.A. By permission of William Morrow(92).

Hawliczkowa, Helena, *Kuchnia Polska.* Copyright by Helena Kulzowa Hawliczkowa. Reprinted by permission of Agencja autorska, sp.z.o.o., Warszawa(158).

Hazelton, Nika, *The Regional Italian Kitchen.* Copyright © 1978 by Nika Hazelton. Published by M. Evans and Company Inc., New York. By permission of Curtis Brown Ltd., New York(96).

Heath, Ambrose, *Good Savouries.* Copyright Ambrose Heath 1934. Published by Faber and Faber Limited, London. By permission of Faber and Faber Limited(137). *Madame Prunier's Fish Cookery Book.* Copyright by Madame Prunier. Published by Hutchinson and Co. (Publishers) Ltd., London, 1938. By permission of A. P. Watt Limited, Literary Agents, London(127).

Henderson, William Augustus, *The Housekeeper's Instructor, Or Universal Family Cook.* Tenth edition. Published in London, 1804(152).

Hewitt, Jean, *The New York Times Large Type Cookbook.* Copyright © 1969 by Jean Hewitt. Reprinted by permission of Times Books, a division of Quadrangle/The New York Times Book Co., Inc.(129, 130).

Isnard, Léon, *La Gastronomie Africaine.* © Albin Michel, 1930. Published by Éditions Albin Michel, Paris. Translated by permission of Éditions Albin Michel(135).

Jakobsson, Oskar (Editor), *Good Food In Sweden.* © 1968 Oskar Jakobsson and Generalstabens Litografiska Anstalt, Stockholm. Published by Generalstabens Litografiska Anstalt, Stockholm. By permission of Generalstabens Litografiska Anstalt(119).

Jans, Hugh, *Sla, Slaatjes, Snacks.* Published by Meijer Pers BV, Amsterdam, 1967. Translated by permission of Meijer Pers BV, Amsterdam(120).

The Junior League of the City of New York, *New York Entertains.* Copyright © 1974 by the Junior League of the City of New York, Inc. Reprinted by permission of Doubleday & Company, Inc.(135).

Kamman, Madeleine M., *When French Women Cook.* Copyright © 1976 by Madeleine M. Kamman (New York: Atheneum, 1976). Reprinted with the permission of Atheneum Publishers(102).

Kenney, A. Herbert ("Wyvern"), *Fifty Lunches.* Published by Edward Arnold, London, 1895(132).

Krüger, Arne and Annette Wolter, *Kochen Heute.* © by Gräfe und Unzer GmbH, München. Published by Gräfe und Unzer GmbH, Munich. Translated by permission of Gräfe und Unzer GmbH(98, 154).

Kulinarische Gerichte: Zu Gast bei Freunden. Sixth Edition 1977. Copyright to German translation by Verlag für die Frau DDR Leipzig. Published by Verlag für die Frau and Verlag MIR, Moscow. Translated by permission of The Copyright Agency of the USSR-VAAP(91, 100, 105).

La Chapelle, Vincent, *The Modern Cook,* Vol. 3. London, 1733(154).

Lagattolla, Franco, *The Recipes that Made a Million.* © Franco Lagottolla 1978. Published by Orbis Publishing Limited, London. By permission of Orbis Publishing Limited(97).

Lamb, Venice, *The Home Book of Turkish Cooking.* © Venice Lamb 1969, 1973. Published by Faber & Faber Ltd., London. By permission of Faber & Faber Ltd.(98).

Lazarque, E. Auricoste de, *Cuisine Messine.* Published by Sidot Frères, Libraires—Éditeurs, Nancy, 1927. Reprinted by Laffitte Reprints, Marseilles, 1979. Translated by permission of Laffitte Reprints(159).

Levy, Faye, *La Varenne Tour Book.* Copyright © 1979 La Varenne USA, Inc. Published by permission of LaToque International, Pennsylvania(114).

London, Sheryl and Mel, *The Fish-Lovers' Cookbook.* Copyright © 1980 by Rodale Press, Inc. Permission granted by Rodale Press, Inc., Emmaus, PA 18049(118).

Lowinsky, Ruth, *Lovely Food.* Copyright © The Nonesuch Press, London. Published by The Nonesuch Press, London, 1931. By permission of The Nonesuch Press Ltd.(93). *More Lovely Food.* Copyright © The Nonesuch Press, London. Published by The Nonesuch Press, London, 1935. By permission of The Nonesuch Press Ltd.(138).

Lyon, Ninette, *Les Oeufs.* Copyright © 1977 by Ninette Lyon and Éditions Arts and Voyages, Brussels. Published by Éditions Arts and Voyages. Translated by permission of Éditions Gamma, Belgium(134, 136, 142).

MacMiadhacháin, Anna, *Spanish Regional Cookery.* Copyright © Anna MacMiadhacháin, 1976. Published by Penguin Books Ltd., London. By permission of Penguin Books Ltd.(151).

Magyar, Elek, *Kochbuch für Feinschmecker.* © Dr. Magyar Bálint. © Dr. Magyar Pál. Originally published in 1967 under the title *Az Inyesmester Szakacs Konyve* by Corvina, Budapest. Translated by permission of Artisjus, Literary Agency, Budapest(114).

Mardikian, George, *Dinner at Omar Khayyam's.* Copyright © 1945 by George Mardikian. Copyright renewed. First published by The Viking Press, New York, 1944. By permission of McIntosh and Otis, Inc., New York(98).

Margittai, Tom and Paul Kovi, *The Four Seasons.* Copyright © 1980 Tom Margittai and Paul Kovi. Reprinted by permission of Simon & Schuster, a division of Gulf & Western Corporation(132, 155).

Marty, Albin, *Fourmiguetto: Souvenirs, Contes et Recettes du Languedoc.* Published by Éditions CREER, F63340 Nonette, 1978. Translated by permission of Éditions CREER(119).

Mascarelli, Benoît, *La Table en Provence & sur la Côte d'Azur.* Published by Jacques Haumont, Paris, 1947(126).

Le Ménagier de Paris *(Traité de Morale et d'Économie Domestique par un Bourgeois Parisien).* Tome II. Composed c. 1393. Reprinted by Slatkine Reprints, Geneva, 1967. Translated by permission of Slatkine Reprints(148).

Menon, *Les Soupers de la Cour (ou l'Art de Travailler Toutes Sortes d'Aliments).* Originally published in 1755 by Guillyn, Libraire, Paris. Reprinted in 1978 by Librairie SOETE, Paris(108, 126).

Meyers, Perla, *The Peasant Kitchen: A Return to Simple Good Food.* Copyright © 1975 by Perla Meyers. Reprinted by permission of Harper & Row, Publishers, Inc.(113). *The Seasonal Kitchen.* Copyright © 1973 by Perla Meyers. Reprinted by permission of Holt, Rinehart and Winston, Publishers(90).

Miller, Gloria Bley, *The Thousand Recipe Chinese Cookbook.* Copyright © 1966 by Gloria Bley Miller. Published by Grosset & Dunlap, Inc., by permission of the author(106).

El Mundo Gastronómico. Published by Damas Grises, La Cruz Roja Colombiana, Cali(93).

Nathan, Joan and Judy Stacey Goldman, *The Flavor of Jerusalem.* Copyright © 1974, 1975 by Joan Nathan Gerson and Judy Stacey Goldman. Reprinted by permission of Little, Brown and Company(96, 103).

Ngô, Bach and Gloria Zimmerman, *The Classic Cuisine of Vietnam.* Copyright © 1979 by Barron's Educational Series, Inc., Woodbury, New York. Reprinted with permission of Barron's Educational Series, Inc.(112).

Nicholas, Jean F., *The Complete Book of American Fish and Shellfish.* Copyright © 1981, CBI Publishing Company, 51 Sleeper St., Boston, MA 02210(127).

Nignon, M. Édouard (Editor), *Le Livre de Cuisine de L'Ouest-Éclair.* Published by L'Ouest-Éclair, Rennes, 1941. Translated by permission of Société d'Éditions Ouest-France, Rennes(110).

Nignon, Édouard, *Les Plaisirs de la Table.* Published by the author c. 1920. Reprinted by Éditions Daniel Morcrette, B. P. 26, 9570 Luzarches, 1979. Translated by permission of Éditions Daniel Morcrette(149).

Norberg, Inga (Editor), *Good Food from Sweden.* Published by Chatto and Windus, London, 1935. By permission of Curtis Brown Ltd., London, agents for the author(119).

Ochorowicz-Monatowa, Marja, *Polish Cookery.* Translated by Jean Karsavina. Copyright © 1958 by Crown Publishers, Inc. Used by permission of Crown Publishers, Inc.(157).

Oliver, Michel, *Mes Recettes.* © Plon, 1975. Published by Librairie Plon. Translated by permission of Librairie Plon, Paris(97, 110).

Olney, Judith, *Comforting Food.* Copyright © 1979 by Judith Olney. Published by Atheneum Publishers, Inc., New York. Reprinted with the permission of Atheneum Publishers, Inc.(133, 140). *Summer Food.* Copyright © 1978 by Judith Olney. Published by Atheneum Publishers, New York. Reprinted with the permission of Atheneum Publishers(109, 143).

Olney, Richard, *Simple French Food.* Copyright © 1974 by Richard Olney (New York: Atheneum, 1974). Reprinted with the permission of Atheneum Publishers(111).

Ortiz, Elisabeth Lambert, *The Complete Book of Caribbean Cooking.* Copyright © 1973 by Elisabeth Lambert Ortiz. Reprinted by permission of the publishers, M. Evans & Co., Inc., New York(124).

Östenius, Asta and Brita Olssen (Editors), *Swedish Cooking.* © 1971 ICA-Förlaget AB, Västerås, Sweden. Published by ICA-Förlaget AB, Västerås. By permission of ICA-Förlaget AB(121).

Paradissis, Chrissa, *The Best Book of Greek Cookery.* Copyright © 1976 P. Efstathiadis & Sons. Published by P. Efstathiadis & Sons, Athens. By permission of P. Efstathiadis & Sons(140, 148).

Peter, Madeleine (Editor), *Favorite Recipes of the Great Women Chefs of France.* Recipe by Christiane Conticiai, Le Parc, Villemomble (Seine-Saint-Denis). Translated and edited by Nancy Simmons. Copyright © 1977 by Éditions Robert Laffont S.A. Copyright © 1979 by Holt, Rinehart and Winston. Reprinted by permission of Holt, Rinehart and Winston, Publishers(122).

Petit, A., *La Gastronomie en Russie.* Published by the author and Émile Mellier, Paris, 1860(120, 144).

Petits Propos Culinaires II, August 1979. Copyright © 1979 Prospect Books, London. Used by permission of the publisher(110—Nathan d'Aulnay, 113—Suad Aljure). © Éditions Albin Michel, 1977. Published by Éditions Albin Michel, Paris. Translated by permission of Éditions Albin Michel(148).

Philippon, Henri, *Cuisine de Provence.* © Éditions Albin Michel, 1977. Published by Éditions Albin Michel, Paris. Translated by permission of Éditions Albin Michel(148).

Plucinska, I., *Ksiazka Kucharska Udoskonalona.* Copyright by author. Poznań, 1945. Translated by permission of Agencja Autorska, Warsaw(137).

Portevin, G., *Ce qu'il faut Savoir pour Manger les Bons Champignons.* (Savoir en Histoire Naturelle, Volume VI). Published by Paul Lechevalier, Éditeur, Paris, 1948. Translated by permission of Éditions Lechevalier(99).

Read, Jan and Maite Manjón, *Flavours of Spain.* Copyright © Jan Read and Maite Manjón 1978. Published by Cassell Ltd., London. By permission of Cassell Ltd.(153).

Ross, Janet and Michael Waterfield, *Leaves From Our Tuscan Kitchen.* Copyright © Michael Waterfield, 1973. Reprinted with the permission of Atheneum Publishers(101).

Rossi, Emanuele (Editor), *La Vera Cuciniera Genovese.* Published by Casa Editrice Bietti, Milan, 1973. Translated by permission of Casa Editrice Bietti(100, 104).

Rossi Callizo, Gloria, *Las Mejores Tapas, Cenas Frías y Platos Combinados.* Copyright © Editorial De Vecchi, S.A., Barcelona, 1980. Published by Editorial De Vecchi, S.A. Translated by permission of Editorial De Vecchi, S.A.(123).

Sahni, Julie, *Classic Indian Cooking.* Copyright © 1980 by Julie Sahni. By permission of William Morrow & Company(95).

Salles, Prosper and Prosper Montagné, *La Grande Cuisine.* Published by Imp. A. Chène, Monaco, 1900(91, 117).

Sarvis, Shirley, *Crab & Abalone.* Copyright © 1968 by Shirley Sarvis and Tony Calvello. Published by Bobbs-Merrill Company, Inc.(130).

Schapira, Christiane, *La Cuisine Corse.* © Solar, 1979. Published by Solar, Paris. Translated by permission of Solar(101, 103).

Scheibler, Sophie Wilhelmine, *Allgemeines Deutsches Kochbuch für Alle Stände.* Published in Leipzig, 1896(120).

Serra, Victoria, *Tía Victoria's Spanish Kitchen.* English text copyright © Elizabeth Gili, 1963. Published by Kaye & Ward Ltd., London, 1963. Translated by Elizabeth Gili from the original Spanish entitled *Sabores: Cocina del Hogar* by Victoria Serra Suñol. By permission of Kaye & Ward Ltd.(134).

Siegel, F. (Translator), *Russian Cooking.* © English translation, MIR Publishers, 1974. Published by MIR Publishers, Moscow. By permission of The Copyright Agency of the USSR-VAAP(97).

Simonet, Suzanne, *Le Grand Livre de la Cuisine Occitane.* © Jean-Pierre Delarge, Éditions Universitaires, 1977. Published by Jean-Pierre Delarge, Éditeur, Paris. Translated by permission of Jean-Pierre Delarge, Éditeur(156).

Stuber, Hedwig Maria, *Ich Helf dir Kochen.* © BLV Verlagsgesellschaft mbH., München, 1976. Published by BLV Verlagsgesellschaft mbH., Munich. Translated by permission of BLV Verlagsgesellschaft mbH.(119, 149).

Tendret, Lucien, *La Table au Pays de Brillat-Savarin.* Published by Librairie Dardel, Chambéry, 1934. Translated by permission of Jacques Grancher, Éditeur(94, 134).

Thiébault, Sylvie, *Tartes Sucrées et Tartes Salées.* © Solar, 1977: Published by Solar, Paris. Translated by permission of Solar(143).

Toulouse-Lautrec, Mapie de, *La Cuisine de Mapie.* Copyright © 1967 by Librairie Jules Tallandier, France (159, 160).

Tracy, Marian, *The Shellfish Cookbook.* Copyright © 1965 by Marian Tracy. Used with permission of the publisher, Bobbs-Merrill Company, Inc.(130).

Uvezian, Sonia, *The Best Foods of Russia.* Copyright © 1976 by Sonia Uvezian. Reprinted by permission of Harcourt Brace Jovanovich, Inc.(112).

Vence, Céline, *Encyclopédie Hachette de la Cuisine Régionale.* © Hachette 1979. Published by Librairie Hachette, Paris. Translated by permission of Librairie Hachette(97).

Vergé, Roger, *Roger Vergé's Cuisine of the South of France.* English Translation Copyright © 1980 by William Morrow and Company, Inc. Originally published in French under the title *Ma Cuisine de Soleil.* Copyright © 1979 by Editions Robert Laffont S.A. Used by permission of William Morrow and Company, Inc.(105).

Voegeling, François, *La Gastronomie Alsacienne.* © by Éditions des Dernières Nouvelles de Strasbourg. Published by Éditions des Dernières Nouvelles d'Alsace-ISTRA. Translated by permission of Éditions ISTRA(150).

Volpicelli, Luigi and Secondino Freda (Editors), *L'Antiartusi: 1000 Ricette.* © 1978 Pan Editrice, Milano. Published by Pan Editrice, Milan. Translated by permission of Pan Editrice(94, 117, 144, 158).

Watt, Alexander, *Paris Bistro Cookery.* Copyright © 1957 by Alexander Watt. Reprinted by permission of Alfred A. Knopf, Inc.(143).

Weber, Dominique, *Les Bonnes Recettes des Provinces de France.* © Bordas, Paris, 1979. Published by Éditions Bordas. Translated by permission of Éditions Bordas(140).

Willan, Anne, *Entertaining: Complete Menus For All Occasions.* English edition by Elisabeth Evans. Copyright © 1980 La Varenne. Printed by permission of the publisher, B. T. Batsford Ltd., London, 1980(91).

Willan, Anne and Jane Grigson (Editors), *The Observer French Cookery School.* Copyright © 1980 by Anne Willan and Jane Grigson. Reprinted by permission of Harold Ober Associates, Inc. and La Varenne, Paris(92, 141, 155).

Willinsky, Grete, *Kulinarische Weltreise.* © 1961 by Mary Hahns Kochbuchverlag, Berlin W. Published by Buchergilce Gutenberg, Frankfurt/Main. Translated by permission of Mary Hahns Kochbuchverlag, Munich(116).

Wolfert, Paula, *Mediterranean Cooking.* Copyright © 1977 by Paula Wolfert. Published by Quadrangle/The New York Times Book Co., Inc., New York. Used by permission of Paula Wolfert and Quadrangle/The New York Times Book Co., Inc.(157).

Wretman, Tore, *Swedish Smörgåsbord.* © Tore Wretman, 1964. Second edition, 1977. By permission of Tore Wretman(118).

Wurtzburger, Janet E. C. and Mac K. Griswold (Editors), *Private Collections: A Culinary Treasure.* Recipe by Edward L. Brewter. Copyright © 1973 by The Walters Art Gallery, Baltimore. Published by permission of the Women's Committee of The Walters Art Gallery, Baltimore(132).

Acknowledgments

The indexes for this book were prepared by Louise W. Hedberg. The editors are particularly indebted to Pat Alburey, Hertfordshire, England; Gail Duff, Kent, England; Elisabeth Lambert Ortiz, London; Ann O'Sullivan, Majorca, Spain; Dr. R. H. Smith, Aberdeen, Scotland; Kunio Yasutake, Alexandria, Virginia.

The editors also wish to thank: Mary Attenborough, Essex, England; Katherine Browne, Sussex, England; Sarah Bunney, London; Josephine Christian, Somerset, England; Liz Clasen, London; Claire Clifton, London; Emma Codrington, Surrey, England; Tony Craze, London; Jennifer Davidson, Berkeley, California; Lindsay Duguid, London; Fiona Duncan, London; Mimi Errington, London; Neyla Freeman, London; Carmel Friedlander, London; Ramona-Ann Gale, Surrey, England; Henrietta Green, Gloucestershire, England; Fayal Greene, London; Gillian Gutman, Surrey, England; Annie Hall, London; Maggie Heinz, London; Stella Henvey, London; Christie Horn, London; Marion Hunter, Surrey, England; Brenda Jayes, London; Rosemary Klein, London; John Leslie, London; Vivian McCorry, London; Pippa Millard, London; Sonya Mills, Kent, England; Wendy Morris, London; Maria Mosby, London; Dilys Naylor, Surrey, England; Jo Oxley, Surrey, England; Joanna Roberts, London; Manuel Rodríguez and José Sánchez, Ivano Greengrocers, London; Michael Schwab, London; Cynthia A. Sheppard, London; Ann Stevenson, London; Stephanie Thompson, Surrey, England; Fiona Tillet, London; J. M. Turnell & Co., London; Tina Walker, London; Nigel Warrington, London; Dr. R. Wootten, Department of Agriculture and Fisheries for Scotland, Aberdeen.

Picture Credits

The sources for the pictures in this book are listed below. Credits for each of the photographers and illustrators are listed by page number in sequence with successive pages indicated by hyphens; where necessary, the locations of pictures within pages are also indicated—separated from page numbers by dashes.

Photographs by Aldo Tutino: 6—bottom, 11-15, 16-17—bottom, 18-19—bottom, 24-31, 34-35, 38—bottom, 39—top right and bottom, 42-51, 54-55—bottom, 60—top left, 64—bottom right, 70—bottom, 71—top center, top right, 75—bottom, 76-77, 88.
Photographs by Tom Belshaw: 7, 8—top, 9, 20, 21—top, 22-23, 32-33, 36-37, 38—top left, 40-41, 52—bottom right, 53—bottom, 55—top, 58—top, 59, 60—top right and bottom, 61-62, 64—top and bottom left, 65, 68-69, 70—top, 71—top left, 78—bottom right, 80-81, 82—bottom, 83—top center and bottom, 86-87.
Other photographs (alphabetically): John Cook, 4. David Davies, 84—bottom right, 85—top right and bottom. Alan Duns, cover, 6—top, 16-17—top, 18-19—top, 52—top and bottom left, 53—top, 56—top and bottom right, 57, 58—bottom, 66-67, 83—top right, 84—top and bottom left, 85—top left, top center. John Elliott, 8—bottom, 10, 21—top, 38—top right, 39—top left, top center, 54—top, 56—bottom left, 71—bottom, 72-74, 75—top, 82—top, 83—top left. Louis Klein, 2. Bob Komar, 78—top and bottom left, 79.
Illustrations: From the Mary Evans Picture Library and private sources and *Food & Drink: A Pictorial Archive from Nineteenth Century Sources* by Jim Harter, published by Dover Publications, Inc., 1979, 91-167.

Library of Congress Cataloguing in Publication Data
Main entry under title:
Hors d'oeuvre.
   (The Good cook techniques & recipes)
   Includes index.
   1. Cookery (Appetizers) I. Time-Life Books. II. Series.
TX740.H6445   641.8′12   82-657
ISBN 0-8094-2943-8   AACR2
ISBN 0-8094-2942-X (lib. bdg.)
ISBN 0-8094-2941-1 (retail ed.)